Latin American Literature

Latin American Literature

Symptoms, risks and strategies of post-structuralist criticism

Bernard McGuirk

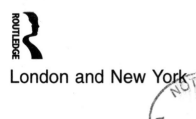

London and New York

First published 1997
by Routledge
11 New Fetter Lane, London EC4P 4EE

Simultaneously published in the USA and Canada
by Routledge
29 West 35th Street, New York, NY 10001

Typeset in Palatino by Keystroke, Jacaranda Lodge,
Wolverhampton

Printed and bound in Great Britain by
TJ Press (Padstow) Ltd, Padstow, Cornwall

British Library Cataloguing in Publication Data
A catalogue record for this book is available from the British Library

Library of Congress Cataloging in Publication Data
McGuirk, Bernard.
    Latin American literature : symptoms, risks, and strategies of
post-structuralist criticism / Bernard McGuirk.
        p.   cm.
    Includes bibliographical references and index.
    1. Latin American literature—20th century—History and
criticism. 2. Criticism—Latin America—History—20th century.
3. Postmodernism (Literature)—Latin America. 4. Politics and
literature—Latin America. I. Title.
PQ7081.M3727   1996
860.9'98—dc20   96–17603
[463'.21]   CIP

ISBN 0–415–07755–9

T 1001296283

we now demonstrate a method
by examples . . . There is not *a*
philosophical method, though
there are indeed methods, like
different therapies.
            Ludwig Wittgenstein

To Elizabeth, Catherine and Siobhán

Contents

Preface

For many Latin Americans there is no such place, let alone a common literature. Utopian or atopian, any emphasis on difference or differences between countries and cultures can never be just literary and the issues raised in this book will derive from a perceived need to address specific cultural encounters which are also always ideological. The range of literatures discussed includes but is not restricted to writings from Argentina, Brazil, Chile, Guatemala, Mexico, Nicaragua and Peru. The critical perspectives, predominantly post-structuralist, embrace the concerns of contemporary Latin American critics as well as those of recent thinkers from other traditions, broadly in the post-Derridan contexts of my own intellectual formation.

The choice of texts is, in the first instance, a personal preference. Always. Yet this book is aimed at readers neither necessarily acquainted with Latin American literature nor expecting to find in it another of the many available general introductions. Unapologetically, the selection reflects the opportunities I have taken to apply insights of post-structuralist critical practice to texts by already well-known Latin American authors and by others likely to become so. It will be obvious to specialists and to non-specialists alike that two writers figure more prominently than any others, the Peruvian César Vallejo (1892–1938) and the Argentine Jorges Luis Borges (1899–1986). But the need for any sense of coverage, of representativeness, disappeared long ago. The literatures of the countries of Latin America can in no convincing sense be said to require projection, a project, in any case, entirely other to the concerns of the present volume. Texts of Rubén Darío, Pablo Neruda, Mário de Andrade, João Guimarães Rosa, Julio Cortázar, Carlos Fuentes and Susana Thénon, amongst others, are approached by taking risks and employing strategies which open up symptomatic differences not only *between* but also *within* cultures. If the necessary interplay between literature and theory has any constant, it will always be the capacity of the one to interrogate the limits and limitations of the other. This book seeks to highlight the differences at play in literature which cultural studies can also explore.

Acknowledgements

I wish to thank Pamela Attenborough who assisted me in the preparation of the manuscript of this book and the following, whose contributions to the evolution of my critical practices have been crucial. Whether as colleagues or interlocutors, doubters or interrogators, at conferences or in conversation, and consciously or not, each has drawn my attention to dimensions or limitations of applying critical theories to literary and cultural texts which I should otherwise have overlooked: Mário Barros, Lena Bergstein, Malcolm Bowie, Anny Brooksbank-Jones, Richard Cardwell, Jean Chapot, Georgiana Colvile, Geoffrey Connell, Francisco Delich, Jacques Derrida, Terry Eagleton, Charlie Feiling, Evelyn Fishburn, Jean Franco, Néstor García Canclini, Daniel Gercke, John Gledson, Marina Heck, James Higgins, Heloisa Buarque de Hollanda, Nelly Kaplan, Tom Kavanagh, Richard King, Diana Knight, Jo Labanyi, David Lagmanovich, Claude Makovsky, Gerald Martin, Walter Mignolo, Mark Millington, Wander Miranda, Sylvia Molloy, Alberto Moreiras, David Murray, Julio Ortega, Christopher Norris, Giovanni Pontiero, Mary Louise Pratt, Robert Pring-Mill, Hamish Reid, Susana Reisz, Solange Ribeiro, Nelly Richard, William Rowe, Silviano Santiago, Nicolau Sevcenko, Samir Shah, Adam Sharman, Julian Shaw, Paul Julian Smith, Eneida Maria de Souza, Judith Still, Ilana Strozenberg, Douglas Tallack, Brian Tate, Arthur Terry, Sultana Wahnon Bensusan, George Yudice, Roberto Ventura, Else Vieira.

Chapter 1 and chapter 2 are extensive reworkings of 'Pre-post Eros: On Reading Love Poetry Before and After Theory: From Pablo Neruda to Susana Thénon', *New Hispanisms: Literature, Culture, Theory*, edited by Mark I. Millington and Paul Julian

Smith, Ottawa Hispanic Studies, Dovehouse Editions, Canada, 1994, pp. 176–209. Chapter 2 includes an analysis of a Cendrars poem which first appeared in French, in 'Autre lieu, autres jeux: la feinte de l'altérité dans *Sud-Américaines' Feuilles de Route*, 26, Grenoble, avril 1992, pp. 9–21. Chapter 3 is an expanded version of the Spanish original '"Yo sé . . . ", "Yo persigo . . . ", "Yo no sé . . . ", El modernismo y la meta-historia de la literatura', *¿Qué es el modernismo? Nueva encuesta, Nuevas lecturas*, edited by Richard A. Cardwell and Bernard McGuirk, Society of Spanish and Spanish American Studies, Colorado, 1993, pp. 339–54. Chapter 4 contains material on Rubén Darío and César Vallejo, first published in 'On Misreading Mallarmé: the Resistance to Modernity', *Literary Theory and Poetry: Extending the Canon*, edited by David Murray, Batsford, 1989. pp. 167–90. Chapter 5 includes an analysis of a poem which first appeared in 'Limenperuguano: Semiosis, Hermeneutics and the Defects of the Romantic Discourse. César Vallejo's *Trilce I*', *Essays in Honour of R. B. Tate*, University of Nottingham, 1984, pp. 71–82, edited by Richard A Cardwell, *Nottingham Monographs in the Humanities*, 1984, pp. 71–82. Chapter 6 includes a short section on narratology which first appeared in Spanish in 'Seminario sobre Jorge Luis Borges', *Actas del Primer Congreso de Semiótica e Hispanismo*, Madrid: CSIC, 1984, pp. 539–46. Chapter 7 is a much expanded version of the Spanish conference paper which first appeared in 'La Semi(er)ótica de la otredad: "El otro cielo"', *Actas del Coloquio Internacional sobre la Americanidad de Julio Cortázar*, Mannheim, 1987, pp. 345–54. Chapter 9 is based on a paper given at the Vth Triennial Congress of the British Comparative Literature Association which appeared in the proceedings as '"Borges and I": Jorge Luis Borges and the "Discerned" Subject', *Romance Studies*, 16, Summer, 1990, pp. 43–9. Chapter 10 contains a central section which first appeared in Spanish in 'Z/Z', *Coloquio Internacional: Escritura y sexualidad en la literatura hispanoamericana*, Madrid: Editorial Fundamentos, 1990, pp. 207–31. The two Penguin volumes from which I have quoted are as follows: Jorge Luis Borges, *Labyrinths*, 1970, translated by James E. Irby and Donald A. Yates; Carlos Fuentes, *Terra Nostra*, 1978, translated by Margaret Sayers Peden.

Fore-word: locating inequality
Post-, trans-, intra-

> Be not afeared: the isle is full of noises,
> Sounds and sweet airs, that give delight
> and hurt not.
>
> *The Tempest*

The relations explored in this book are the transactional effects of inequality. Might not the very possibility of equality function as an inappropriate (utopian) notion? Might even to imagine equality be a dangerous diversion from the varying pressures, rhythms and demands of *hic et nunc* inequalities? At the same time, might the idea of 'unlearning' privilege be viewed as (irrelevantly) utopian, absorbing energies which might be redirected to the urgencies of post-colonial, trans-national, intra-marginal negotiations? The questions to be addressed, then, will derive from a perceived need to interrelate post-structuralisms and histories, to extrapolate from the observable differences which none the less give mutual relevance to separate and coherent cultural specificities. My encounters with Latin American literatures will be symptomized, in the Machereyan sense, by selective though always ideological gaps; in the Derridan perspective of my own intellectual formation, it will have been necessary to run the risks of the strategies pursued.

One point of entry, one key, to the question of negotiable discourses of Utopia is the question of place, of spaces, and when in doubt as to where to begin an initial strategy is the approach Jacques Derrida has described thus: '*We must begin wherever we are . . . .* It is impossible to justify absolutely a point of departure. *Wherever we are*: in a text where we think we are' (1976, 162). Thus, by way of some personal, professional, national and cultural contextualization to this book, I choose to begin within the institutionality of British academe or the text in which I think I am. In reading a selected range of texts from (or on) Latin America in the last one hundred years, I am afforded the opportunity to examine current intellectual practices not only within my own but also within other cultures and, indeed, meditate on what, in 1940, the Cuban Fernando Ortiz, and, in 1982, the Uruguayan Ángel Rama termed *transculturation*.

The United Kingdom, in terms of its response to 'foreign' theories, has moved hardly at all from the 1970s' stance of, at best, reticence, at worst, rejection. The 1992 Cambridge Derrida farrago (was he 'worthy' of an honorary degree?) echoed the earlier MacCabe affair or, more amusingly, in my own case brought to mind the comment of a Hispanist colleague on my return to teaching within the British system after several years spent studying and teaching in Paris. 'You made two basic mistakes,' he said, 'first, going to France, second, coming back. In short, though there is a national context of Anglo-Saxon philosophical contempt for the supposed normative inexactitude of such as Derrida's 'tour de Babel' slipperiness of word-play, it is obvious that such a reaction goes well beyond ideas. Ideologically, UK institutions have at best tolerated but rarely if ever absorbed theoretical practices – much less their political implications. Since the death of Franco, Spanish academe has inexorably dropped many of the cautions regarding theory that once bedevilled its conservative praxes. Chairs of literary and critical theory proliferate, new journals provide a forum of debate and publications to a generation of critics informed, either directly or via the many translations available, of the major currents in contemporary thought. In this respect, Spain has rapidly caught up not only with an already relatively advanced Portugal (ever alert to Paris) but also with broadly *au fait* (e.g. Sarlo, Ludmer, Molloy, García Canclini) Spanish American and, particularly, sophisticated Brazilian critical practices (e.g. de Campos, Merquior, Santiago, Schwarz). We should not be surprised, perhaps, by the crosscurrents which have fertilized the North American dimension of the discipline, given the contribution of Latin American critics to US institutions. There is, however, a concomitant danger: that of colonization. The case of Ángel Rama's difficult ride in and eventual exclusion from US academic debate was symptomatic of an ever-lurking inequality in North–South encounters, although in the United States the reaction of the establishment was considerably more subtle than in Britain. From an early stage a new theoretical elite, far from rejecting the ideas of formalism, structuralism and the proliferating theories of post-structuralism – from Derrida to Kristeva, from Macherey to Foucault, from Lacan to Deleuze and Guattari – consistently and professionally absorbed, experienced and, all too often, sanitized (before re-packaging) the continental imports. I think particularly, in this respect, of Jonathan Culler, the successful popularizer of *la nouvelle critique*, or the Yale School critics who colonized Derrida (irrecuperably?) as a trans-Atlantic or even *mid*-Atlantic figure, as 'theologized' – a great irony, since it was Derrida himself who first proclaimed that 'the age of the sign is essentially theological'. Remember, however, that in *Of Grammatology* he continued: 'Perhaps it [the age of the sign] will never *end*. Its historical *closure* is, however, outlined' (Derrida 1976, 13–14). In the hands of the North American deconstructors, Derrida, deified, it seems would never end, though the historical, ideologically subversive, *present* Derrida, has often been the victim of a very clearly outlined closure. He might thus be rendered harmless. Perhaps the most cynical expression of both Anglo and Anglo-American academic responses to literary theory was the humorous novel of David Lodge (formerly of the University of Birmingham), *Small World* (Lodge 1984). Here, theory itself became the ultimate *logos*, the transcendental signifier in a post-theological academic world in which the pilgrimage was replaced by the annual conference circuit. In this small world, this microcosm of the age-old quest for Truth, structuralism, Marxism, phenomenology, deconstruction, reader-response theory *et al.* struggled for supremacy, each offering the promise of at least revelation, and, for the *cognoscenti* (the academics and the critics) and even for the acolytes (the post-graduate students), the guarantee of salvation. What I am describing here are competing brands of a very North American fundamentalism, a religion of text rather than of theology, and an activity of the market-place rather than of the spirit, a loyalty and servitude to no God but to 'God's own Country'.

The thread of theological reference throughout this account of literary–critical activity of the last two decades both in the United Kingdom and in the United States weaves an all too deconstructible fabric. For the liberal humanist (theological)

enterprise constantly trades in metaphors of growth, development, quest for maturity, refined sensitivity and independence.
Yet for each positive reading of the metaphors there is the absent,
suppressed negative. Just as *growth* also means cancer or tumour,
development for Britain and the United States has often implied
under-development for the countries of Latin America; a *quest
for maturity* often neglects childhood, adolescence and adulthood
in favour of the moribund policies of octogenarians; a *refined
sensitivity* may appreciate, may even stretch out to stroke, the
beautiful bird singing just beyond the cell-bars; finally, *independence* has often hinged on the benefits derived from dependence-
economies elsewhere, conveniently situated in the 'back-yard',
the 'legitimate sphere-of-influence' of, say, Nicaragua, Grenada
or Panama. All these, then, are but deconstructible metaphors
of the 'prison-house' of liberal humanism and its late twentieth-
century literary critical colonies.

The Anglo-Saxon literary establishment, in these two decades,
has not only learned to live with the continental luxury imports of
critical theory but has cleverly turned the insights and practices
of the structuralist and post-structuralist enterprises to its own
ends and purposes. While extremely cautious of the anti-humanist
pretensions of High Structuralism, the academic institutions,
both in the United Kingdom and in the United States, did recognize the respectability of structuralism's 'scientific' procedures.
When, however, post-structuralism emerged, as a legacy of structuralism's insistence on relational differences between objects
rather than on the quest to analyse the object itself, the majority of
those academics and critics who showed any interest whatsoever
did so with a view to exploiting either the element of the play
of differences (i.e. play as self-indulgent game) or the obsessive
return to deconstructible metaphors *within* the text, as if those
metaphors were never more than linguistic/textual relations,
never anchored, nor anchorable, in social reality. In short, as
Fredric Jameson's famous title suggests, the prison-house of
liberal humanism was but one dimension of *The Prison House
of Language* (Jameson 1972). If the house of the Lord has many
mansions, that occupied by the latter-day Anglo-Saxon deconstructors was all too often the kindergarten, where clever
but adolescent minds built, demolished and rebuilt labyrinthine
constructions with the building-blocks of an intellectual nursery.
Deconstruction had thus, all too often, become a compulsive

habit, a masturbatory repetition masquerading as the only *jouissance* possible.

Understandably seeking alternatives to such antics, many critics have sought, in modishly titled successors such as New Historicism, Gender Studies or Cultural Studies, critical practices which purport to enter into dialogue with others, with other cultures, even with other theories. Yet, in the institutional context of the universities where such 'strategies of conversion' *à la* Bourdieu take place, they have sometimes become umbrella terms under which theoretical issues may shelter without specificity. Paradoxically, the rush to politically correct labelling can easily conceal a perilous disregard for the particular which is not so much utopian as atopian. In this respect, such critical practices conform to a markedly capitalist aspiration: namely, the abolition of particular spaces. Atopianism, however, obviously operates, ever paradoxically, in the *here* and *now*. Though resigned to the location of such a present in a territory policed by economies of restriction, we may still pose the question as to whether there can be a way out of the prison-house. Or has the key been thrown away for ever?

Obviously the *Prison House of Language* may be subverted, if not entirely demolished, by a new linguistics. In this area, an important contribution has been that of Mary Louise Pratt, whose proposals for a 'linguistics of contact' are of acute relevance to this discussion. She has attacked the linguistic community which constantly presents itself as a 'nation': adult, monolingual, mono-dialogic. She has questioned linguistic research on speech interaction which stresses 'order', where breakdown is seen as *dis*order. In this linguistics, only 'legitimate' moves are recognized; 'protest' is excluded; child language is seen as 'deficient' adult language; medical discourse is judged by efficiency of scientific objectives rather than by patients' needs; the linguistic community is too often revealed as anthropocentric; in short, any lack of consensus is seen as a *loss*. Such a linguistics ignores *dystopias*; ignores multi-linguicity, ignores immigration within strong states, ignores women, ignores classroom discourse, ignores working-class practice, ignores all non-homogeneity. This 'old' linguistics might be replaced by a linguistics of *contact*: contact of, and across, boundaries; across, and not within, lines of separation. Such a 'new' linguistics, for Mary Louise Pratt, would have rejected, for instance, apartheid defined as 'segregation', would have rejected it as apartheid's representation *of* itself *to* itself. For what if apartheid were conceived of as a 'particular form of togetherness' – a zone of contact which 'showed up', rather than 'hid', the interaction of black servant with white master/mistress? Such a linguistics might now address directly the question of whether the black *middle*-class speaker aspires to, appropriates, or intervenes in, white discourse. In such a linguistics, the 'slipperiness' of signifiers would be a given, as would the inevitable asymmetry between reception and production (Pratt 1987, 48–66).

It is worth recalling that Mary Louise Pratt is known both as a socio-linguist and as a Latin Americanist. And the closeness of her proposals to those of several Brazilian theorists is, I suggest, illuminating in the present context:

> We can oppose (or, at least, to 'ventilate' this dominance, contrapose, in the musical sense of the word 'counterpoint') a modal, differential nationalism. In the former case, one seeks the origin and the *parousic* itinerary of a national Logos, seen as a point. This is an episode of the Western metaphysics of presence, transferred to our tropical latitudes, one which does not take into account the final meaning of this transfer. A chapter to be added to the Platonizing logocentrism which Derrida, in *Of Grammatology*, submitted to a lucid and revealing analysis, not insignificantly at the instigation of two ex-centrics, Fenellosa, the anti-sinologist, and Nietzsche, the shatterer of certainties. In this instance, one seeks to locate the moment of incarnation of the national spirit (logos), obscuring the differential (the disruptions and infractions, the margins, the 'monstrous') to define better a certain privileged course: the straight line this logophony traces across History. The moment of this zenith (comparable to the organic blossoming of the tree) coincides with that of the *parousia* of this logos, in full flower within the domestic courtyard. Yet, when it comes time to describe this entified substance – the 'national character' – one is reduced to a 'half-portrait', watered-down and conventional, where nothing is characteristic and the reconciliatory patro-centrism must resort to hypotheses to sustain itself.
>
> (de Campos 1986, 45)

Haroldo de Campos thus characterizes discursive activities as following that double trajectory, that toing-and-froing, that shuttle, of a practice which settles on no one word, much less a binary pair, preferring – opting – to perform in the space of *trans-*. *Trans-* is the ever-mobile 'third term' of such a theory. Thus *trans*portation, *trans*lation, *trans*culturation (all familiar starting-points within the disciplines of linguistics, Latin American Studies, Cultural Theory) act only as initial points of reference in, for example, the post-modern translation aesthetics developed recently by the Brazilian critic Else Vieira. Her meditation on 'double plagiarism'/'double appropriation' is disconcertingly close both to Baruch Spinoza's notion of *becoming* and to Gilles Deleuze's phenomenon of 'double capture'. Vieira's *consumption* of Augusto de Campos' 'my way of loving them is by devouring them. Or translating them' (Vieira 1995, 10) in no way exhausts the possibility of seeing *Antropofagia* as also a re-digesting of Spinoza and Deleuze:

> As the lover changes, so does the object of his love: someone who is loved is not the same person that he was before he was loved. This double change is true of 'becoming' as a general principle; Deleuze calls the phenomenon 'double capture', whereby both terms in the relation of love take on qualities of the other (though each maintains its independent identity) .... This then is double-capture: there is an asymmetrical taking-on of new properties, without any sort of fusion, for both are caught in a single process of becoming .... 'Becoming' is not therefore a relation of opposition, of *either x or y*, but rather a matter of encounter, of capture, of *x and y*.
>
> (Jenkins in McGuirk 1989, 102–3)

Though the impact of Haroldo de Campos' claims has been perhaps most observable in the field of post-modern translation theory, it is important to stress that *within* Latin America debates comparable to the polemics developed elsewhere in recent years by such as Spivak, Bhabha and Said have been both as heated and as relevant to cultural and literary theories as they have been to linguistics. However, the theories and literary practices of such as the de Campos brothers have also been countered, famously, by the critique of the prominent Brazilian Marxist Roberto Schwarz. Most notably in 'Marco histórico' of 1985, recently reproduced in John Gledson's translation, as 'A Historic Landmark' in *Misplaced Ideas* (Schwarz 1992, 187–96), the notions of Augusto and Haroldo de Campos are subjected to a searching examination:

Others, and that includes me, will see the poem as the nth example of a key trick played by the concretists, always concerned to organize Brazilian and world literature so that it culminates in them, a tendency which sets up a confusion between theory and self-advertisement as well as being provincial nonsense . . . . In an extreme and unjustified leap, in which he transforms calamity into liberty, Haroldo explains that, given the impasse between Imperialism and Bureaucratic dictatorships, both of them equally dreadful, poetry is now entering into a 'post-utopian' world, one of the 'pluralization of possible poetics'. The situation has got better because it has got worse, so to speak . . . . Behind the globalized form of the real, from which contradictions, differences, and other marks of concrete reality are missing, maybe there is an element of indifference . . . . Bringing together total ambition and total lack of definition, the 'everything' blends the inadequacies of messianic utopianism and the self-sufficiency of a bureaucracy which promises nothing. However that may be, as far as the poet is concerned, poetry no longer lives in a situation of impasse, but in a world which it has transformed and will go on transforming (what for?).

(Schwarz 1992, 191–5)

John Gledson himself, in a perceptively balanced commentary on Schwarz's polemic with the Concretist de Campos, adds:

It would be easy to see Roberto Schwarz as a pessimist. He certainly is unwilling to ignore the brute facts of mass poverty and exploitation which have plagued Brazil's past and continue to plague its present. One can feel his anger at those who try to argue, with singularly contorted logic and deafness to the calls of common sense, that things are better because they are worse: because Brazilians have always imitated, but are now told there is no reason to think that imitations are inferior to the things they copy, they are suddenly in the vanguard.

(ibid., xix)

For Gledson, the 'sleight of hand' whereby 'suddenly, the periphery becomes the centre' will never convince an 'enlightened materialist' such as Schwarz that 'differential nationalism' transferred 'to our tropical latitudes' (in Haroldo de Campos' words) can be anything other than a dangerous and irresponsible 'slipperiness', not only of signifiers *à la* Mary Louise Pratt, but also of that 'rarified realm of absolute desires' where all that 'is left is the abstract gesticulations of the desire to transform, wrapped up in attractive lettering' (ibid., 195).

Are we to be locked again into the long familiar tensions of a Nietzsche–Marx binary? As an extension and corollary of the *Prison House of Language* (and the cell of traditional translation), the *Prison House of Criticism* might be evaded by an analysis that, instead of regarding the growth and development of 'human subjects' within the confines of literature, would investigate what Terry Eagleton has called the production of certain *forms of subjectivity* judged appropriate to the society in question. Basically, such a literary-critical practice takes as read, as well as spoken, such basic Bakhtinian notions as dialogics and heteroglossia. Far from assuming univocality, or even an essentially ambiguous, *un*grounded vocality, in a literary text, such a criticism has to assume that at play is always a multivoicedness, while constantly asking 'which voices?' – but, in short, ever resisting the possibility of the univocal, political, institutionalized 'voice', ever resisting interpretative closure.

Within such critical practices, and in the studies in this volume, the *Prison House of Symbol*, or symbolic systems, might be subjected to the deconstructive procedures which reveal all such systems, be they theological, gnostic, mythological, materialist, psychoanalytical or pragmatic, to be dangerously hermeneutic. Thus, for example, a Freudian, Lacanian or Kristevan-feminist analysis – while useful – ought never to be, for criticism, a writing-cure, equivalent to the talking-cure notion of the psychoanalyst's consulting-room. For 'cure', or 'explanation', suggests, inevitably, that there was something 'wrong', 'deficient' or 'completable', in the first place, in the 'patient'/'text'. All desire for movement, change, redistribution of power or meaning, would thus be only interpretable as Oedipal compensation, forever erected as the master-signifier, be it in Freudian, Lacanian, Kristevan or any other symbolic discourse. Under the lock and key of such institutionality, it is difficult to escape the hermeneutic shadow of many psychoanalytical practices as they are currently applied to literary criticism.

Admittedly, there is no reason why psychoanalytical criticism should not be subjected to the same subversive operations as any other deconstructible hermeneutic – and there is some evidence to suggest that the Anglo-Saxon tradition has glimpsed a way out of 'lack' discourses in the work of Barbara Johnston and (vicariously) Toril Moi. For these writers, as for others such as Christopher Norris, Terry Eagleton and William Ray, criticism might have to recognize its position in the margin of literary activity, but can never be content with – indeed, must struggle against – marginality, or its complacent conversion into an ivory-tower comfort. In the *Prison House of Institutionality* many critical practices have been reluctant to take on board the implications of Michel Foucault's investigations. For each of the practices I have mentioned – linguistic, translational, literary-critical, psycho-analytical – and, no less, Latin American Studies is always, too, an institution, subject to the codes and house-rules of its own hierarchy. All too often, the institution disguises its practice(s) behind its theory/theories, consciously or unconsciously forgetting the inseparability of theory and practice. Inevitably, the circle closes in the constant self-assertion, and re-establishment, of the metaphysics of presence.

Ironically, as I suggested earlier, Derrida has been attacked for providing the deconstructors with a methodology of 'play'. The accusation is based on an inadequate, false reading of Derrida, a bandwagon jumped on most recently and, in my view, risibly, by Mario Vargas Llosa, improbable spokesman for the 'patrimony of everyman':

> As for Jacques Derrida, every time I have tried to face his obscurantist prose and his asphyxiating literary analyses, I have had a feeling I was wasting my time . . . . Responsibility and intelligibility go hand in hand with a certain conception of what literary criticism is about, with the conviction that the scope of literature extends to all human experience, because it reflects that experience and contributes decisively to the shaping of it. It ought to be everyman's patrimony, an activity fed by the common resources of the species, to which we can turn in search of order when we seem to be sinking in chaos.
>
> (Vargas Llosa 1994, 8)

The political history of Latin America is littered with nostra 'to which we can turn in search of order when we seem to be sinking in chaos'. But why should Derrida be so threatening? Derrida's notion of *différance* (with an *a*), I shall argue, is structuralist *différence* (with an *e*) *at work.* What is at issue, in the politicizing of structuralist practice, in the era of 'post-', is precisely a matter of strategy and risk. It is not enough merely to identify trace and supplement; it is necessary to make them *work* against institutionality. In short, deconstruction ought to be symptomized not by method but by practice, not by a binary plenitude of difference and substitution but by a dynamic play of differences – a dialectics. As such it cannot easily be consigned to the past in favour of a critical methodology which opts for a socio-historical grounding in some less slippery medium of cultural analysis. For it inhabits the very dialectical intention of every such methodology.

For many critics of Latin American literature and culture, even those who have taken the trouble to tackle the difficulties of both imported and local models of post-structuralist criticism, old binaries prove irresistible. Deconstructive practice, in such cases, is but a moment, a passing ripple on the deep pool of subjectivity which, when the surface settles, reflects again a familiar yearning for truth, a knowable subject and an undifferentiated ethical code of moral values – for 'everyman'. For such critics, on the one hand properly suspicious of master discourses (where the sign, however polyvalent, ultimately points to, say, a concrete, economic reality), on the other hand too easily fall victim to post-modernist 'micro' discourses *à la* Baudrillard where it is 'symbolic' value that, primarily, derives from the sign. Paradoxically, in the context of a post-modern mass culture, a 'pursuit of signs' for its own sake, aspiring beyond referentiality, re-enacts that aesthetic of Symbolism embodied in Mallarmé's 'le vide papier que la blancheur défend'. Rather apocalyptically (frenetically, at least), an ineffable, uninscribable 'blankness' of totalizing symbol is embraced. Consciously or not, the theological enterprise – albeit thoroughly post-Nietzschean inasmuch as unanchored in a specific God – none the less survives as a rhythm, a trajectory, a pulse of transcendentalism. Such a version of permanently deconstructive sign-play is a misapplication of Derrida, a blunting – through over-use – of the radical edge, a deification even more damaging than the reification performed by those who see deconstruction as latter-day formalism.

Anglo-Saxon – and, specifically, Rortian – caution regarding 'going transcendental' *is* a healthy reaction to the irrelevantly, the unradically theoretical. Yet, too often, that caution is passed off as 'natural' or 'common sense' empiricism. Anglo-Saxon (and Vargas Llosan) criticism might do better to indulge in a *dialectical* model of meaning, as proposed, more optimistically than in the case of Roberto Schwarz, by William Ray, though, as Ray himself points out, it would be an exercise in self-contradiction to argue the permanent truth of such a model. Ray does warn that 'analytic discourse is as self-differing, its truths as slippery as any literary work' – and, concomitantly, commitment (or resignation) to such a model of criticism will inevitably threaten both camps, the historicists and the out-and-out theorists. A radical *use* of post-structuralist insight, however, might characterize the 'conflict' between them as both necessary and irresolvable: 'functioning as a purge, dialectical practice uses the logic of each system of (coercive) authority to demonstrate that system's shortcomings'. When Ray goes on to comfort 'those who fear the revolution (because) they have already missed it', he is suggesting no more than that, as critics, we are *all* post-structuralists, implicated, consciously or not, willingly or not, in that dialectical process which defines critical practice as always 'historical' but never 'history' itself (Ray 1984, 206). In short, textuality *is* the constant and radical dialectical play of the difference(s) between text and context. Criticism is but the constant tracing and supplementing (or another version) of that textuality.

I shall end this Fore-word, however, not on such an abstraction but, rather, with a proposal for the kind of readings of Latin American literatures in the wake of post-structuralism and postmodernism which, perhaps, has not (yet) been the most prevalent. The Argentine sociologist Francisco Delich has recently proposed a fascinating mode of reconceptualizing binarist habits in his provocatively titled 'The Cemetery of Theory', in an as yet unpublished paper from 'Redirections: Cultures, Media, Theory', a colloquium held in Córdoba, Argentina, in 1992. With specific reference to Latin America and, in particular, to Paraguay, he comments on the feasibility of regarding the relation of the individual or group to the *state* and to *society* other than through the Hegelian dialectic of *public* versus *private* (as if in an extension of another questionable but traditional division: namely, that of body and soul). He reminds us that the notion of 'public' space begins, in the Old Testament, with David. In the Jews' encounter with God, no difference existed between public and private; the only conceptual distinction to be made was that of sacred and profane. When, however, David is questioned by the 'public', it is for personal reasons (over the death of Uriah, the husband of Bathsheba: II Samuel 12). Delich argues that, in one case at least, the emergence of the 'public good' is clearly marked, though God continues to be the guarantor of that good. Now, in the case of the Guarani, he further reminds us, proselytization was accepted with equanimity, *except* for the idea of an all-seeing God – the unacceptable implication of which is the abolition of privacy. In both cases, parabolically, there is a tension between competing public and private interests; in both cases, focus is shifted to the *particular* interest of an individual or group, each defined by the interaction, or complementarity, of the polarities.

The threat of an all-seeing God as, no less, that of more recent missionaries, has hardly receded in the particular social contexts of modern Latin America. At the time of writing, in 1996, 'the text in which I think I am' has been subjected to many revisions, many re-writings, some less superficial than the *boutade* interventions of such posturing but still too influential literary demagogues as Vargas Llosa. A recent attachment to the Centro Interdisciplinar de Estudos Contemporâneos in Rio de Janeiro afforded me the chance to witness a range of projects focused on urban minorities, each notable for the rigorous attention given to the interaction of groups, and of individuals, with larger-scale political movements. If I had some sense of a panopticon at work, it came from an all-too-familiar source, not from a specific institution but from the encroaching *effects* of a recent paradigm shift being imported from the United States. The prevailing vogue for cultural studies emerged as a strategy of conversion whereby Latin American*ists* preached to Latin Americans on the virtues of establishing a North–South dialogue with the 'Cultural Studies of the Americas' as an object of investigation.

Proselytization and fundamentalism often go hand in hand – in this case, with requests for direct access to the father. As a visiting UK academic, did I think that the ideas of Richard Hoggart still had valency and relevance for Latin American social relations today? And was the work of Stuart Hall a transferable model? This sensible concern for a back-to-basics grasp of 'cultural studies' as a historically contextualizable political and intellectual movement arose from circumspection as to blanket *usages* of the term recently filtered southwards. 'New Historicism', 'hybridity', 'cultural studies' were buzz-words that echoed through the conference rooms of the universities at the very moment that, outside, in the streets of the cities and of the small towns, the public-address systems blared the message of the *Igreja Universal do Reino de Deus*. A much-discussed practical academic project was the setting-up of an electronic network, a cyber-space, no doubt, for locating inequalities. I learned, too, that the net (of the works) of 'Bishop' Edir Macedo was being cast as far as Brixton, in south London. More than two thousand 'temples' (sometimes converted cinemas of a pre-1950s' popular culture) established world-wide since the founding of the Church in 1978; a *Rede Record* to combat *Rede Globo*; an obligatory percentage levy of adherents' earnings. An apt and obvious candidate for the cultural study of its signifying practices, its discursive processes and its media constructions. I returned to the United Kingdom just in time to catch (*Desert Island Discs*) the horror of Hoggart and (*Start the Week*) the hesitation of Hall regarding current (mis-)appropriations of the term 'Cultural Studies'. Academics belching undigested theories of the last thirty years had taken over; the emphasis was ever more on the signifying and ever less on the practice.

Amidst the blare of public and private address-systems, however, the particular quality of many projects on Latin America could be heard. The Rio-based CIEC and an equivalent enterprise at the São Paulo Fundação Memorial da América Latina were ones I witnessed at first hand. A notable record of reciprocal ventures, since 1984, with Argentina, Uruguay, Brazil, Chile and Paraguay, organized by the Latin American Studies Center of the University of Maryland, now includes the ambitious 'Una Cultura para la Democracia' project. In the United Kingdom, at the University of London, King's College, a strong research and publishing focus has been developed at the Centre for Latin American Cultural Studies. Since 1992, the Nottingham Post-graduate School of Critical Theory has participated in an 'Intercultural Transfer' project with the National University of Córdoba, Argentina, and the Federal University of Minas Gerais, Brazil, amongst others, bringing together in joint research and publishing activities, historians, sociologists, economists, psychoanalysts, philosophers and literary critics.

I have chosen to reflect on the difference between the mere label 'cultural studies' and the painstaking intellectual commitment implied by the effective analysis of particular cultures, because of the danger of seeing the practice of critical theory as being inimical to the pursuit of political and historical questions. Locating inequalities will always be of a greater urgency than the analysis of texts, be they literary, cinematic or cultural. But what cultural studies are not also critical studies? Principally, I suggest, those that opt for messages which, however loudly blared, cannot be allowed to conceal the ideological *and* the theoretical infrastructure that they exploit. As for critical theory, at least in the various forms of it practised in this book, it will operate ever inseparably from the discursiveness of cultural expression. I await the counters of those who would, and will, contest my argument that we are all post-structuralists.

In the mode of contemporary theoretical meditation, it is to another Judaic speculation that I now turn: namely, to the thinking of Emmanuel Levinas, and to the possibility of a discourse which counters the restricting dualism of material versus transcendental. In a reversal of that trajectory which I have outlined as a shift from public and private towards the particular, Levinas ponders the construction of Self in Other/Other in Self as an identity which *begins* with the 'particular'. In 'Phenomenology of Eros', he writes:

> The not-yet-being is precisely not a possible that would only be more remote than other possibles. The caress does not *act*, does not grasp possibles. The secret it forces does not inform it as an experience; it overwhelms the relation of the I with itself and with the non-I. *An amorphous future where it escapes itself and loses its position as a subject.*
>
> (Levinas 1969, 259; my italics)

In such a discourse, the public/private, body/soul, national/foreign, material/transcendental categories – undermined, in turn, by de Campos, Vieira, Delich, and so on – cannot effectively operate. For the Brazilian critic and novelist Silviano Santiago, Latin American literature occupies a particular space of *in-betweenness* (*entre-lugar*) which, in his overtly Derrida-derived proposal, invites the reader to study the cultures of the continent in a *hic et nunc* perspective which defies the rigidity of any fixed critical position. Santiago's evocation of Latin America as a writing-space which is but seemingly empty is, there can be no doubt, not only a direct reference to Machereyan symptomatic gaps but also a corollary to the Foucault-derived arguments of

Ángel Rama to which I return in the final chapter. Equally, his exploitation of the terms 'temple' and 'site of clandestinity' are reminders of the *violent hierarchies* which – as perhaps the first importer of the work of Derrida into Brazil (especially in *Glossário de Derrida* of 1976) – Santiago seeks to remind us, operate not just in literature. For such hierarchies derive from, even depend on, dominant presences and the politics of dominance – institutions of very variable clandestinity: in short, a post-colonial complexity of Latin American, and specifically, Brazilian social constructs and ideologies. I would situate Santiago's writing, in this context, as one of the epigraphs to this chapter might suggest, and, returning to my point of departure, against that preponderance of readings of Derrida which has focused on the (Graeco-Roman) Heideggerian to the (wilful?) exclusion of the (Judaic) Levinasian. In the terms of this discussion, the *particularity* of Levinas' construction of Self in Other/Other in Self not only echoes a Spinozerian 'becoming' of heterodox mysticism but also reminds us of the closeness of Levinas' writing, at times, both to the particularity of much *écriture féminine* and to Derrida's *Spurs*. The interlocking facets of many post-structuralist and post-modern discourses, of supposed disparity but, on investigation, of mutually enriching – and unsettling – dynamics, I would suggest, compose a mosaic. Subjected to reading, re-reading, citation and translation, these discourses might be transformed into a different conceptual pattern, one of ever-shifting lines, a constant re-enactment of Proustian *tremblement de contours*. Thus, to take but another French blur, it may have become commonplace to read Kristeva in Derrida, Derrida in Irigaray, and Irigaray in Levinas. What is less frequently observed, in this shuttle effect of *inter*- and *intra*-textualities, is the threads and patterns woven by such Latin American critical theorists as Santiago, de Campos, Schwarz and, above all, Ángel Rama. Rama's metaphor of 'weavers in the grand historical workshop of Latin American society' has recently been re-appropriated by Adriana Pagano as follows: 'the envisaged goal is to map the diversities articulated into a global network, to write the literary history of the sub-continent while posing questions of its own chronology and periodization, to re-enact differently the colonial Utopian project not of discovering but of *writing* Latin America' (Pagano, in press).

How, then, is the encounter with the other to be represented? The trace of Mauss which emerges from the following might have been written by any (or all) of these scriptors, be they Latin American or other(wise). In fact, the intervention, the particular tremble (not to say *frisson*), is Luce Irigaray's: 'The gift has no goal. No for. And no object. The gift – is given. Before any division into donor and recipient. Before any separate identities of giver and receiver. Even before the gift' (Irigaray 1992, 73). Just as I have made the claim for overlapping (or, to re-use a by now familiar Brazilian metaphor, mutually feeding) critical discourses, I would argue, too, that the Levinasian focus I have chosen is but one mode whereby cultures and societies might be theorized differently. Rather than the utopian horizontal of materialism, or the religious verticality of transcendentalism, a *trans-jectory* of movement both *across* frontiers and through the *up*lift of self in other, other in self, becomes operative. Through such *trans*lation the writing self is to be located in writing others – multi-epigraphically, mosaically . . .

Derrida has insisted in recent years that deconstruction is a political rather than a textual operation – that it is by touching solid structures, 'material' institutions, and not merely discourses or significant representations, that deconstruction distinguishes itself from analysis or 'criticism'.

Terry Eagleton

The *dream of an order* served to perpetuate power and to conserve the socio-economic and cultural structure which that power guaranteed. And, further, it was imposed on whichever discourse opposed that power, obliging it to pass first through the *dream of another order*.

Ángel Rama

Play is the disruption of presence. . . . Play is always play of absence and presence, but if it is to be thought radically, play must be conceived of before the alternative of presence and absence. Being must be conceived as presence or absence on the basis of play and not the other way round.

Jacques Derrida

Between sacrifice and play, between prison and transgression, between submission to the code and aggression, between obedience and rebellion, between assimilation and expression – there, in that seemingly empty space, its temple and its site of clandestinity, there, the anthropophagous ritual of Latin American literature is performed.

Silviano Santiago

I called to him several times. And I said what I was so eager to say, to state formally and under oath. I said it as loud as I could: 'Father, you have been out there long enough. You are old ... Come back, you don't have to do it any more ... Come back and I'll go instead. Right now, if you want. Any time. I'll get into the boat. I'll take your place.' And when I had said this my heart beat more firmly. He heard me. He stood up. He manoeuvred with his oars and headed the boat toward me. He had accepted my offer. And suddenly I trembled, down deep. For he had raised his arm and waved – the first time in so many, so many years. And I couldn't ... In terror, my hair on end, I ran, I fled madly. For he seemed to come from another world. And I'm begging forgiveness, begging, begging.

João Guimarães Rosa

A 'war of position' is where you advance on a number of different positions at once. . . . The real break comes not from inverting the model but from breaking free of its limiting terms, changing the frame.

Stuart Hall

Nothing is further from *Eros* than possession.

Emmanuel Levinas

POST SCRIPTUM?

Lest the mosaic appear too Mosaic, I might both echo and extend Susan Handelman's lapidary (or tiled?) statement and say: *It is not only* 'the Jew [who] will not abandon Scripture for Logos' (Handelman 1987, 106). She goes on to cite Derrida on Levinas: 'Are we Jews? Are we Greeks? We live in the difference between the Jew and the Greek, which is perhaps the unity which is called history. We live in and of difference, that is, in hypocrisy' (ibid., 153). An alternative (Greek?) metaphor for the problematic of locating multi-cultures emerged strongly in the sixteenth century – a response, no doubt, in part, to the proliferating encounters with 'new' worlds: *isolario.* The 'island books' of Renaissance cartographers textualized the world as an infinite series of floating units of singular force – but, also, of pulling power, of influence, on each other. In the mosaic, or the islands, of my epigraphs, Jews meet (Graeco-Roman?) Celt, Uruguayan, Brazilian, Jamaican. If the chapters which follow seem to offer but alternative readings, my own fragmented textualities, it may be as a result of the wish to avoid, in my engagement with locating inequali*ties,* the *isola*tions of labelling practice. Whether, at moments, I shall have inhabited translation, criticism, psychoanalysis, literature or a range of theories, it ought not to have been to leave, successively, one insulated praxis for another; to have missed the structure of the floating islands which constitutes, without unifying, the cartography. Most important of all, I ought to have remembered that the cartography is the discourse, that Latin America, the world, is not like that, is not that representation: 'And what is the legitimacy, what is the meaning of the *copula* in this proposition . . . : "Jewgreek is Greekjew. Extremes meet"?', continues Derrida (1976, 153). I might ask, in turn, with Guimarães Rosa, *'Can* I take your place?' Literature highlights the differences that cultural studies explore.

WORKS CITED

Campos, Haroldo de. 'Europe under the Sign of Devoration', *Latin American Literary Review*, 25 (Jan.–June 1986), 42–60.

Derrida, Jacques. *Of Grammatology*, trans. G. Spivak. Baltimore, Md: Johns Hopkins University Press, 1976.

Handelman, Susan. 'Jacques Derrida and the Heretic Hermeneutic', in *Displacements: Derrida and After*, ed. Mark Krupnick. Bloomington: Indiana University Press, 1987.

Irigaray, Luce. *Elemental Passions*, trans. Joanne Collie and Judith Still. London: Athlone Press, 1992.

Jameson, Fredric. *The Prison House of Language*. Princeton, NJ: Princeton University Press, 1972.

Jenkins, Timothy, in McGuirk, Bernard. 'On the Trajectory of Gnosis: St. John of the Cross, Reverdy, Derrida, Levinas', in *Pierre Reverdy 1889–1989*, ed. Bernard McGuirk (*Nottingham French Studies*, 28, 2, (1989)).

Levinas, Emmanuel. *Totality and Infinity*, trans. A. Lingis. Pittsburgh: Duquesne University Press, 1969.

Lodge, David. *Small World*, London: Secker and Warburg, 1984.

Pagano, Adriana. 'Literary Theory in Latin America', in *The Encyclopaedia of Latin American Literature*. London: Fitzroy Dearborn (in press).

Pratt, Mary Louise. 'Linguistic Utopias', in *The Linguistics of Writing*, ed. Nigel Fabb *et al*. Manchester: Manchester University Press, 1987 (pp. 48–66).

Rama, Ángel. *La ciudad letrada*. Hanover: Ediciones del Norte, 1984.

Ray, William. *Literary Meaning*. Oxford: Blackwell, 1984.

Santiago, Silviano. 'O entre-lugar do discurso latino-americano', in *Uma literatura nos trópicos*. São Paulo: Perspectiva, 1978 (pp. 11–28).

Schwarz, Roberto. *Misplaced Ideas: Essays on Brazilian Culture*, trans. and ed. John Gledson. London and New York: Verso, 1992.

Vargas Llosa, Mario. 'Staring into the Abyss', *Sunday Times*, 8–9, 24 April 1994.

Vieira, Else Ribeiro Pires. 'Towards a Minor Translation', in *Inequality and Difference in Hispanic and Latin American Cultures*, ed. Bernard McGuirk and Mark I. Millington. Lewiston, Queenston and Lampeter: Edwin Mellen Press, 1995 (pp. 141–52).

Wright, Elizabeth. *Psychoanalytical Criticism: Theory in Practice*. London: Methuen, 1984.

Chapter 1

Pre-

Sewing up meaning: a liberal humanist closure of Pablo Neruda's 'Oh vastness of pines'

The devil dances in an empty pocket

There will always have been a pre-. A metaphysics of presence will not tolerate the blank space. Thus, while the fifteenth-century adage of the devil's dancing in an empty pocket might be said to invert a traditional ethic's insertion of God into the void, it is none the less a tell-tale (tail?) pointer to that construction of originary male presence which underlies all Western discourse. We might well have been reminded, as recently as 1983, that: 'Western philosophy . . . has yearned for the sign which will give meaning to all others – "the transcendental signifier". . . . A great number of candidates for this role – God, the Idea, the World Spirit, the Self, substance, matter and so on – have thrust themselves forward from time to time' (Eagleton 1983, 131). How, though, has such a metaphysics operated in lyric poetry? When a poet writes, when a reader reads, what devilish constructions are thrust into textuality?

In seeking to illustrate the manner in which literary-metaphysical constructions have tended to perform to a predominantly male beat or rhythm, an oft-aired debate of the last two decades, I have opted for a recent and particularly perceptive analysis of the issue by Susan Winnett. In her 1990 essay 'Coming Unstrung: Women, Men, Narrative and Principles of Pleasure', Winnett outlines a model for narrative fiction which is, however, pertinent to lyric poetry. She opens in strikingly subversive fashion:

> I would like to begin with the proposition that female orgasm is unnecessary . . . . Women's pleasure can take place outside or independent of, the male sexual economy whose pulsations

determine the dominant culture, its repressions, its taboos, and its narratives, as well as the 'human sciences' developed to explain them.

(Winnett 1990, 505)

Winnett's enquiry into the explanatory paradigms, though not specifically pitched at the functioning of the erotic in the lyric, raises 'the issue of the difference between women's and men's reading pleasures' (ibid., 505). For my purposes, before showing in Chapter 11 how Susana Thénon's poetry 'works on the difference' (Cixous 1977, 480), it is necessary to exemplify, by recourse to a canonical male love-poem, the projection of a given sexual economy into a totalizing structure, a universalizing world-view. Of the many available examples, I have chosen a Chilean text, and a particularly well-known case, poem III of Pablo Neruda's *Veinte poemas de amor y una canción desesperada / Twenty Love Poems and a Song of Despair*, first published in 1924. This choice might lay me open to the charge of making Neruda the most obvious of easy targets, primarily because any reading might detect in his early work a strong masculist bias, as most critics have been ready to observe; and, in this respect, I would agree with Christopher Perriam and Paul Julian Smith regarding the self-subverting nature of Neruda's flagrant *machismo*. The case I shall argue, however, is that such a poem as 'Ah vastedad de pinos ...' is a particularly successful lyrical construct, which may be seen to operate as a sophisticated elaboration not merely 'undone' by but performing a strong role within the libidinal economy I wish to highlight.

Before reading the poem, however, it is worth taking into account the prime caveat of Susan Winnett:

We all know what male orgasm looks like. It is preceded by a visible 'awakening', an arousal, the birth of an appetency, ambition, desire or intention. The male organ registers the intensity of this stimulation, rising to the occasion of its provocation, becoming at once the means of pleasure and culture's sign of power. This energy, 'aroused into expectancy', takes its course toward 'significant discharge' and shrinks into a state of quiescence (or satisfaction) that, minutes before, would have been a sign of impotence. The man must have this genital response before he can participate, which means that something in the time before intercourse must have aroused him. And his participation generally ceases with the ejaculation that signals the end of his arousal. The myth of the afterglow – so often a euphemism for sleep – seems a compensation for the finality he has reached. . . . A refresher course in the fundamentals of structuralism should suffice to remind us that the 'erotic in human nature' has to be understood within its various determining contexts if the concept is to be productive (what is 'the erotic'? how do we define the 'human nature' in which we locate 'the erotic'? is 'human nature' a cultural ['human'] or a biological ['nature'] construct?). And even if we have become wary of the generic 'man in society', we still might need to be reminded that such generalizations in such contexts indicate that the pleasure the reader is expected to take in the text is the pleasure of the man.

(Winnett 1990, 506)

I shall now test, with reference to the Neruda poem, the applicability of both Winnett's description of tumescence/ detumescence, and her warning regarding the generalization of reading the erotic. Put differently, what might a 'man in society', indeed, a liberal-humanist reading look like?

III

Ah vastedad de pinos, rumor de olas quebrándose,
lento juego de luces, campana solitaria,
crepúsculo cayendo en tus ojos, muñeca,
caracola terrestre, en ti la tierra canta!

En ti los ríos cantan y mi alma en ellos huye
como tú lo desees y hacia donde tú quieras.
Márcame mi camino en tu arco de esperanza
y soltaré en delirio mi bandada de flechas.

En torno a mí estoy viendo tu cintura de niebla
y tu silencio acosa mis horas perseguidas,
y eres tú con tus brazos de piedra transparente
donde mis besos anclan y mi húmeda ansia anida.

Ah tu voz misteriosa que el amor tiñe y dobla
en el atardecer resonante y muriendo!
Así en horas profundas sobre los campos he visto
doblarse las espigas en la boca del viento.

(Neruda 1967, 88)

[Oh vastness of pines, sound of waves breaking,/slow play of light, solitary bell,/twilight falling in your eyes, darling,/ terrestrial conch-shell, in you the earth sings!/In you the rivers sing and my soul flees in them/as you desire and wherever you wish./Mark out my path on your bow of hope/and I shall loose in delirium my flight of arrows./About me I am seeing your waist of mist/and your silence hounds my persecuted hours,/and you are with your arms of stone transparent/ where my kisses anchor and my humid anxiety nestles./Oh your mysterious voice which love tints and bends/in the evening resonant and dying!/Thus in profound hours over the fields I have seen/the ears of grain sway in the face of the wind.]

The poem opens, in philosophical parlance, with 'perceptions of the external world', the generalized sweep of a horizon (in no sense recognizably Chilean), but one which is organized according to the prosodic dictates of the chosen verse form. An interlocking construction, hemistich by hemistich, consisting of sight and sound semantic divisions, is established in the first line as the fulcrum of the poem's balance, a pattern which is to be maintained throughout. The invasion of an as yet unspecified (and as yet ungendered) consciousness, by waves visual and auditory, triggers an internalizing of the initial perception. The illusion that swaying immensity and pent-up sighs derive from Nature projects erotic rhythms as simply 'occurring', a context-less, culture-free, spontaneous phenomenon. The specific sight and sound effects of line 2 are slowed down and individualized ('solitaria'); (fore-)play of light, peal of striking clapper within orifice of bell.

In line 3, the play of outer/inner is maintained in the shift from 'crepúsculo' to 'ojos', an ingenious trope of shifting focalization not into the eyes of the beholder but, rather, into the eyes of the beloved ('muñeca' operates as a term of affection equivalent to 'frívola', 'presumida', 'linda'). The device is, of course, traditional – 'your eyes are my eyes'. Here, however, the proximity of near eye-to-eye contact enables the lover to see the reflection of the outer world in the mirror of the woman's pupils. And proximity of vision rapidly gives way to proximity of sound. 'Caracola terrestre' of line 4 operates on at least three levels. First, the holding of sea-shell to ear; second, the Gongorine but also *modernista* oxymoron of marine life on land; third, the stylistic evasion of the taboo word 'concha'/'cunt' in the euphemism 'caracola'/'conch'. In combination, these devices convey not just contrastive outer/inner repetitions, but the interpenetration of bodies in which the sounds of the earth sing out in throbbing pulsation.

A shift from solid ('tierra'), to liquid ('ríos') in line 5, marks a semantic flow (erotics) in tune with the poem's rhythmic flow (poetics). For the second quatrain, far from having the eight pauses of the first, has only two. Punctuation cannot now be allowed to interrupt the breathlessness of approaching climax, the shift of control from 'mi alma' to the purported desire and will of a previously notably passive 'tú'. Thus, the metaphor of lines 7–8 operates ambivalently. In male terms, the huntsman's firing at his quarry the delirious arrows of Cupid's bow is reversible if 'arco de esperanza' is read as the open arch of expectation of a receptive female principle in coital aperture. Thus, expulsion/reception may *seem* to be in equilibrium, though the active verb 'soltar' and the imperative 'márcame' are male-delivered, by contrast with the two subjunctives a line earlier attributed to the 'muñeca', a doll-like figure, passive indeed under the weight of both prosodic and semantic effusion.

The third quatrain opens on a hesitant rhythm, the prosaic fall of 'en torno a mí' giving way to a protracted present continuous tense in 'estoy viendo'. Momentum has been lost, and vision is blurred. For it is not 'tu cintura' which is misty – rather, the perception of it, because the eyes of the beholder are either misted with emotion or merely glazed in trance. Whichever, an archetypal, male, *post-coitum triste* transfers and redistributes senses both emotional and corporal within the hitherto consistent left/right–visual/auditory patterning of the text. 'Tu silencio' comes to inhabit the site of previously subjective visuality in the first hemistich; in its place on the right there is no longer a perception of sound but, rather, an awareness of hounding in 'perseguidas'. This change of mood has, additionally, been prepared by the word 'acosa', an unmistakable accusation of relentless pursuit which, far from echoing the huntsman's enthusiastic chase, conveys a note of bothersome pestering. Thus, the previous order has been invaded by an extraneous, unwelcome intrusion into the sight-and-sound controlling mechanisms of male perception. And the key to this development is the first appearance, explicitly, of time ('horas'). Now, a strong awareness of otherness is manifest in 'y eres tú', dexterously separated from the claim of transparency by the delay of the epithet to the end of the line and the juxtaposition of 'brazos de piedra' and 'transparente', an illusory oxymoron. The play of solidity and insubstantiality emerges as having been falsely projected towards the female principle; in fact, it derives from the sudden sense of insecurity of a male persona involved in a double search for haven and protection. The images of line 12 re-introduce the land/sea–dry/wet transitions of the poem's opening phase; for the points of contact with the woman's body are, first, lingering, anchoring kisses, and second, moist interiority of a still nestling 'ansia' ('anxiety' but also 'desire'). The tense mood of breathless vulnerability is reinforced by a maintained punctuation pattern which at once reproduces the uninterrupted flow of the previous quatrain but, this time, in a carefully constructed set of elisions in 'a' ('mi húmeda ansia anida'), contrastively drags out prosodically the burdensome temporal consciousness operating at the semantic level.

In the final quatrain, 'tu voz' replaces 'tu silencio'. Again, an auditory version of alterity occupies the site of previously visual subjective perception; again, the shift is complemented by an emotive reaction which attributes mystery, or unattainability, or impenetrability, to the other. An ingenious image-cluster is employed now, in the final sequence of the poem, as effectively as was the 'caracola terrestre' conceit of the opening quatrain. For 'que el amor tiñe y dobla' exploits visuality ('teñir'/'to change the hue of, to tint') and auditivity ('doblar'/'to ring out'). Furthermore, 'tiñe y dobla' resembles but departs from the set phrase 'tañe y dobla', the ringing and pealing of bells; 'dobla' also means 'doubles up', 'is repeated' (a harbinger of the meaning to be exploited in the final line). Thus, love, 'el amor', is attributed with the power of multiply altering and confusing perception though, already, a synaesthetic technique has been preparing, too, for the re-working of the poem's opening. The lone voice, amidst the fusion of colour and sound, parallels the solitary bell set against the slow play of light of line 2. As 'atardecer' harks back to 'crepúsculo', as 'resonante' picks up the echoing 'campana', a suggestive possibility is prompted. In the time it has taken for the bell's peal to ring out and fade away, the prelude to, the climax of, and the reaction after coitus have all been textualized; or, stated in

reverse, the poem has been sexualized. Whichever version is preferred, the apostrophized end-word to the process is 'muriendo!'
– a classic transition from Eros to Thanatos, physical escape,
in sex, from temporal preoccupation; metaphysical escape, in
poetry, from mortality.

The final couplet of the text shifts the focus from present to
past via the generalizing adverb 'así'; specific action is superseded by the absorption of its significance, though the perception
is still borne on the vehicle of male visuality in 'he visto'.
Justification of the notion that meditation on time is in itself
profound ('en horas profundas') depends on the most traditional
of tropes, the return to Nature. Organically, this process depends
on the cyclical evocation of the wind's bending the crops, a
natural counterpart to culture's scythe in the passage of the
seasons. Psycho-sexually, the rise and fall of the 'espigas', or ears
of grain, evokes the equivalent performance of the male member,
the more so here since a second meaning of 'espiga' is the clapper
of a bell, further echoed in the transference of 'boca' from
'campana' to 'viento'. In short, the poem turns full circle in the
technical return to a broad sweep of perceptions of the external
world, restoring a general, universal horizon of spatio-temporal
reference after the personalized experience contained in the 'eye'
of the poem. Yet the question which arises in the shift of *topoi*
from the erotic to *tempus fugit* is precisely 'Whose eye?'.

At this point, returning to a generic 'man in society' and mis-
chievously re-phrasing Susan Winnett, we might in retrospect
proclaim that, having read a successful example of male love-
poetry, 'We would like to *end* with the proposition that male
orgasm is *necessary*.' Notwithstanding the complexity of poetic
tropes and devices, the relationship between focalizer and the
external reality of Nature may be described not only as pathetic
fallacy but also, demonstrably, as aesthetic 'phallus-ery'. Why
should this be so and what are the implications of such a reading
for alternative discourses of love?

The question 'Why?' relates partly to the poet's use of 'Nature's
vast frame' (Shelley) as an analogue of mind which has come to be
known as 'organicism'. M. H. Abrams long ago pointed out that
such organicism derives from a theological model. God creates
and expresses his 'mind' in and through nature: similarly, the
poet creates and expresses *his* mind in and through the poem,
fostering 'the doctrine that a poem is a disguised self-revelation,

in which its creator, "visibly invisible", at the same time expresses and conceals himself' (Abrams 1953, 65–6). In the instance of the Neruda poem, however, self-expression would appear to apply rather more than self-concealment. For what is more obviously concealed is woman, not only as textual 'object' but, Winnett would argue, as reading subject:

> the issue of women's reading pleasure has not attracted the attention it should: for the male critic, the sexual pleasure of reading would seem to take place within a nexus of homo-social arrangements in which 'the marriage of true minds' is an affair 'between men', as Eve Sedgwick has put it. In this system, woman is neither an independent subjectivity nor a desiring agent but, rather, an enabling position organizing the social fiction of heterosexuality . . . . And this realization does nothing but make it all the more frightening to contemplate the obstacles our own education has placed in the way both of women's conceiving (of) their own pleasure and of men's conceding that female pleasure might have a different plot.
>
> For if we do now pursue the analogy between the representability of the sex act and a possible erotics of reading, we find a woman's encounter with the text determined by a broad range of options for pleasure that have *nothing to do* (or can choose to have nothing to do) with [these] notions of representability.
>
> (Winnett 1990, 507; her italics)

In the context of this book, I am perhaps less concerned with the plurality of notions of representability, by now a post-structuralist cliché, than with the pedagogical resonance of encounters with (Latin American) literature involving 'a broad range of options for pleasure'. The very word *pleasure*, when broached in the context of the function of criticism, has too often triggered polemics locked into a Nietzsche-versus-Marx binarism which, it seems, is still strongly operative in the discipline called Hispanic Studies. Impassioned attacks on the work of Paul Julian Smith and Mark Millington, Hispanists who have opted for the pleasure but also for the relevance of applying insights of *la nouvelle critique* in their own practices, have recently been made by Malcolm Read, basically on the grounds of class analyses, and through selective misapplication of the Marxist critiques of such as Terry Eagleton (Read 1993, 257–75; 1995,

91–100). The rub, however, is that, in the same essay on Perry Anderson from which I took an epigraph for my 'Fore-word: locating inequality', Eagleton also asserted:

If dialogue between Marxism and post-structuralism is difficult, then it is in part because of a difference in historical timescale – because they do not quite inhabit the same epochal dimension. Perhaps one can best formulate this by suggesting that it is not so much that Marxism cannot accept much of what post-structuralism has to tell it, but that it cannot accept it yet.

(Eagleton 1985, 8)

It is in that *entre-lugar*, that *entre-tiempo*, that the chapters which follow have been written – between *pre-* and *post-*, and before I take up the question of 'a woman's reading pleasure' (in the script of the Argentine Susana Thénon) – exploring modes of deferral whereby Latin American literature will be shown to resist reductivist binarisms and polarities (in a post-script *sine qua non*).

WORKS CITED

Abrams, M. H. *The Mirror and the Lamp*. New York: Oxford University Press, 1953.
Cixous, Hélène. 'Entretien avec Françoise van Rossum-Guyon', *Revue des sciences humaines*, 168 (1977), 479–93.
Eagleton, Terry. *Literary Theory: An Introduction*. Oxford: Blackwell, 1983.
—— 'Marxism, Structuralism, and Post-structuralism', *Diacritics* (Winter, 1985), 2–12.
Neruda, Pablo. *Veinte poemas de amor y una canción desesperada*, in *Obras completas*. Buenos Aires: Losada, 1967 (pp. 85–106).
Perriam, Christopher. 'Metaphorical *Machismo*: Neruda's Love Poetry'. *Forum for Modern Language Studies*, 24 (1988), 58–77.
Read, Malcolm. 'Classing Race and Gender: Readings of "The Male (Capitalist) Order"'. *Siglo XX/20th Century*, 11.1–2 (1993), 257–75.
—— 'On Location', *Siglo XX/20th Century*. 13.1 (1995), 91–100.
Smith, Paul Julian. *The Body Hispanic: Gender and Sexuality in Spanish and Spanish American Literature*. Oxford and New York: Oxford University Press, 1989.
Winnett, Susan. 'Coming Unstrung: Women, Men, Narrative and Principles of Pleasure', *Publications of the Modern Language Association of America*, 105.3 (1990), 505–18.

Chapter 2

Eurocentrism and the male gaze in Brazil
Other place, other plays: the ploy of alterity in Blaise Cendrars' *South Americans*

If gender was the principal issue at stake in the previous chapter, it will be raised again now in a context of marked cultural and racial difference. For the moment, I choose to continue to analyse the problems posed in the context of lyric poetry. At about the same time as Neruda was to displace his Chilean perspective to Burma and, subsequently, to Spain, so a Swiss-French eye was gleaning, and re-projecting, its very influential if peculiar vision of Brazil.

At play is Eurocentrism and, specifically, the construction of 'otherness' in a little-known poem-sequence of Blaise Cendrars. Reading between the lines, I shall address a sub-text to be taken less literally than laterally; or Latin Americanly, for it will soon become clear that the name of the game in Cendrars' *Sud-Américaines* is the play of marginality.

We are confronted here with two forms of displacement. The one, from the 'centre' to the West, the literal journey to 'Utopialand' (Cendrars' own word for Brazil) made first in 1924, from Paris to São Paulo, and then subsequently in 1926, 1927, 1928 and 1929, later in 1934, 1935, and finally in 1953. The second displacement occurs in the non-literal and non-essential sense of a post-structuralist alternative to Hegelian *Aufhebung*, or the reconciliation of differences:

A great deal is at stake in the newly important (dis-)place of displacement. In Derrida's writing, displacement almost always figures as an alternative to Hegelian *Aufhebung*, the sublation by means of which contradictions are transcended. Under the new (post-Hegelian) dispensation, in the reign of difference (as opposed to identity) there will be no more grand claims, no more leapfrogging beyond stubborn conflicts to false reconciliations.

(Krupnick 1987, 2)

At first glance, these *Sud-Américaines*, tail-piece to *Feuilles de route*, and first published in late 1926, might appear to constitute but another instance of verbal photography, of those 'post-cards destined for my friends', the mere 'little stories without pretension but very intimate, notably evocations of people' of the poet's own description. Certainly, mainstream Cendrars criticism has largely ignored the invitation to penetrate the intimacy, the personal evocations of these poems, perhaps content to share Cendrars' reported initial naive delight in the exoticism of 'the country which belongs to no-one' (Eulálio 1986, 42). Conceived of thus, Cendrars' first contact with South America would be a consummated rendezvous with his personal 'Nevernever land'; a bridging of the gap between the French capital and a brave New World. Monique Chefdor, for instance, succinctly encapsulates the context:

Disgruntled as he was by the dictatorial tyranny which he thought Dada and Surrealism were exerting on poetry, Cendrars was seduced by the youthful enthusiasm of these South American poets and artists.... Exhilarated by the dynamism of Brazil, Cendrars postponed once more his decision to renounce poetry .... These poems were composed as 'travel notes' carrying a step further [his] desire to do away with literary devices and purge the poetic idiom of all affectation .... With the exception of a handful of poems ... and possibly the series on South American women, his poems are not verbal picture postcards. They are more informed by his own feelings along the journey than by an exotic aesthetics of diversity .... By the end of his poetic cycle Cendrars has achieved his goal to write 'without ostentation, simply, true, as one lives'.

(Chefdor 1980, 57–60)

For at least one critic, then, in Baudelairean terms, 'Là, tout n'est qu'ordre et beauté/luxe, calme et volupté'/'There, all is but order and beauty, luxury, calm and voluptuousness'. Where the present analysis differs from this view, however, is over the opposition of an 'exotic aesthetics' and the poet's 'own feelings'. The difference, I suggest, lies not so much between as *within*.

The name Blaise Cendrars has long been associated with that explosion of avant-garde literary activity in poetry, prose, the cinema and the plastic arts which, in Brazil, began with the celebrated *Semana de Arte Moderna / Week of Modern Art* in 1922 and which, in one of its key documents, the *Manifesto Pau Brasil / Brazil Wood Manifesto* of 1924, hails Cendrars as principal inspiration of the following:

Uma sugestão de Blaise Cendrars:
Tendes as locomotivas cheias, ides partir.
Um negro gira a manivela do desvio rotativo em que estais.
O menor descuido vos fará partir na direção
oposta ao vosso destino.

(Eulálio 1986, 34–5)

[A suggestion of Blaise Cendrars: Your locomotives are full, you're about to set off. A black turns the lever of the controls where you're standing. The slightest lack of attention will send you off in the opposite direction from your destination.]

While two of the foremost poets of the generation, Manuel Bandeira and Mário de Andrade, comment respectively on the 'violence' and the 'explosion' of Cendrars' impact upon Brazilian art (Eulálio 1986, 29), it is his close friend Oswald de Andrade who pens the Manifesto and leads the *Pau Brasil* tendency. With the woman artist Tarsila do Amaral, Oswald returns to Brazil from Paris 'quase com os olhos estrangeiros amantes do exótico do europeu que os "guiava", Cendrars no caso'/'almost with foreign eyes, with a love for the exotic of the European who was "guiding" them, of Cendrars, in fact'. And this is the crux of the question of reciprocal influence, for, as W. Mays writes: 'Cendrars a donc découvert l'Amérique, l'Amérique du Sud, particulièrement le Brésil. . . . Mieux que cela, il a fait découvrir le Brésil à nombre de Brésiliens qui l'ignoraient'/'Cendrars thus discovered America, South America, particularly Brazil . . . . Better still, he made a number of Brazilians who didn't know it discover Brazil' (Mays 1925, 11). In short, *Pau Brasil* is a clearcut case of Eurocentrism operating not between but within continents. As one critic of Cendrars, Jay Bochner, has pointed out:

Cendrars was able to provide them with one thing at least. The conviction that the roots of their modernism had to be autochthonous, to be found in authentic Brazil .... *The discovery working for both the Frenchman and the Brazilian.*

(Bochner 1978, 69; my italics)

The context of *Sud-Américaines*, then, is that general fetishization of 'the primitive' which, as Alexandre Eulálio claims, makes of Brazil 'un immense laboratoire culturel ... un attrait irrésistible sur Cendrars'/'an immense cultural laboratory ... an irresistible attraction for Cendrars' (Eulálio 1986, 23–4). For Oswald de Andrade, both in *Pau Brasil* and in the subsequent 'Anthropophagy' phase, a parallel if more extreme primitivism provides the vehicle for his notorious attack on academic and respectable values, and his search for poetry within the Brazilian vernacular. A key question, before any close examination of the text of *Sud-Américaines* begins, is to what extent either author – but specifically Cendrars – is able to shed pre-established modes of fetishization in constructing his vision(s) of Brazil. Is the so-called 'new objectivity' of, say, Cendrars' *Kodak* (also of 1924) conceivable? Can poetry ever capture a photographic (or mirror) state without providing a stage on which are performed not only the exoticisms but also the eroticisms – indeed, the strange pathologies which, paradoxically, Cendrars himself would subsequently ascribe to a series of Brazilian 'portraits', in his prose writings? What always needs to be questioned, above all, however, in Homi Bhabha's formulation, is the mode of presentation of otherness.

I

La route monte en lacets
L'auto s'élève brusque et puissante
Nous grimpons dans un tintamarre d'avion qui va plafonner
Chaque tournant la jette contre mon épaule et quand nous
    virons
dans le vide elle se cramponne inconsciente à mon bras et se
penche au-dessus du précipice
Au sommet de la serra nous nous arrêtons court devant la
    faille géante
Une lune monstrueuse et toute proche monte derrière nous
«Lua, lua!» murmure-t-elle
Au nom de la lune, mon ami, comment Dieu autorise-t-il ces
gigantesques travaux qui nous permirent de passer?

Ce n'est pas la lune, chérie, mais le soleil qui en précipitant
les brouillards fit cette énorme déchirure
Regarde l'eau qui coule au fond parmi les débris des
    montagnes
et qui s'engouffre dans les tuyaux de l'usine
Cette station envoie de l'électricité jusqu'à Rio

[The road rises in hairpin bends/ The automobile ascends
brisk and powerful/We climb in a roar of an aeroplane ceiling
out/Every bend throws her against my shoulder and when
we veer/in the void she clutches unconsciously on to my
arm/and leans over the precipice/At the summit of the *sierra*
we pull up short before the gigantic drop/A monstrous moon
rises close behind us/'Lua, lua!' she whispers/In the name of
the moon, my friend, how does God allow/the giant works
which let us pass?/It's not the moon, darling, but the sun
which in bringing down/the mists made this great slit/
Look at the water flowing at the bottom/among the debris
of the mountains/and plunging into the pipes of the power
plant/This station sends electricity all the way to Rio]

On the literal level, the opening section of the poem sequence has
sufficient local reference to evoke, for instance, the spectacular
panorama of the *Dedo de Deus/Finger of God* mountain range
which lies between Rio de Janeiro and Teresópolis, one of the
chic summer retreats of nineteenth-century Brazilian royalty
and, latterly, of the high *bourgeoisie*. Psychically, the ascent of the
strikingly phallic peaks on the exhilarating trajectory of dizzying
hairpin bends constructs a parallel to exotic local colour – the
erotic focal 'other' of a male gaze. The male gaze, in this case as
ever, is constructed from a set of clichés which might even be
read as a checklist of Futurist shibboleths – automobile/aeroplane,
speed/height, power/vertigo, electricity and hydro-generation.
Less historically specific, however, is the culturally powerful
binarism at play in the attitude to a murmuring 'elle' – awestruck
at the authority of an omnipotent God, giant mountains and a
day-time moon – on the part of a condescending focalizer operating knowledge versus ignorance, wisdom versus innocence.
In hindsight, therefore, the rise 'en lacets' has bound together
(*enlacés*?) woman 'as signifier for [a] male other', and the 'man
[who] can live out his fantasies and obsessions through linguistic
commands' in Laura Mulvey's classic definition (1975, 7). As a

Latin Americanist, my first reaction to Cendrars' text is to situate it within that tradition of Eurocentric writing which, as Mary Louise Pratt noted of Alexander von Humboldt's *Personal Narrative of Travels to the Equinoctal Regions of the New Continent* of 1816, has as 'one of his principal discursive strategies . . . to reduce America to landscape and marginalise its inhabitants . . . . In [their] eroticism, [their] dramatisation of contact . . . these sentimental texts are characteristically dialogic in the Bakhtinian sense: they represent the Other's voices in dialogue with the voices of self and often tender the Other some credibility and equality' (Pratt 1986, 147–51).

II

Libertins et libertines
Maintenant nous pouvons avouer
Nous sommes quelques-uns de par le monde
Santé intégrale
Nous avons aussi les plus belles femmes du monde
Simplicité
Intelligence
Amour
Sports
Nous leurs avons aussi appris la liberté
Les enfants grandissent avec les chiens les chevaux les
oiseaux au milieu des belles servantes toutes rondes et
mobiles comme des tournesols

[Libertins and libertines/Now we can assert/We are someone of the world/Total health/We who have the most beautiful women in the world/Simplicity/Intelligence/Love/Sports/ We have also taught them liberty/The children grow up alongside the dogs the horses the birds/amongst the lovely servant girls as round and mobile as sunflowers]

In the second sequence, 'some credibility and equality' are illusorily promoted by 'Libertins and libertines'. In the sudden avowal of the new status of 'nous', free-thinking *citoyen du monde*, healthy, simple, intelligent, lover, sportsman, there emerges an unmistakably Riefenstahl-like racial stereotyping, albeit here a fusion of European and native characteristics which can ill disguise the consistent condescension of 'Nous leurs avons aussi appris la liberté' – all 'they' needed in their Douanier Rousseau closeness-to-nature of flora and fauna. Further echoes of Humboldt, further evidence of why Cendrars saw Brazil as perhaps the last chance for the reinvigoration of 'l'homme blanc', and of his own remarkable psychic investment in the country (Roig 1988, 273–98).

III

Il n'y a plus de jalousie de crainte ou de timidité
Nos amies sont fortes et saines
Elles sont belles et simples et grandes
Et elles savent toutes s'habiller
Ce ne sont pas des femmes intelligentes mais elles sont très
    perspicaces
Elles n'ont pas peur d'aimer
Elles ne craignent pas de prendre
Elles savent tout aussi bien donner
Chacune d'elles a dû lutter avec sa famille leur position
    sociale
le monde ou autre chose
Maintenant
Elles ont simplifié leur vie et sont pleines d'enfantillages
Plus de meubles plus de bibelots elles aiment les animaux
les grandes automobiles et leur sourire
Elles voyagent
Elles détestent la musique mais emportent toutes un phono

[There is no more jealousy fear or timidness/Our girl-friends are strong and healthy/They are beautiful and simple and big/And they all know how to dress/These are not intelligent women but they are very perspicacious/They have no fear of loving/They aren't afraid to take/They also know how to give/Each of them must have fought with their family/for their social position the world or something else/Now they have simplified their lives and are full of child-like ways/No more furniture no more knick-knacks they love animals/great automobiles and their smile/They travel/They detest music but all carry a gramophone]

If the third section opens with a burst of utopic release from repression built on jealousy, fear or timidity, a racial safety-factor must guarantee untainted 'amies . . . fortes et saines'. And the chosen women have learned how to dress *chic* (despite their lack of intelligence) . . . for a certain (native?) craftiness or 'perspicacité' or/and their struggle for social position (note that the class reference is broached but dropped immediately) have gifted them with a child-like simplicity. They have learned to cast aside the trinkets of bourgeois culture, loving exteriors not interiors, kinesis not stasis, modern sound not (traditional) music.

IV

Il y en a trois que j'aime particulièrement
La première
Une vieille dame sensible belle et bonne
Adorablement bavarde et d'une souveraine élégance
Mondaine mais d'une gourmandise telle qu'elle s'est libérée
    de la mondanité
La deuxième est la sauvageonne de l'Hôtel Meurice
Tout le jour elle peigne ses longs cheveux et grignote son
    rouge de chez Guerlain
Bananiers nourrice nègre colibris
Son pays est si loin qu'on voyage six semaines sur un fleuve
recouvert de fleurs de mousses de champignons gros comme
des œufs d'autruche
Elle est si belle le soir dans le hall de l'hôtel que tous les
    hommes en sont fous
Son sourire le plus aigu est pour moi car je sais rire comme
    les abeilles sauvages de son pays
La dernière est trop riche pour être heureuse
Mais elle a déjà fait de grands progrès
Ce n'est pas du premier coup que l'on trouve son équilibre
    et la simplicité de la vie au milieu de toutes les
    complications de la richesse
Il y faut de l'entêtement
Elle le sait bien elle qui monte si divinement à cheval et qui
fait corps avec son grand étalon argentin
Que ta volonté soit comme ta cravache
Mais ne t'en sers pas
Trop
Souvent

[There are three I love particularly/The first/An old lady

sensitive beautiful and good/Adorably talkative and with majestic elegance/Worldly but with such a sweet tooth that she has freed/herself from worldliness/The second is the wild savage of the Hotel Meurice/All day long she combs her long hair and dabs on her rouge/from the house of Guerlain/Banana trees black nurse humming birds/Her country is so far away that you have to travel six weeks on a river/covered with flowers with mosses with mushrooms as big as/ostrich-eggs/She is so lovely each evening in the hotel lobby that all the men are mad for her/Her sharpest smile is for me for I know how to laugh like/the wild bees of her country/The last one is too rich to be happy/But she has already made great progress/It's not first time round that you find your balance/and the simplicity of life amidst all the complications/of being rich/You have to have persistence/She knows as much she who rides so divinely and/is at one with her great Argentine stallion/May your will be like your whip/But don't use it/Too/Often]

Close inspection of the fourth section throws up a quick-fire portrait-gallery of gender stereotypes. First, the big-hearted if ageing whore – reminiscent in her combination of *gourmandise* and *bavardage* of Sander Gilman's classification of 'Black Bodies, White Bodies: Towards an Iconography of Female Sexuality in Late Nineteenth-Century Art, Medicine and Literature'. For here is the Brazilian equivalent of the Hottentot Venus:

When the Victorians saw the female black, they saw her in terms of her buttocks and saw represented by the buttocks all the anomalies of her genitalia. In a mid-century erotic caricature of the Hottentot Venus, a white, male observer views her through a telescope, unable to see anything but her buttocks.

(Gilman 1986, 238)

Cendrars is more subtle, more modern . . . the telescope has been replaced by a kaleidoscope peep show, which now throws up the 'sauvageonne de l'Hôtel Meurice', desirable barbarian who, despite hotel living, is set amongst 'bananiers nourrice nègre colibris' – a Carmen Miranda look-alike who, in the scopophilic perspective of the poem, breaks the Eurocentric binds not only of the house of Guerlain but also in a re-working of the exotic myth of Mallarmé's 'l'antique Amazone'. Notable here is the juxta-position of 'tous les hommes' and 'moi' – favoured because a 'wild-bee laugh' (improbable sting in this psycho-sexual tale) sets the focalizer apart (according to him) from the generalized scopophilia. The third woman, a thoroughly up-to-date addition to the mother-whore pairing, none the less threatens but momen-tarily to break with 'the silent image of woman still tied to her place as bearer of meaning, not maker of meaning' (Mulvey 1975, 7). For this *arriviste*, 'qui monte si divinement à cheval', re-broaches the question of social class only to emphasize the decadent attraction of the class, power and money struggle of a very *fin de siècle* version of an urban(e) 'belle dame sans merci', or a 'Belle de jour', perhaps, asked to go gentle on the whip!

V

Il y en a encore une autre qui est encore comme une toute
    petite fille
Malgré son horrible mari ce divorce affreux et la détention
    au clôitre
Elle est farouche comme le jour et la nuit
Elle est plus belle qu'un œuf
Plus belle qu'un rond
Mais elle est toujours trop nue sa beauté déborde elle ne sait
    pas encore s'habiller
Elle mange aussi beaucoup trop et son ventre s'arrondit
    comme si elle était enceinte de deux petits mois
C'est qu'elle a un tel appétit et une telle envie de vivre
Nous allons lui apprendre tout ça et lui apprendre à
    s'habiller
Et lui donner les bonnes adresses

[There's yet another one who is still like a little girl/ Despite her horrible husband their frightful divorce and her imprisonment/in the cloister/She's as untamed as day and night/She's lovelier than an egg/More beautiful than a ring/ But she's always too naked her beauty is overflowing she still doesn't know how to dress/She also eats too much and her belly is rounded as/if she were just two months pregnant/ For she has such an appetite and such a lust for life/We'll teach her all that and teach her how to dress/And give her the knack]

In part five, the gallery extends to the portrait of a child–woman. After the rival male (the horrible divorced ex-husband) has been debased, a seductive tension of wildness versus vulnerability, of animality versus fertility, develops into the overt clash of cultures, Eurocentric surfeit of clothes versus 'native' excess of nakedness. Though the return to a surfeit of eating initially serves as a reminder of 'la vieille's' over-indulgence, what bursts forth *à la Tampopo*, *La Grande Bouffe*, or *The Cook, the Thief, his Wife and her Lover*, is the psycho-sexual desire to possess and to reproduce not only a child, but a divided, multiplied self – hence the all too obvious pun on 'enceinte de deux petits *mois*' (my italics). Finally, 'Nous allons lui apprendre tout ça' makes of the key sexual act an unnameable 'absent' term. '*Ça'[it; id]*, fulfilment of *male* appetite and the will to live on via offspring, is not shared with 'her' but condescendingly offered as yet more 'masculine' knowledge. Once again, as Laura Mulvey has shown, 'in a world ordered by sexual imbalance, pleasure in looking has been split between active/male and passive/female. The determining male gaze projects its fantasy onto the female figure, which is styled accordingly. In their traditional exhibitionist role, women are simultaneously looked at and displayed so that they can be said to connote *to-be-looked-at-ness*. Woman displayed as sexual object is the leitmotif of erotic spectacle: from pin-ups to strip-tease, from Ziegfeld to Busby Berkeley . . . [to Blaise Cendrars] she holds the look, plays to and signifies male desire' (Mulvey 1975, 11).

VI

Une
Il y en a encore une
Une que j'aime plus que tout au monde
Je me donne à elle tout entier comme une pepsine car elle a
    besoin d'un fortifiant
Car elle est trop douce
Car elle est encore un peu craintive
Car le bonheur est une chose bien lourde à porter
Car la beauté a besoin d'un petit quart d'heure d'exercice
    tous les matins

[One/There's one more/One that I love more than anything in the world/I give myself to her whole as a pepsin for she needs/a pick-me-up/For she's so sweet/For she's still a little too timorous/For happinesss is something very hard to bear/ For beauty needs a little quarter-hour's exercise/Every morning]

And what of the final portrait, that of 'Une que j'aime plus que tout au monde' of the sixth section? Final example of male munificence; receptacle for the circumlocutory release of effervescent fluid, the life-giving 'pepsine', man's quintessential gift, since the 'fortifiant' is really 'moi' – this time overt, undisguisedly one, the great 'I'. Yet this climax of self-bestowal is coyly followed by four modes of explanation: 'car . . . , car . . . , car . . . , car . . . '; a wholly inadequate 'explication de sexe' since the complements in each case are concessive – 'trop', 'un peu', 'chose bien lourde', 'besoin', successive pointers to lack, insufficiency, supplementability, whence the final ambivalence of 'Car la beauté a besoin d'un petit quart d'heure d'exercise tous les matins'. Is this to be read as a supplementary, male (i.e. fifteen-minute) matutinal coition? Or is it a pre-Jane Fonda version of toning exercises carried out in preparation for the next visit of, and subjection to, homo-scopophilia?

VII

Nous ne voulons pas être tristes
C'est trop facile
C'est trop bête
C'est trop commode
On en a trop souvent l'occasion
C'est pas malin
Tout le monde est triste
Nous ne voulons plus être tristes

[We don't want to be sad/It's too easy/It's too silly/It's too comfortable/One has the chance too often/It's not wicked/ Everyone is sad/We don't want to be sad any longer]

By the time, in sequence seven, of the return of 'nous', it must be asked if – after the so-called 'profils libertins des sud-américaines'/'libertine profiles of South American women' (Eulálio 1986, 52) – a new male gazer has emerged. It would seem not. For the final verses are archetypally the *post-coitum triste* of a focalizer/possessor infected not only by 'tristesse' but also by the most banal of desires to avoid banality.

Lest it appear that poor Blaise is the sole butt of a gender/race/class critique, I now draw attention to two parallel Brazilian examples of the clichéd masculist vision. First, that of Cendrars' closest Brazilian poet collaborator Oswald de Andrade, founder of the Anthropophagy school of extreme primitivism, attacking academic values and respectability and seeking poetry within the Brazilian vernacular:

CIVILIZAÇÃO PERNAMBUCANA

As mulheres andam tão louças
E tão custosas
Que não se contentam com os tafetás
São tantas as jóias com que se adornam
Que parecem chovidas em suas cabeças e gargantas
As pérolas rubis e diamantes
Tudo são delícias
Não parece esta terra senão um retrato
Do terreal paraíso.

(in Pontiero 1969, 36)

[PERNAMBUCO CIVILIZATION

The women are so smart/And so costly/That they're not content with taffetas/So many are the jewels with which they adorn themselves/That they seem to have rained on their heads and throats/The pearls rubies and diamonds/All are delights/This land seems nothing but a portrait/Of heaven on earth.]

Roberto Schwarz, writing in 1988, describes the *Pau Brasil* programme as trying to give 'a triumphalist interpretation of our backwardness . . . Local primitivism would give back a modern sense to a tired European culture . . . Oswald de Andrade [used the anthropophagy] metaphor of "swallowing up" the alien: a copy, to be sure, but with regenerative effect. Historical distance allows us to see the ingenuousness and conceit contained in these propositions . . . . How can one fail to notice that the *Antropófagos* like the nationalists take as their subject the abstract Brazilian, with no class specification?' (Schwarz 1988, 84). In Oswald de Andrade's poem, one side of an unmediated binary, *woman*, adorned by an equally undifferentiated polarized epithet of the 'self'/'other' spectrum, namely, *Brazilian*, bears the whole weight of a classic idealization. This heaven-on-earth portrait of the 1920s differs from the utopianism of the earliest, so-called, *discoverers* of the Americas only in so far as ideal place, *locus amoenus*, is substituted by unreal race, or *focus a man has*, the vision of perfect, native woman. From *El Dorado* to *La Dorada*? Or yet another case (after Cendrars) not of discovery but of *invention*?

A problematic example of what Schwarz goes on to describe as the 'programmatic innocence of the Anthropophagists' is Manuel Bandeira's short poem 'Irene no céu', from *Libertinagem*:

IRENE NO CÉU

Irene preta
Irene boa
Irene sempre de bom humor.

Imagino Irene entrando no céu:
– Licença, meu branco!
E São Pedro bonachão:
– Entra, Irene. Você não precisa pedir licença.
(in Pontiero 1969, 67)

[IRENE IN HEAVEN

Irene black/Irene nice/Irene always good-humoured./I imagine Irene going to Heaven:/'May I? Mister white man!'/ And good old St Peter:/'Come in, Irene. You don't need to ask.']

Paradoxically, this poem dates from 1930, for, already in 1924, Manuel Bandeira had written scathingly of Oswald de Andrade, thus:

O seu primitivismo consiste em plantar bananeiras e pôr de cócoras em baixo dois ou três negros tirados da antologia do Sr. Blaise Cendrars.
(Eulálio 1986, 46)

[His primitivism consists of planting banana-trees and beneath, on their haunches, two or three blacks taken from M. Blaise Cendrars' anthology.]

And in 1926, another critic, Plínio Delgado, could write:

> Tomamos o Brasil como tema só porque o Sr. Blaise Cendrars
> fêz uma poesia sobre um negro. Temos a visão sêca e formal
> de nossa terra.
>
> (Eulálio 1986, 46)

> [We take Brazil as a theme only because M. Blaise Cendrars
> wrote poetry about a black. We have a dry and formal vision
> of our land.]

Which brings me back, full circle, to displacement. As Roberto
Schwarz puts it: 'The basic scheme is as follows: a tiny élite
devotes itself to copying Old World culture. . . . As a result, literature and politics occupy an exotic position, and we become
incapable of *creating things of our own that spring from the depths of
our life and history*. . . . But why not reverse the argument? Why
should the imitative character of our life not stem from forms of
inequality so brutal that they lack the minimal reciprocity . . .
without which modern society can only appear artificial and
"imported?"' (Schwarz 1988, 85 and 89; his italics). It need hardly
be pointed out that Schwarz's critical insight here is the most
overt of echoes – notably in the italicized imperative of the
need for a Brazilian aesthetics *springing from within* – of Mário de
Andrade's 1922 formulation of the problematic. The challenge of
achieving, in art, that other reciprocity, the equipoise of exterior
and interior representation of modernity, was, after all, the pulse
and rhythm of *Paulicéia desvairada*:

> Escrever arte moderna não significa jamais
> para mim representar a vida actual no que tem
> de exterior; automóveis, cinema, asfalto. Se
> estas palavras frequentam-me no livro não é porque pense
> com elas escrever moderno, mas porque sendo meu livro
>   moderno,
> elas têm nele sua razão de ser.
>
> (in Pontiero 1969, 9)

> [To write modern art no longer means/for me to represent
> present-day life in its/external features; automobiles, cinema,
> asphalt. If/these words appear frequently in my book it's not
> because I think/with them I'm writing modern, but because,
> my book being modern,/they have in it their reason for being.]

Viewed thus, the *avant-garde* cannot, could not, be imported. In Pascalian terms, and at the risk of displacing theology, it could be argued that Brazil would not have been seeking modernity had it not already found it. Or, rephrasing Mário, the writer does not so much write the modern as be written by it. In this respect, imported 'culture' rapidly assumes an air as dated as the nineteenth-century, or *fin de siècle*, bourgeois preoccupation mocked by Jules Laforgue or Mário de Andrade, by Frenchman or Brazilian, alike:

Eu insulto o burguês! O burguês níquel
o burguês-burguês!
A digestão bem feita de São Paulo!

O homem-curva! O homem-nádegas!
O homem que sendo francês, brasileiro, italiano,
é sempre um cauteloso pouco-a-pouco!

Eu insulto as aristocracias cautelosas!
Os barões lampeões! os condes Joões! os duques zurros!
que vivem dentro de muros sem pulos;
e gemem sangues de alguns milréis fracos
para dizerem que as filhas da senhora falam o francês
e tocam o 'Printemps' com as unhas!
                                    (in Pontiero 1969, 21)

[I insult the bourgeois! The nickel-bourgeois/the bourgeois-bourgeois!/The well-made digestion of São Paulo!/The belly-man! The bum-man!/The man who being French, Brazilian, Italian,/is always a cautious little-by-little./I insult cautious aristocracies!/The robber-barons! The count Johns! The donkey-bray dukes!/who live within walls they don't have to jump;/And sigh up bloods of some weak *milréis* [sovereigns]/ to say that the lady's daughters speak French/and play 'Printemps' with their nails!]

The valency of this 1922 debunking of the Ubu-like pot-bellied Europhile wheezingly preening and prancing before the effete daughters of the *nouveaux riches* persists, both sociologically and linguistically. The poem hovers on the brink of cultivated indecency, parodying the saying:

Eu sou o gato maltês
Toca pouco e fala francês.

[I am the Maltese cat/Playing little and talking French.]

From Puss-in-Boots to pussy in cahoots is but a small jump (into bed) with a rich *gata*. At issue, then as now, is the *tension* of invitation and rejection, performed in Mário's text much as the masculist shibboleths mocked in contemporary feminist writings are, to some extent, re-affirmed (or at least re-voiced) as they are undermined. 'Ode ao burguês', then, comes to *include* an imprecation to exclusion:

Fora! Fú! Fora o bom burguês!
        (in Pontiero 1969, 22)

[Off! Shoo! Be off with the good bourgeois!]

But the fat cats, the lampooned *lampeões*, play on . . . .
As if in prolepsis of the insight later to be encapsulated so pithily by Derrida's 'we can pronounce not a single destructive proposition which has not already had to slip into the form, the logic, and the implicit postulations of precisely what it seeks to contest' (Derrida 1972, 280), Mário plays the game of unveiling, of discovering, the play of outer–inner in the streets of São Paulo, in his 'Descobrimento':

Abancado à escrivaninha em São Paulo
Na minha casa da rua Lopes Chaves
De sopetão senti um friume por dentro.
Fiquei trêmulo, muito comovido
Com o livro palerma olhando pra mim.
Não vê que me lembrei que lá no norte, meu Deus!
    muito longe de mim

Na escuridão ativa de noite que caiu
Um homem pálido magro de cabelo escorrendo nos olhos,
Depois de fazer uma pele com a borracha do dia,
Faz pouco se deitou, está dormindo.

Ésse homem é brasileiro que nem eu.
        (in Pontiero 1969, 22–3)

[Crouched at my desk in São Paulo/At my house in the rua Lopes Chaves/In a trice I felt a chill inside me./I shivered, deeply moved/With the stupid book looking at me./Can't you see that I was remembering that up there in the North, my God!/very far from me/In the active blackness of nightfall/ a pale thin man with his hair in his eyes,/Having wrapped himself in the remains of the day,/Has just turned in and is sleeping./That man's as Brazilian as I am.]

Here, in 1927, the meditative strain evident in Schwarz's troubled commentary on literature and politics occupying an exotic position is foreshadowed by Mário de Andrade. The result, in this case, more resembles politico-artistic *conscience* than poetic *consciousness*. Thus, a (limiting) binary is established between 'me' and 'him'; I *this* Brazilian, he *that* Brazilian... with a striving for dialogue, an ironic highlighting of difference *between* as inseparable from an experience of difference *within*. The implication of 'Ésse homem é brasileiro que nem eu' still renders self *and* other rather than self *in* other, however, as the locus of personal and national identity. In Schwarz's terms, it does not yet 'reverse the argument', but merely sets up the possibility of encounter, of dialogics.

By way of conclusion, I would suggest that such reversals are not only possible, but may, indeed, be achieved with gentleness and humour. The final poem I wish to highlight, by Carlos Drummond de Andrade, dates from 1930:

INICIAÇÃO AMOROSA

A rede entre duas mangueiras
balançava no mundo profundo.
O dia era quente, sem vento.
O sol lá em cima, as folhas no meio,
o dia era quente.

E como eu não tinha nada que fazer vivia namorando as
    pernas morenas da lavadeira.
Um dia ela veio para a rede,
se enroscou nos meus braços,
me deu um abraço,
me deu as maminhas
que eram só minhas.

A rede virou,
o mundo afundou.

Depois fui para a cama
febre 40 graus febre.
Uma lavadeira imensa, com duas tetas imensas, girava no
    espaço verde.

(Drummond de Andrade 1965, 10)

[AMOROUS INITIATION

The hammock between two mango-trees/Was swinging in the
world so deep./The day was hot, windless./The sun up
there,/The leaves between,/The day was hot./And since I'd
nothing to do I spent my life in love with the dark legs of the
washer-woman./One day she came to the hammock./Curled
up in my arms,/Gave me a cuddle/Gave me her boobies/
All to myself./The hammock tipped,/The world dipped./
Afterwards I went to bed/With fever 40 degrees fever/A huge
washer-woman, with two huge tits, twisted/in green space.]

Viewed at a distance of more than sixty years, the poem may be
read as virtually a blueprint of how to pastiche and deflate the
inherited strains of intra-colonialism. Indolently slung between
binaries not just of a self-indulgent tropicalism but, less explicitly, also of a class-consciousness illusorily suspended between
casa grande (plantation-house) and *senzala* (slave-quarters), the
male subject rapidly falls victim of his inherited fantasizing.
Though gentle, the mockery of Drummond's poem allows little if
any room for a Gilberto Freyre style vision of patriarchalism,
much less for the uncritical nationalism of *ufanismo*. If ambiguity
of intention on the part of the *morena* remains open for just long
enough for the poem to mime the hammock-swing rhythms of a
lulling sensualism, the comic and bathetic shift from 'maminhas'
to 'só minhas' triggers the overturning of such presumptious
droit de seigneur-ism. The reader is left to ponder whether the
fevered hallucination on which the poem ends is any more or less
realistic than the fever-pitch image-making of Brazilian sexuality
out of which the text and the publicity have grown.

The process of self-realization, in this poem, as distinct from
the narcissistic self-construction which fixes identity in a mirror-
state, *à la* Cendrars, but also *à la* young Neruda, divulges rather

a restless, unfulfilled, performative subject constructing identity on a *mirror-stage*. The point is that the construction of an identity for the self is again inseparable from the construction (or is it deconstruction?) of a gendered identity for the reader. The poem has every ingredient of eroticism as exoticism ... but the heat haze produces an illusion which is self-delusion. The rising temperature of male sexuality which momentarily threatens to melt down the implicit differences of gender, colour, class and economies of a post-colonial relation is suddenly turned upside-down. Whereas Cendrars' construction of women in *Sud-Américaines* may be viewed as the staging of other place at the site of other plays, other ploys ... or '*pseudo*-américaines', and Mário's insight represents an early *prise de conscience*, Drummond's performance turns on the twist of subjectivity, alterity, exoticism and eroticism, the deflating siting of the 'je' very firmly on its rear. Just as Mário drew on popular culture for the *gato maltês* saying, Drummond exploits here that international cliché of inverted libidinal daydream:

> Two in a hammock
> Attempted to kiss
> When all of a sudden
> They landed like this

REAR-MIRROR

Self-realization and self-mockery, however, are not at the end of any tail. For a prehensile capacity to turn back on one's hang-ups – the image of an ever-exotic Brazil, for example – in no way abolishes the ambivalent rhythms of an unfulfilled desire. Even after the frontiers of linguistic difference have been breached, and forty years after Cendrars' displacement to 'Utopialand', the Vienna-born Ernst Jandl's sound-poem 'Calypso' (Jandl 1966, 12), compulsively re-performs the apparently irresolvable, and still observably pleasurable, ploys of other = women ... but (for me) not yet. To the deferred pleasures of *nondum* I shall return, however, in Chapter 8, in discussion of Carlos Fuentes' *Terra Nostra*. Meanwhile:

> CALYPSO
> ich was not yet
> in brasilien

nach brasilien
wulld ich laik du go

wer de wimen
arr so ander
so quait ander
denn anderwo

ich was not yet
in brasilien
nach brasilien
wulld ich laik du go

als ich anderschdehn
mange lanquidsch
will ich anderschdehn
auch lanquidsch in rioo

ich was not yet
in brasilien
nach brasilien
wulld ich laik du go

wenn de senden
mi across de meer
wai mi not senden wer
ich wulld laik du go

yes yes de senden
mi across de meer
wer ich was not yet
ich laik du go sehr

ich was not yet
in brasilien
yes nach brasilien
wulld ich laik du go

WORKS CITED

Bhabha, Homi, 'The Other Question . . . ', *Screen*, 24–6, (1983), 18–36.
Bochner, Jay. *Blaise Cendrars: Discovery and Re-Creation*. Toronto: University of Toronto Press, 1978.

Carteret, John-Grand. *Die Erotik in der französischen Karikatur*, trans. Cary von Karwarth and Adolf Neumann. Vienna: 1909.

Cendrars, Blaise. *Œuvres complètes*. Paris: Pléiade, 1967.

Chefdor, Monique. *Blaise Cendrars*. Boston: Twayne, 1980.

Derrida, Jacques. *Writing and Difference*, trans. A. Bass. London: Routledge and Kegan Paul, 1978.

Drummond de Andrade, Carlos. *Antologia poética*. Lisboa: Ática, 1965.

Eulálio, Alexandre. 'L'Aventure brésilienne', *Travaux de la Faculté des Lettres et Sciences Humaines de l'Université de Rennes*, 5 (1986), 19–55.

Gilman, Sander L. 'Black Bodies, White Bodies: Towards an Iconography of Female Sexuality in Late Nineteenth-Century Art, Medicine and Literature', in *Race, Writing and Difference*, ed. Henry Louis Gates Jr. Chicago and London: University of Chicago Press, 1986, 223–61.

Jandl, Ernst. *Laut und Luise*. Stuttgart: Reclam Universal-Bibliothek, 1966.

Krupnick, Mark (ed.). *Displacement: Derrida and After*. Bloomington: University of Indiana Press, 1987.

Mays, W. 'Chez Blaise Cendrars', *Le Journal littéraire*, 3 January 1925.

Mulvey, Laura. 'Visual Pleasure and Narrative Cinema', *Screen*, 16:3 (1975), 7.

Pontiero, Giovanni (ed.). *An Anthology of Brazilian Modernist Poetry*. Oxford: Pergamon, 1969.

Pratt, Mary Louise. 'Scratches on the Face of the Country: or, What Mr Barrow Saw in the Land of the Bushmen', in *Race, Writing and Difference*, ed. Henry Louis Gates Jr. Chicago and London: University of Chicago Press, 1986, 138–62.

Roig, Adrien. 'Blaise Cendrars et le Brésil: Le grand film brésilien, la traduction de A *Selva*, Le «Morro Azul» et la «Tour Eiffel Sidérale»', *Portugal, Brésil, France: Histoire et culture* (1988), 273–98.

Schwarz, Roberto. 'Brazilian Culture: Nationalism by Elimination', *New Left Review*, 167 (1988), 77–90.

Chapter 3

On the meta-history of literature
'I know . . .', 'I seek . . . ', 'I know not . . .':
modernismo, modernidad and the poetics of
discontinuity

> The traditional devices for constructing a comprehensive view of history
> and for retrieving the past as a patient and continuous development
> must be systematically dismantled. Necessarily, we must dismiss those
> tendencies that encourage the consoling play of recognitions . . . . History
> becomes 'effective' to the degree that it introduces discontinuity into our
> very being.
>
> Michel Foucault

While it has become fashionable in the wake of the structuralist
revolution to speak, and write, of the 'discourse of history,' there
is little evidence to suggest that the insights developed by
Hayden White, Roland Barthes and Michel Foucault, for instance,
have been rigorously applied to *literary* history. It is still canonical
to consider literary history as a succession of '-isms', without
questioning that positivist assimilation of individual writers and
works into conveniently described blocks or movements as other
than a natural or innocent scholarly activity. Why should this
be so?

First, it is perhaps easier to identify the common preoccupations
and comparable styles of successive generations of writers and
artists than to emphasize the differences between them. Second,
a tradition of literary history has been accepted by scholars and
literary critics as the normal and efficient mode of situating
and presenting literatures both national and universal. Third, a
propensity to categorize recurrent themes and parallel forms
has brought a by no means specious aura of scientific profession-
alism to the scholarly treatment of literature as an institution.
Fourth, and crucially, the use of literary historical bracketing
and categorization can be periodically reviewed, so that yester-
year's assumptions concerning similarity and difference provide

the material of healthy debate and re-appraisal. All these factors and more have been shown to apply to the phenomenon called *modernismo*. In short, the term is at best unstable, at worst misleading. Not only is *modernismo* notoriously anachronistic when set alongside 'modernism', internationally, but the thematics of *modernismo* have also been shown to be unprogressive, not to say backward-looking, both in a purely literary and in a socio-ideological sense.

The survival of the term *modernismo* as in any way useful or even meaningful is an issue to be debated both specifically and as part of the general problematic of the discourse of literary history in both Spain and Spanish America. What does, what can, the term mean? What is at stake in its retention and application? In this chapter, I wish to address both a case-study of comparative textual analysis – namely, poems by Bécquer, Darío and Vallejo – and the problems posed by an uncritical use of literary history. In the process, I hope to question a causalist progression of continuity, proposing an alternative construct whereby (literary) history may be mapped according to the contours of its markedly troped but disguisedly discontinuous discourse.

GUSTAVO ADOLFO BÉCQUER AND META-HISTORY

The theoretical model I shall refer to here is Hayden White's *meta-history*, and the text analysed will be that of a supposed Spanish precursor of Hispano-American *modernismo*, Gustavo Adolfo Bécquer's *Rima I*. Basically, White's thesis draws attention to the interferences in the construction of historiography of ideological, generic and stylistic considerations. The historian selects, arranges, explains and ideologizes always in a hermeneutic manner.

Interpretation thus enters into historiography in at least three ways: aesthetically (in the choice of a narrative strategy), epistemologically (in the choice of an explanatory paradigm), and ethically (in the choice of a strategy by which the ideological implications of a given representation can be drawn from the comprehension of current social problems) (White 1978, 69–70). For White, all history-writing, including literary history, is metahistorical, constructed upon the basic tropes of metaphor, metonymy, synecdoche and irony. Constantly redeploying these tropes, literary history refers at once to literary texts and to itself.

In the following analysis of *Rima I* (Bécquer 1954, 439), I shall be using, perforce, both an inherited literary history and, concomitantly, received tropes, part of an interpretative strategy which, as the term *hermeneutic* suggests, situates a given text in a more generalized schema, as part of a *progression*, historical, ethical, generic and stylistic:

> Yo sé un himno gigante y extraño
> que anuncia en la noche del alma una aurora,
> y estas páginas son de este himno
> cadencias que el aire dilata en las sombras.
>
> Yo quisiera escribirlo, del hombre
> domando el rebelde, mezquino idioma,
> con palabras que fuesen a un tiempo
> suspiros y risas, colores y notas.
>
> Pero en vano es luchar; que no hay cifra
> capaz de encerrarlo, y apenas, ¡oh hermosa!,
> si, teniendo en mis manos las tuyas,
> pudiera, al oído, cantártelo a solas.

[I know a hymn gigantic and strange/which announces in the night of the soul a dawn,/and these pages are of that hymn/cadences which the air disperses in the shadows./ I should like to write it,/taming man's rebellious, mean language/ with words that were at once/sighs and laughter, colours and notes./But it is to fight in vain; for there is no cipher/capable of containing it, and if only, oh beautiful!,/ holding your hands in mine,/I could, in your ear, sing it to you alone.]

Generically, the keynote 'Yo . . . ' situates this *rima* in a tradition of egocentric lyricism, *historically* consistent with a pose of Romantic bravado launched by 'Yo sé . . . '. An affirmation of epistemological certainty is based on that knowledge which derives from art, in this case, 'un himno gigante y extraño' which, *metonymically*, endows the persona with special access to a transcendent and exotic, quasi-religious, medium of expression, akin to the exaltation and disproportion of mainstream Romantic rhetoric as conceived in the Dionysian tradition of musicality, irrationality, suffering and love-worship – in the terms, that is, of Nietzsche's Apollonian–Dionysian binary of poetic impulses. *Generically*, too, an Orphic mission of annunciation combines with the traditions of prefatory poem and *ars poetica*, proclaiming the *aesthetic* of fading, evanescent lyricism both of this poem and of 'estas páginas' (the *Rimas* which follow). Thus far, the testimonial function of poetry is confidently expounded in the indicative mood. Concomitantly, the *metaphoric* 'aurora' of rebirth and hope is chanted within a present darkness which echoes, at once, the mystic 'noche del alma' and a prevailing Romantic *ethic* of negativity and loss of guiding faith.

However, the confident opening note of the poem and of the collection is subjected to a twofold transformation. The swelling hymn is composed of cadences which not only herald an *ars poetica* comparable to 'de la musique avant toute chose'/'music before all else' and 'rien n'est plus cher que la chanson grise'/ 'nothing is more cherished than the grey song', but also are subject to that process of *fadeur* identified by Jean-Pierre Richard as the organizing phenomenology of Verlaine's verse (Richard 1955). Here, the equation of 'páginas' with 'cadencias que el aire dilata en las sombras' functions, first, temporally, as a logical and chronological transition from 'noche' to 'aurora,' an archetypally Baudelairean 'Crépuscule du matin' when the artist, after the long night's struggle to write, contemplates the 'fading' of his own inspiration, as of the *reveille*, in the synaesthetic play of sound and sight, of wind and light:

La diane chantait dans les cours des casernes,
Et le vent du matin soufflait sur les lanternes . . .
Et l'homme est las d'écrire.
(Baudelaire 1961, 99)

[The reveille resounds across the barracks square,/and the morning wind blows on the lanterns. . . . And the man is tired of writing.]

Second, stylistically, Bécquer's 'theme', the special insight or privileged knowledge of the poet, fragments and is diffused into the first synaesthetic effects, which are to be exploited fully in the following stanza. To pursue for a moment the *metonymic* trope, the 'himno gigante y extraño' of Romanticism can be seen to have undergone a transformation. For what emerges from the metonym 'cadencias que el aire dilata en las sombras' is the 'idée même et suave' of Symbolism: not accidentally does 'musicalement se lève' figure in Bécquer's version of an aesthetic of convoked absence (Mallarmé 1945, 857).

The shift from Romantic to Symbolist mode is both conveyed and echoed in the transition from 'Yo sé . . . ' to 'Yo quisiera . . . ', a change of mood, too, syntactically (indicative to subjunctive) and psychologically (conviction to aspiration). And the object of Bécquer's aspiration, echoing so precisely Mallarmé's dilemma, is writing itself. Traditionally 'tamable', ever subordinate to thought or content, the medium of expression, 'el idioma', is now perceived as 'rebelde, mezquino', the more galling in the light of a further Mallarméan insight: 'ce n'est pas avec des idées qu'on fait [de la poésie] mais avec des mots'/'it is not with ideas that [poetry] is made but with words' (Mondor 1941, 684). The stylistic trope at play here, then, in White's terms, is *irony*. The notion of 'domando' (or the possibility of expressing 'los extravagantes hijos de mi fantasía'/'the extravagant children of my fantasy' (Bécquer 1954, 45) is revealed as an *impossibility* twice over. Synaesthetic fragmentation, in the opening stanza, is inferred; in the second stanza it is preferred, since it is seen to offer a surer way of conveying the content of the poetic imagination. In short, Bécquer's poem broaches referentiality itself as the crucial theoretical problem to be tackled, though never overcome, in the *Rimas*. There can be *no* fusion, 'a un tiempo', of those very 'suspiros y risas, colores y notas' which characterize the collection's content with 'las palabras', which constitute its form. Hence the most prosaic of resignations, 'Pero en vano es luchar': a further *irony*, given that this is the prefatory poem of the *Rimas*, a collection announced in failure as doomed to failure. A further comparison with Mallarmé is irresistible. *Plusieurs sonnets* opens with a similar admission of failure, albeit an inestimably more complex rendering of the theme of the impossibility of writing:

Quand l'ombre menaça de la fatale loi
Tel vieux Rêve, désir et mal de mes vertèbres,
Affligé de périr sous les plafonds funèbres
Il a ployé son aile indubitable en moi.
                    (Mallarmé 1945, 67)

[When the shadows threatened of the fatal law/Such an old

Dream, desire and ill of my vertebrae/Afflicted by perishing under the funereal ceilings/It folded its indubitable wing over me.]

And it is *a synecdoche* which completes the ironic insight: 'que no hay cifra capaz de encerrarlo'. The cipher, as in the case of Baudelaire's hieroglyph, survives but half-broken, evoking syn-aesthetic correspondences yet, ultimately, failing to communicate unmediated thoughts and emotions. Again, mere knowledge of the 'hymn' of art cannot render the poet 'déchiffreur de l'univers'/'decipherer of the Universe'. The alternative is meek – 'y apenas' – and, belatedly, lapses into a Romantic ethic of love-worship, expressed, however, in an anti-Romantic style, *decrescendo*. For the apostrophe '¡oh hermosa!' is bracketed by 'apenas' and 'si,' subject precisely to the impossibility that has been the theme of the poem. Merely glimpsed, the love-object, absent from the text until now, is attenuated on either side of its conception, hemmed in, defined, obliterated, replaced by gram-matical doubt, by the never-to-be-realized subjunctive mood. As a consequence, the humble, murmured, private, phatic act, merely imagined, far from achieved, stands in the most ironic counterpoint to the opening chant of projected knowledge. The collapse of a theologically derived medium, 'himno', into a putative discourse of private, unvoiced, whispered but direct communication is, furthermore, an illusion. For, rephrasing Foucault, the poem 'becomes effective to the degree that it intro-duces discontinuity into our very being' (Foucault 1984, 88). And the discontinuity here is a lapse into non-written, possibly even non-voiced, whispered, communication – 'si, teniendo en mis manos las tuyas/pudiera, al oído' – in short, a dream of non-referentiality. Bécquer, as the *Rimas* begin, clings to the possi-ble physical consolation of 'la chair' not yet revealed as 'triste, hélas', even if already juxtaposed with the failed communicative medium of 'les livres' – though Mallarmé's version of satiety is expressed from the readerly, as distinct from Bécquer's writerly, point of view: 'la chair est triste, hélas, et j'ai lu tous les livres/Fuir là-bas fuir!'/'the flesh is sad, alas, and I have read all the books/To flee, over there, to flee!' (Mallarmé 1945, 67).

RUBÉN DARÍO AND THE ANXIETY OF INFLUENCE

The 'introduction into our very being of discontinuity' is a notion inconceivable – as Foucault would be the first to concede – without a norm of continuity. Such a norm, in this case, would be the continuity of literary influence. The model I shall employ here, however, is a theory of influence which contests 'normal' acceptance of literary precedents and predecessors, substituting a vision of anguished struggle against 'priority', against strong paternity. It is Harold Bloom's theory regarding the anguished 'misreading' on the part of a successor-poet of the influential texts of a 'strong' precursor. Bloom's theory is 'dramatized' in *The Anxiety of Influence* and *A Map of Misreading*, not only major works concerned with poetic theory but also important analyses of the development of Romantic rhetoric in the English tradition. My use of the model here will be but partial, since my concern is to show how, in the literary history of *modernismo*, Rubén Darío's aesthetic swerves away, in Bloomian terms, from the unacceptable insights of such a strong precursor poet as Bécquer. In the next chapter, I shall discuss in detail the technical application of Bloom's ratios to Darío's 'misreading' of Mallarmé. In this instance, my analysis of 'Yo persigo una forma . . . ' will be concerned rather with the problems of 'metahistory' already broached:

> Yo persigo una forma que no encuentra mi estilo,
> botón de pensamiento que busca ser la rosa;
> se anuncia con un beso que en mis labios se posa
> al abrazo imposible de la Venus de Milo.
>
> Adornan verdes palmas el blanco peristilo;
> los astros me han predicho la visión de la Diosa;
> y en mi alma reposa la luz como reposa
> el ave de la luna sobre un lago tranquilo.
>
> Y no hallo en mí sino la palabra que huye,
> la iniciación melódica que de la flauta fluye
> y la barca del sueño que en el espacio boga;
>
> y bajo la ventana de mi Bella-Durmiente,
> el sollozo continuo del chorro de la fuente
> y el cuello del gran cisne blanco que me interroga.

[I pursue a form not found by my style,/pansy [thought] bud which seeks to be the rose;/with a kiss placed on my lips it announces itself/to the impossible embrace of the Venus de Milo./Green palms adorn the white peristyle;/the stars have foretold to me the vision of the Goddess;/and in my soul the light rests as does/the bird of the moon on a tranquil lake./ And I find only the word which flees,/the melodic initiation which flows from the flute/and the boat of dream [sleep] which floats in space;/and below the window of my Sleeping Beauty,/the continual sobbing of the fountain's flow/and the neck of the great white swan which interrogates me.]

As in my analysis of the Bécquer poem, I shall apply to Darío's sonnet White's categories of interpretation: namely, the aesthetic, the epistemological and the ethical. Furthermore, I shall comment on the tropes of literary history which the individual poem exploits, not only metaphor, metonymy, synecdoche and irony but also the Bloomian additions of hyperbole and metalepsis.

Aesthetically, it will be recalled, a writer opts for a 'narrative strategy' in response to the existing literary history which is the context of all writing. Here, Darío's response to Bécquer's 'en vano es luchar; que no hay cifra' constitutes both a 'narrative strategy' and a Bloomian *clinamen* or 'swerve'. It is one of pursuit and, as such, initiates a sonnet-pattern which conforms closely to the Bloomian 'Scene of Instruction' in terms both of meta-literary history and of psychology:

> The young poet is seized by an older poet's power (election), whereupon ensues an agreement of poetic visions (covenant), followed by the choice of a counter inspiration or muse (rivalry), after which the apparently liberated ephebe offers himself as the true manifestation of the authentic poet (incarnation); eventually the latecomer comprehensively revalues the precursor (interpretation) and ultimately recreates him in a new way (revision).
>
> (Leitch 1983, 130–1)

Accordingly, having elected to pursue a literary form of expression commensurate with poetic inspiration, Darío establishes a covenant with a literary-historical tradition of the poet–seer/ *voyant*/*vidente* yet swerves from the rival insight of, say, Bécquer, by introducing a third term, 'estilo', into the 'fondo–forma' schism. Inspired by the seemingly new concentration on style, the liberated ephebe proceeds to elaborate on 'estilo' as the true manifestation of poetic authenticity incarnate. Eventually, this swerve serves to interpret the precursor text as not having gone far enough, thus performing a revision of the earlier poem.

In order to show how this aesthetic strategy is constructed into the epistemological choice of an explanatory paradigm of literary history, it is possible to follow the tropes of Darío's sonnet-cum-'Scene of Instruction'. As in Bloom's model, *tropes of action* ('which exibit a language of need and powerlessness') are set against *tropes of desire* ('which display a language of possession and power') (Leitch 1983, 136). Here, however, the latter, the 'tropes of desire', consequent upon 'Yo persigo . . . ', are but few, and are contained within the sonnet's quatrains. Hinging on 'annunciation' (quatrain 1) and 'prediction' (quatrain 2), these tropes operate, for example, as follows: the *synecdoche* of 'botón de pensamiento', but one instance of humble beauty aspiring to superior form, a pansy desirous of the perfection of the rose; the *metalepsis* (or metonymical substitution of one word for another) of 'pensamiento que busca ser la rosa', where thought also aspires to a similar formal perfection; and the *hyperbole* of 'los astros me han predicho la visión de la Diosa', a cosmic guarantee of religious consummation.

By contrast with these but few tropes of desire, tropes of action abound. Concomitantly, a pose of 'possession and power' is revealed as such by multiple evidence of 'need and powerless-ness', as follows. *Metonymically*, 'mi estilo' names writing itself – yet writing constitutes an inevitable delay in the direct pursuit of Darío's particular concept of formal beauty (as expressed, hyperbolically, in 'la visión de la Diosa'). Thus, while it is true to say that the 'forma'/'estilo' division appears to swerve away from Bécquer's problematic but direct struggle with language as the impossible referent, this instance of discontinuity with the precursor is not, however, a radical discontinuity. For Darío's writing, his 'estilo', is revealed as 'peristilo', a peri(phrastic) style which, as decoratively as the overgrown columns which surround a Greek temple, serves but to obfuscate a glimpsed repository of the God(dess)head. In short, for Darío, the ethic is ever obscured by the aesthetic, or the aesthetico-erotic.

Ironically, then, in Darío's pursuit of an ethic (a *modernista* version of the Grail?) the 'blanco peristilo' is not white but blank.

Metaphorically, though consistent with Michael Riffaterre's notion of a poem's 'repressed matrix' (1978, 19) – it is the 'temple of art' of his own writing, of *modernismo* itself, that confounds Darío's *aesthetics* (his 'choice of a narrative strategy'). His *epistemology* (his 'choice of an explanatory paradigm') is, however, never as 'real' as Bécquer's ('oh, hermosa') putative woman. Darío's experience of love-worship is inscribed in a series of written, literary, mythical figures – the Venus de Milo, the Diosa and the Bella-Durmiente – phantoms of the unreal consummation enshrined for ever in art, religion and dream. Darío's *ethics* (his choice of a strategy by which the ideological implications of a given representation can be drawn from the comprehension of current social problems) are not, in fact, drawn but perimetral. The 'interroga' which ends the sonnet is not a question-mark but a symbol, not a metaphysical, ethical, anguish but, as will become clear in Chapter 4, and in unmistakable Bloomian terms, an 'anxiety of influence', the ego-centred, Oedipal anguish of a Darío concerned with his self-image as a poet, aesthetic 'ephebe' inadequate to the *epistemological* challenge of the precursor Bécquer.

CÉSAR VALLEJO AND THE INSTITUTION OF MARGINALITY

The third and final theoretical model on which I wish to draw, in this case-study of meta-historical literary discourse, is that of Michel Foucault himself. Most aptly, Foucault's contribution to our understanding of the discursive practices which, cumulatively, constitute 'literary history' centres on that very epistemological challenge which, I shall argue, though ultimately daunting for Darío, is taken up more successfully by César Vallejo. In short, Vallejo is confronted, in his early poetry in particular, not only with the general epistemological problem of Bécquer's 'rebelde, mezquino idioma' but also with the culturally specific 'inheritance' of Darío's Hispano-American *modernismo*. To follow Vallejo's transition from *Los heraldos negros* (1918) to *Trilce* (1922) is to witness his struggling emergence from the strait-jacket of a received poetic discourse yet, at the same time, to realize the impossibility of writing outside a conceptual framework (*epistémé*) of the literary history of the *fin de siècle*. Far from being a chronological continuity, a causality, much less a succession of metaphysical or philosophical fashions or adherences, the *epistémé* (basically a structuralist conceptualization of inter-related, sometimes complementary, sometimes conflictual layers of meaning) is characterizable by discursive discontinuity and resistance. Foucault himself explains it thus: 'by *epistémé* we mean, in fact, the total set of relations that unite, at a given period, the discursive practices that give rise to epistemological figures, sciences, and possibly formalized systems. . . . The *epistémé* is not a form of knowledge [*connaissance*]' (Foucault 1974, 191). Further: 'the *epistémé* is a specifically *discursive* apparatus' (Foucault 1983, 197).

It is this paradoxical dependence on 'institutionality' on the part of the writer seeking a personal space or 'margin' in which to perform that brings my analysis close to the tenets of Foucault and, in particular, to his notion of 'transformation'. Though typically post-structuralist in highlighting differentiality rather than continuity in the history of institutions, Foucault's thought, for my purposes here, will be discussed more narrowly. I shall seek to apply his typology of 'transformation' – namely, the stages of 'derivation', 'mutation' and 'redistribution' (1972, 33) – to Vallejo's inherited discourse of *modernismo*, itself a power-ful institution, itself a dominant body of rules, shibboleths, necessities and exclusions:

> Hay golpes en la vida, tan fuertes . . . ¡Yo no sé!
> Golpes como del odio de Dios; como si ante ellos,
> la resaca de todo lo sufrido
> se empozara en el alma . . . ¡Yo no sé!

> Son pocos; pero son . . . Abren zanjas oscuras
> en el rostro más fiero y en el lomo más fuerte.
> Serán tal vez los potros de bárbaros atilas;
> o los heraldos negros que nos manda la Muerte.

> Son las caídas hondas de los Cristos del alma,
> de alguna fe adorable que el Destino blasfema.
> Esos golpes sangrientos son las crepitaciones
> de algún pan que en la puerta del horno se nos quema.

> Y el hombre . . . Pobre . . . pobre! Vuelve los ojos,
> como cuando por sobre el hombro nos llama una palmada;
> vuelve los ojos locos, y todo lo vivido
> se empoza, como charco de culpa, en la mirada.

> Hay golpes en la vida, tan fuertes . . . ¡Yo no sé!

[There are blows in life, so strong . . . I don't know!/Blows like
that of the hatred of God; as if in the face of them,/the hang-
over of everything ever suffered/became stagnant in the soul
. . . I don't know!/They are few; but they're real . . . they open
up dark flaws/in the proudest face and on the strongest
back./They'll be perhaps the colts of barbarous Atillas;/or the
black heralds sent to us by Death./They are the deep falls of
the Christs of the soul,/Of some adorable faith which Fate
blasphemes./Those bloody blows are the cracklings/of some
bread which at the oven door burns on us./And man. . . .
Wretched . . . wretched! Glances around, just as when over the
shoulder we hear someone clapping;/glances madly round,
and everything already lived/goes stagnant, like a pond of
guilt, in the gaze./There are blows in life, so strong . . . I don't
know!]

This, the first of *Los heraldos negros*, not only occupies a key
position (as was the case with Bécquer's *Rima I* and Darío's
closing poem of *Prosas profanas*) but also acts as an overture to the
collection, broaching the themes and motifs, the style and
rhetoric, of the poetry to follow. The most obvious formal feature
of a poem which, thematically and rhetorically, *derives* from the
stylized, resigned, never-to-be-answered interrogative on which
'Yo persigo una forma . . . ' ended, is the 'bracketing' device of its
opening and closing, apparently identical, lines. 'Inside' these
brackets (and in Foucauldian terms) we are confronted with a
derivation – 'golpes'. These blows are but few, yet recognizably
and gloomily Romantic: 'el odio de Dios', 'la resaca de todo lo
sufrido' and the concomitant potential of the soul for nothing
but stagnation. So much for the poem's theme and a response
to it, namely, ' . . . ¡Yo no sé!'. Thus far, Darío's structure or
'institution' of non-response is hardly disturbed. What, then, of
the rhetoric chosen to embody and convey these all too familiar,
Romantically derived insights? Here, irrefutably, a predominantly *modernista* discourse operates:

> Abren zanjas oscuras
> en el rostro más fiero y en el lomo más fuerte.
> Serán tal vez los potros de bárbaros atilas;
> o los heraldos negros que nos manda la Muerte.

The archaeology of Vallejo's knowledge, here, encompasses
past, present and future suffering, both intensely physical and,

teleologically speaking, divinatory and eschatological. As a consequence of such strong awareness of pervasive, historically unavoidable fatality, the Christian element, broached initially by 'el odio de Dios' and, arguably, by a doom-laden inversion of guardian angels in 'los heraldos negros', finds expression in the full-blown alexandrine legacy of the couplet:

Son las caídas hondas de los Cristos del alma,
de alguna fe adorable que el Destino blasfema.

Clearly re-enacted is the *derived* rhetoric of *modernismo*'s 'canto de vida *sin* esperanza', notwithstanding the nostalgic, 'adorable', attribution to 'some' kind of ethical imperative in 'alguna fe'.

If the *derivation* of Vallejo's poem is that of the expression of a soul-state, the *mutation* involved in its specific expression is equally traceable in the terms of Foucault's theory of a 'conceptual framework' in which literary utterance must perform. Vincent Leitch, in his strikingly concise *Deconstructive Criticism*, addresses the issue in an analysis on which I shall draw in the pages which follow: 'Foucault typically emphasises accidents, not universal rules, surfaces, not depths; multiplicities, not unities, flaws, not foundations; and differences, not identities' (Leitch 1983, 143–4).

To make of these binary oppositions a provisional checklist with which elements of Vallejo's poem may be shown to conform illustrates the point: the accidental shifts from 'golpes' (undefined) through 'las caídas hondas de los Cristos del alma' (theological discourse) to 'las crepitaciones / de algún pan que en el horno se nos quema' (tantalizingly sudden loss of the 'bread of life'). Thus does the 'accident' triumph over the 'universal rule' of 'alguna fe'; thus does Destiny 'blaspheme'.

The 'surface' effect of 'crepitaciones' supersedes the tired *de profundis clamavi*, the age-old 'depth' of 'las caídas hondas'. Thus, multiplicities rather than the most traditional of 'unities' ('*las* caídas' / '*los* Cristos') at one and the same time abound and fragment, a notable mutation of the singular 'Dios'. Flaws ('zanjas') undermine the derived discourse of Christian 'foundation'. Finally, language itself is turned inside-out as the 'positive' metaphor of herald, millennial standard-bearer of promised light and salvation in the Judaeo-Christian tradition, is suddenly stripped of all such 'identity'; shown up, in *difference*, as but one of 'los heraldos negros que nos manda la muerte'. The 'list',

however, is never complete; for, by a process of endless enchain-
ment, comes a return to that Law of the Accidental inscribed on
the most constellated, most exploding of multifaceted tablets,
in *Un Coup de dés* . . . , by Mallarmé. For Vallejo, one clap of the
hands will never abolish hazard. The accident of Creation is not
to be digested, not to be understood, merely to be registered,
momentarily, 'en la mirada', before turning into a stagnant pool
of guilt.

It may well be the case that Vallejo, like Foucault in Leitch's
reading, ultimately 'produces forms of order as disorder – not
instances of disorder as order' (Leitch 1983, 144). For this is the
law of *mutation*, linked to *derivation*, of course, by the third stage
in Foucault's typology of transformation: namely, *redistribution*.
This third and 'main conceptual weapon in the assault' upon any
construction of a comprehensive view of (literary) history, may
also be the most difficult to grasp:

> At the outset of *The Archaeology of Knowledge*, Foucault situates
> his enterprise amid similar projects in contemporary psycho-
> analysis, linguistics, and anthropology – all of which unleash
> *discontinuity* into their respective realms of discourse. Just as
> these disciplines have *decentered* the 'subject' in relation to the
> laws of his desire, the forms of his language, and the rules of
> his actions and myths – demonstrating that man cannot
> explain his sexuality or Unconscious, his system of language,
> nor the patternings of his fictions or deeds – so archaeology
> decenters 'man' in relation to the (unacknowledged) regular-
> ities and discontinuities of his history, showing that man is
> unable to account for the formation or transformation of his
> discourse – the operative rules of the *epistémé*. The decentering
> strategies of archaeology, like those of related contemporary
> disciplines, deliberately carry forward a critical effort at dis-
> lodging 'consciousness' as the founding concept and ground
> of all human sciences.
>
> (Leitch 1983, 152–3)

The inability to 'account for the formation and transformation
of his discourse' may be claimed to derive from 'false' institutions or repositories of knowledge. Thus, in Vallejo's poem, the
opening sequence of negativity, the first '¡Yo no sé!', may be
indelibly associated with Christian resignation to and before the
mysteries of life. By the end of the poem, '¡Yo no sé!' has been

decentred not only in thematic terms – namely, away from a theological discourse – but also linguistically. For no two utterances can ever be identical, no two utterances can occupy, or derive from, the same context. Time has passed, the poem has expressed that temporal, experiential shift and, in the process, the 'archaeology' decentres the subject ('Yo') of the enunciation. Thus does Vallejo's poem conform to the strategy of 'deliberately carry[ing] forward a critical effort at dislodging "consciousness" as the founding concept' of science, of knowledge. Thus does the text put the notion of refrain under erasure. In the opening poem of *Los heraldos negros*, the 'repetition' of the first line in the final line brings not continuity and unity but *discontinuity* and *difference*.

At this early stage in Vallejo's poetic practice, then, the *epistémé* against which his writing performs – however tentatively – is the 'densely regulated nineteenth century' (Leitch 1983, 144) discourse of *modernismo*. The inherited rules are the rules of a *written* discourse, an artefact as sophisticatedly literary as Darío's 'Yo persigo una forma ... ', a sonnet in which the operative 'archaeology' seems less discursive than directed towards Grecian temples. In Vallejo, an 'expanding will to knowledge' (ibid., 147) prompts a marked restlessness within the strait-jacket, a crying to get out of 'institution' which will only be fully heard in *Trilce*. At this stage, the struggle is to find a voice, an individual expression of material presence in an orality – a transposed speech-act – denied by an unyielding *écriture* inherited from even the restless, highly self-conscious, dissatisfied 'whisper' embryonically disclosed by Bécquer's *Rima I*.

'Finding a voice', however, is as subject to rule and to institution as to any thematic or stylistic aspect of literary history: 'the rules of utterance for an era, which underlie its discourses, are subject to determinable historical formations and transformations. Between what can grammatically and logically be said and what is actually said lies an entire domain of epochal discourse, which can be accounted for neither by linguistics, nor by logic, nor by antiquarian history. Other utterances are disallowed through regulation' (ibid., 147).

The *archive* of discourse upon which Foucault's battery of transformational typology concentrates its deconstructive power will be, increasingly, in the case of César Vallejo, the emergence of orality. Granted the history and, equally, given the necessary transformation which – for Michel Foucault, as for Hayden White, as for Harold Bloom – occurs with each successive instance of intertextual *misprision*, Vallejo will re-enact endlessly the *topos* of this chapter's title: the pursuit of (non-)knowledge. The richness of Vallejo's 'archive', however, is its ever-growing experimentation, its insistent dismantling of the rigidly stylized writing tradition from which it derives. Soon, a stuttering, ever less certain expression of, at least, 'yo persigo', 'yo no sé' will emerge in *Trilce IX* (72):

Vusco volvvver de golpe el golpe . . .
Busco volvver de golpe el golpe . . .
Fallo bolver de golpe el golpe.

[I zeek to go vvvack blow for blow . . . ./I seek to go vvack blow for blow . . . ./I fail to co . . . back blow for blow.]

Derivation is the trajectory of pursuit; *derivation*, too, is the repeated 'blows'. Transformation and redistribution, it should now be clear, do not occur separately, artificially, as mere categories of Foucauldian analysis but, rather, inseparably, dynamically, within the stammering grandeur of a reticently revoiced tradition. The 'stages' of pursuit, despite the apparent anti-climax of 'Fallo . . . ', resist, however, a reading of total failure into Vallejo's enterprise. For the final 'flaw' ('zanja oscura' or 'zanja clara'?) of 'bolver' bodes a radical discontinuity, a forceful oral interference in an enclosed system of written literariness. In short, Vallejo's rewriting of *modernismo* forces (literary) history to become 'effective to the degree that it introduces discontinuity into our very being'. Which is where – in our epigraph – we came in. Or is it?

An epigraph, like a refrain, is unrepeatable, may resound only in difference (as, in Chapter 9, I shall argue in relation to subjectivity). Analogously, instances of writing will ever resist that fitting into compartments of instantly recognizable literary history which, generation after generation, 'period' specialists tend to operate. By recuperating poetic discourse into Romanticism, Parnassianism, Symbolism, *modernismo* and the like, such critics purport to construct, block by block, the pantheon of continuity. While this tendency encourages, in Foucault's words, 'the consoling play of recognitions', such consolations, such constructions, when unblocked, resemble not so much literary history as poetry itself.

In conclusion, the meta-historical reading of literary eras or modes, as explored in this chapter, may be viewed as ever reflexive. An institutionalized, usually academic, decision regarding the drawing of boundaries will rebound; compartments will come apart; '-isms' be schisms. *Modernismo* will exist as a category only for the categorically determined.

> Effective history . . . will uproot its traditional foundations and relentlessly disrupt its pretended continuity. This is because knowledge is not made for understanding; it is made for cutting.
>
> Michel Foucault

WORKS CITED

Baudelaire, Charles. *Les Fleurs du mal*. Paris: Pléiade, 1961.

Bécquer, Gustavo Adolfo. *Obras completas*. Madrid: Aguilar, 1954.

Bloom, Harold. *The Anxiety of Influence*. New York and London: Oxford University Press, 1973.

—— *A Map of Misreading*. New York, Toronto and Melbourne: Oxford University Press, 1975.

—— *Figures of Capable Imagination*. New York: Seabury, 1976.

Darío, Rubén. *Prosas profanas y otros poemas*. Madrid: Castalia, 1983.

Foucault, Michel. 'Réponse à une question: History, Discourse and Discontinuity'. *Salmagundi* 21.229 (1972), 33.

—— *The Archaeology of Knowledge*. London: Tavistock, 1974.

—— *Power/Knowledge*. Brighton: Harvester Press, 1983.

—— 'Nietzsche, Genealogy, History', in *The Foucault Reader*, ed. Paul Rabinow. Harmondsworth: Penguin, 1986.

Leitch, Vincent B. *Deconstructive Criticism: An Advanced Introduction*. London: Hutchinson, 1983.

Mallarmé, Stéphane. *Œuvres complètes*. Paris: Pléiade, 1945.

Mondor, Henri. *Vie de Mallarmé*. Paris: Gallimard, 1941.

Murray, David. (ed.) *Literary Theory and Poetry: Extending the Canon*. London: Batsford, 1989.

Richard, Jean-Pierre. *Poésie et profondeur*. Paris: Editions du Seuil, 1955.

Riffaterre, Michael. *Semiotics of Poetry*. London: Methuen, 1978.

Vallejo, César. *Obra completa*. Madrid: Alianza, 1986.

—— *Trilce*. Madrid: Cátedra, 1991.

White, Hayden. *Tropics of Discourse: Essays in Cultural Criticism*. Baltimore, Md: Johns Hopkins University Press, 1978.

Chapter 4

Reading, misreading and the resistance to modernity

On misprision and intertextuality: from Rubén Darío to César Vallejo

If one recalls Mallarmé's repeated insistence on poetry's abolition of simple referentiality . . . one begins to suspect that the traditional reading of Mallarmé's nonreferentiality is inadequate.

Barbara Johnson

Barbara Johnson claims, in *The Critical Difference*, that 'what is revolutionary in Mallarmé's poetics is less the elimination of the "object" than [the] construction of a systematic set of self-emptying, non intuitive meanings'. She also insists, however, that '"leaving the initiative to words" is not as simple as it sounds' (1985, 53). Taking her analysis further and accepting the invitation to see how later *poets* have read Mallarmé, I wish to concentrate on the word 'traditional'. First, I shall return to the poem by Rubén Darío discussed in the previous chapter and, expanding on his incapacity to absorb fully the implications of Mallarmé's break with traditional epistemology, I shall try to show how César Vallejo, in *Trilce*, requiring to respond to Mallarmé *through* Darío, but with the paradoxical consciousness of 'Fallo bolver' echoing loud, challengingly reads the latter's misreading. The general question of poetic and, by extension, literary influence will be examined, and, as the reference to misreading in my title suggests, I shall be assessing Harold Bloom's ratios of misprision against Vallejo's agonic struggle to deliver modernity.

Following Bloom's tenets that poems lie primarily against three adversaries – themselves, other poems, time – I shall echo this trio with three critical approaches: textual criticism, intertextuality, influence study. While my aim will be to operate all three together, the more general psychoanalytical implications of Bloomian analysis can also be drawn out.

First, Bloom's claim that the 'dialectic of influences reveals that literature itself is founded upon rivalry, misinterpretation, repression, even plain theft and savage misprision' (Bloom 1976, xii) can be viewed in the broader context of a North American reaction against *merely* textual criticism – both the New Critical and 'Verbal Icon' variety of Bloom's own early conditioning (Brooks, Wimsatt, Trilling *et al.*) and later, structuralist, equivalents. The technical and formal nature of my concerns in juxtaposing the Darío sonnet with one by Mallarmé should by no means exclude speculation on intentionality; indeed, might serve to remind us, as Frank Lentricchia has it, that 'the human writes, the human thinks, and is always following after and defending against another human' (1980, 333). A Bloomian analysis might provide an antidote to the French-style deconstructions of the previous chapter and even to that 'anti-humanistic plain dreariness of all those developments in European criticism that have yet to demonstrate that they can help in reading any one poet whatsoever' (Bloom 1973, 13). Equally, Lentricchia is not slow to counter Bloom's humanism on the grounds of Freudianism: 'Bloom's version of the self denies freedom and individuality as it dooms the subject to one activity – the endless and endlessly evasive expression of father-figure anxieties over which it has no control and which finally it cannot evade' (1980, 336). The *limitations* of theory, of theories, I shall also highlight by recourse to Vallejo's experimentalism.

This aporia brings me to the second question, that of Bloom's use of intertextuality. There can be no doubt that Bloomian analysis is post-structuralist in its conforming to certain basic propositions concerning the nature of literary language. Such analysis conforms to the commonplace of *le déjà écrit*, for instance, in the formulation of Tzvetan Todorov: 'No statement exists without the intertextual dimension. Whatever the object of the word, that object, in one way or another, has always already been said; and one cannot avoid encountering discourses held upon that object' (1984, 62). Moreover, Bloomian analysis performs according to Antoine Compagnon's theories of citation: 'To write, since it is always to rewrite, is no different from citing. Citation, thanks to the metonymic confusion over which it presides, is reading and writing; to read or to write is to perform an act of citation' (1979, 34). It is even possible to set Bloomian analysis within a Derridan context, since, again, it performs according to the claim that 'we can pronounce not a single destructive proposition which has not already had to slip into the form, the logic, and the implicit postulations of precisely what it seeks to contest' (Derrida 1978, 280). Thus, in my Mallarmé–Darío example, the potential Freudian dimension of the 'son'-inheritor-ephebe's proposed 'destruction' of the 'father'-precursor-master would be but another, inevitable, failure of the attempt to construct a metaphysics of presence, of self-presence. The fact that, as I shall show in the juxtaposition of the two poems, poetic meaning is always dialectical, poetic expression always an 'anxiety' for originality in a non-unique discourse, merely confirms, conforms with, repeats with a difference, the differentiality of Derrida's deconstruction of Western metaphysics in general and of self-identical subjectivity in particular.

My third category is influence study itself. What kind of text is that of Harold Bloom, what kind of text is this, my own, 'influence study' of Mallarmé and Darío? For Bloom, the answer is clear, if habitually 'strong' (and most un-modest): poetry criticism always parallels poetry in its antithetical dialectical relationship with previous criticism and with poetry. For Bloom, 'all criticism *is* prose poetry'. As such, criticism cannot escape a dialectical reciprocity which constantly defers its own status or 'presence'. What I am writing at this present moment differs from, but is deferred towards, both precursor critics and poets:

> I do not believe that poetic influence is simply some thing that happens, that it is just the process by which ideas and images are transmitted from earlier to later poets. On that view, whether or not influence causes anxiety in the later poet is a matter of temperament and circumstance. Poetic influence thus reduces to source-study.
>
> (Bloom 1976, 9)

Time and again an influence may be traced or asserted; yet influence study generally proves inconclusive to the extent that it remains at the level of established fact. Far more interesting is the question of how influence works and why. In this respect, the work of Bloom has both revitalized and rendered more systematic the 'influence' approach. My intention here is to apply in detail Bloom's so-called 'revisionary ratios' to a poem already visited differently, 'Yo persigo una forma', thereby testing a counter-reading to that based on Hayden White's critique and the (literary) meta-histories of the last chapter; then to argue that Darío's poem constitutes a creative 'misreading' of Mallarmé's 'Mes bouquins refermés sur le nom de Paphos'. I begin with what may be considered as the notoriously prolix Bloom's most succinct statement of his methodology:

> The first principle of the proper study of influence, as I conceive it, is that no strong poem has sources and no strong poem merely alludes to another poem. The meaning of a strong poem is another strong poem, a precursor's poem which is being misinterpreted, revised, corrected, evaded, twisted askew, made to suffer an inclination or bias which is the property of the later and not the earlier poet. Poetic influence, in this sense, is actually poetic misprision, a poet's taking or doing amiss of a parent-poem that keeps finding him, to use a Coleridgean turn-of-phrase. Yet even this misprision is only the first step that a new poet takes when he advances from the early phase where his precursor floods him, to a more Promethean phase where he quests for his own fire, which nevertheless must be stolen from his precursor. I count some half-dozen steps in the life-cycle of the strong poet, as he attempts to convert his inheritance into what will aid him without inhibiting him by the anxiety of a failure in priority, a failure to have begotten himself. These steps are revisionary ratios.
>
> (1976, 9–10)

The six ratios, by now classical or notorious according to one's attitude to Bloom, are *Clinamen*, *Tessera*, *Kenosis*, *Daemonization*, *Askesis* and *Apophrades*. I shall give Bloom's definition of each in the course of my application and would only add that I have chosen to apply them in an order slightly different from the above. This is not a random choice but one dictated by the development of Darío's sonnet. Thus, I have arranged my discussion of the Bloom ratios according to their occurrence in a *linear* reading of 'Yo persigo una forma' in juxtaposition with Mallarmé's 'Mes bouquins refermés sur le nom de Paphos':

> Mes bouquins refermés sur le nom de Paphos,
> Il m'amuse d'élire avec le seul génie
> Une ruine, par mille écumes bénie
> Sous l'hyacinthe, au loin, de ses jours triomphaux.

Coure le froid avec ses silences de faux,
Je n'y hululerai pas de vide nénie
Si ce très blanc ébat au ras du sol dénie
A tout site l'honneur du paysage faux.

Ma faim qui d'aucuns fruits ici ne se régale
Trouve en leur docte manque une saveur égale:
Qu'un éclate de chair humain et parfumant!

Le pied sur quelque guivre où notre amour tisonne,
Je pense plus longtemps peut-être éperdument
A l'autre, au sein brûlé d'une antique amazone.

(1945, 76)

[My books shut on the name of Paphos,/It amuses me to choose with my spirit alone/A ruin blessed by a thousand foams/Far off, beneath the hyacinth of its triumphant days./ Let the cold run with its sickle silences,/I shall not lament an empty refusal/If this most white revel on the earth's surface deny/To any site the false landscape's honour./My hunger that is satisfied with no fruits here/Finds in their learned lack an equal savour:/Let one burst with flesh human and odorous!/ My foot on some serpentine andiron where our love stirs the fire,/I think longer perhaps with desperation/Of the other, of the burnt breast of an ancient Amazon.]

(Translation: Hartley 1965, 102–3)

Yo persigo una forma que no encuentra mi estilo,
botón de pensamiento que busca ser la rosa;
se anuncia con un beso que en mis labios se posa
al abrazo imposible de la Venus de Milo.

Adornan verdes palmas el blanco peristilo;
los astros me han predicho la visión de la Diosa;
y en mi alma reposa la luz como reposa
el ave de la luna sobre un lago tranquilo.

Y no hallo en mí sino la palabra que huye,
la iniciación melódica que de la flauta fluye
y la barca del sueño que en el espacio boga;

y bajo la ventana de mi Bella-Durmiente,

el sollozo continuo del chorro de la fuente
y el cuello del gran cisne blanco que me interroga.

(177)

[I pursue a form not found by my style,/pansy [thought] bud
which seeks to be the rose;/with a kiss placed on my lips it
announces itself/to the impossible embrace of the Venus de
Milo./Green palms adorn the white peristyle;/the stars have
foretold to me the vision of the Goddess;/and in my soul the
light rests as does/the bird of the moon on a tranquil lake./
And I find in me only the word which flees,/the melodic initiation which flows from the flute/and the boat of dream [sleep]
which floats in space;/and below the window of my Sleeping
Beauty,/the continual sobbing of the fountain's flow/and the
neck of the great white swan which interrogates me.]

The two sonnets, both final poems in their respective volumes,
embody as 'events', a moment of 'bouquins refermés' ('books re-
closed'). Mallarmé's poem echoes the closure of his collection
in the abrupt finality of its opening line. The dismissively low
register of 'bouquins' (cf. 'livres'), furthermore, only serves to
underline the relative unimportance of *Poésies*, as of any book
read at the fireside, when compared to Mallarmé's dreamed-of
project of 'The Book, spiritual instrument' (1945, 369).

Mallarmé's dissatisfaction with traditional literature – the mere
'bouquins' reminiscent of Verlaine's dismissive 'And all the rest
is literature' (326) – none the less permitted him to envisage what
it might achieve: 'I believe that literature will furnish us with a
Theatre, whose representations will be the true modern cult; a
Book, explanation of man sufficient for our most beautiful
dreams' (1945, 875–6). I wish to argue that the perceived gap
between Mallarmé's own *style*, in *Poésies*, and the *form* of his
'dream-project' allows for one of Darío's major strategic revisions
of Mallarmé in 'Yo persigo una forma'. I shall therefore consider
briefly Mallarmé's pursuit of an adequate form of expression.

The difficulty of reading Mallarmé ought to be stressed from
the outset, since any claims regarding Darío's 'misprisions' must
be seen in the context of the notorious, cultivated discontinuities
of thought and expression which constitute Mallarmé's style.
Malcolm Bowie best summarizes the challenge involved:

The double effect required to allow Mallarmé's gaps their full
disjunctive and destructive power, yet at the same time remain

attentive to the multitude of invisible currents which pass back and forth between the separated segments, will strike many readers as inexcusably arduous and unrewarding... such moments are of the essence in Mallarmé... the type of the modern artist... intent on breaking up ready-made *Gestalten* and smooth surface textures in order to compel his audience to look elsewhere for artistic coherence, to venture beneath the surface into the difficult, undifferentiated world of unconscious process, to interrupt the easy flow of horizontal perception with strenuous excursions into multi-level, all at once verticality.

(1978, 8, 16)

If the Symbolist aesthetic may best be summarized in Mallarmé's formulation 'to paint not the thing but the effect which it produces' (1959, 137), then the closing of literature on the 'nom de Paphos', in this instance, provides a telling example of the form that aesthetic implies: 'To *name* an object, is to suppress three quarters of the enjoyment of the poem, which consists of guessing little by little: to suggest it, there is the dream. It is the perfect use of this mystery which constitutes the symbol' (ibid., 869). Thus, to cease reading on the very name of Paphos takes attention away from historical fact or mythical association. Far from pondering or re-working the *ideas* prompted by a mention of the shrine of Aphrodite on Cyprus, founded by the Amazons, the sonnet struggles against that 'easy flow of horizontal perception', as Bowie suggests, indulging in its quatrains precisely those 'strenuous excursions' of a fanciful proposition posed only to be negated, a conditionally evoked vision of past glory revealed as a sham by the intrusive cold draught of the present fireside setting. While the quatrains proceed, disjunctively, by means of negations, to *le faux* (= 'the false'; cf. 'la faux' = 'the sickle'), underlining the impossibility of even imaginative access to a historically irrecuperable 'paysage', the tercets construct that 'multi-level, all-at-once verticality' of Mallarmé's most explicit savouring, *in a poem*, of an aesthetic of convoked absence. But to this I shall proceed, in detail, as I follow Darío's swerve away from the Mallarméan model. Meanwhile, suffice it to recall the celebrated parallel, *in prose*, of Mallarmé's aesthetic of absence:

Je dis: une fleur! et, hors de l'oubli où ma voix relègue aucun contour, en tant que quelque chose d'autre que les calices sus,

musicalement se lève, idée même et suave, l
bouquets.

[I say: a flower! and, out of the forgetfulness
banishes any contour, inasmuch as it is some
known calyxes, musically arises, an idea its
the one absent from all bouquets.]

For it is against an aesthetic of the precedence
the idea, of convoked absence over physical (
physical presence, that we can see Darío reactir
the first of Bloom's revisionary ratios, *clinamen*.

CLINAMEN

Clinamen, which is poetic misprision proper. The later poet
swerves away from the precursor, by so reading the parent-
poem as to execute *a clinamen* in relation to it. This appears
as the corrective movement of his own poem, which implies
that the precursor poem went accurately up to a certain point,
but then should have swerved, precisely in the direction that
the new poem moves.

Darío's sonnet follows that of Mallarmé in closing a 'bouquin'
(*Prosas profanas*) on a note of insufficiency. However, it does so
with a corrective desire to modify, or swerve away from, the
Symbolist aesthetic. Whereas Mallarmé plays with the traditional
content/form distinction whereby the latter first abolishes
the former before itself being superseded by the abstraction
'absence', Darío introduces, as suggested in the previous chapter,
'style' into the existing dichotomy. Whereas the very objective of
Mallarmé's poem is the ironic destruction of the notion that
poetic form can express content *as presence*, Darío's sonnet, in its
first line, re-establishes form as the object of a quest rendered
constantly vain, frustrated by the inadequacies of a personal
style. *Absence*, therefore, is by no means a necessary condition, let
alone the objective in itself, for Darío's sonnet implies already,
from the opening line, a pursuit of transcendence which time
and again, in his later poetry, will take the form of a desperate
logocentrism, if not a full-blown ethical teleology. For the
moment, however, 'Yo persigo una forma' swerves away from

the Mallarméan notion that 'it is not with ideas that one makes sonnets but with words' (cf. Bécquer in Chapter 3) by effectively re-opening his own book on a *thought*: the thought that the putative marriage of 'style' and 'form' might indeed bear the fruit of an as yet unattained artistic ideal. In this respect, of course, he is very much the inheritor of an earlier generation of Romantics and Parnassians and, perhaps most of all, of the Wagnerian ideal of *Gesamtkunstwerk* – as, indeed, subsequent elements of Darío's sonnet will suggest. In short, and in Bloomian terms, Mallarmé has absorbed such a heritage 'accurately up to a certain point, but then should have swerved precisely in the direction that the new poem moves'. It would appear then, initially, that Darío is unable to accept the non-theological trajectory and implications of Mallarméan aesthetics, perhaps detecting, even at so short a distance, what Malcolm Bowie argues three-quarters of a century later:

> Mallarmé occupies a special place in the modern tradition. Among French poets of the nineteenth century he was the most adventurously and the most trenchantly agnostic: his powers of doubt played not only upon the time-honoured theologies and theodicies of Europe, but upon those new, secular cults of beauty and 'the Spirit' of which he is popularly thought to be an uncritical exponent.

> (Bowie 1978, 4)

For an author shortly to write of El Arte 'Ego sum lux et veritas et vita', such an intuition as Mallarmé's could offer no comfort.

TESSERA

> *Tessera*, which is completion and antithesis. The later poet antithetically completes the precursor, by so reading the parent-poem as to retain its terms but to mean them in an opposite sense, as though the precursor had failed to go far enough.

The terms 'retained' in the Darío poem but meant 'in an opposite sense' are the terms of *absence*: 'impossible embrace'. The sense, however, is that of unfulfilment, of regret, as distinct from the convoked, the desired, non-presence of 'burnt breast'. That is to say, Darío's *clinamen* involves the inability or reluctance to accept *le docte* ('the learned'), the core of Mallarméan cerebrality which renders 'equal' absence and presence. Darío's aspiration fuses the aesthetic and the sensual in his opening quatrain (although, as I shall show in discussion of *apophrades*, it does retain, inseparably, an element of the cerebral in the double sense of *pensamiento* as: 'thought', 'pansy'). Crucially, his sonnet is constructed not upon a missing term as is Mallarmé's 'dream', but, rather on objective correlatives of his own 'reverie', as concrete, in one instance, as 'the boat of dream'. Mallarmé eschews the 'here' in the passage towards 'lack'; Darío never leaves the 'here', or the 'here below'. A Romantic archetype of *seaward* evasion (the 'real') is forever commingled with a Symbolist *mental* evasion (the 'unreal').

In this case, *tessera* operates to the extent that 'the precursor had failed to go far enough' in developing sensuality, elevating the erudite and the cerebral, perhaps even the spirit, above and beyond Darío's equally important 'hunger' for the fruits of sensuality. Hyperaesthesia, far from attainable through a domestic, fireside reading, in the armchair, amusedly, and at will, is pursued, in Darío's case, through an altogether different iconography of synaesthesia – 'rose', 'kiss', 'lips', 'announces itself' and 'embrace' – however unattainably.

DAEMONIZATION

> *Daemonization*, or the movement toward a personalized Counter-Sublime, in reaction to the precursor's Sublime. The later poet opens himself to what he believes to be a power in the parent-poem that does not belong to the parent proper, but to a range of being just beyond that precursor. He does this, in his poem, by so stationing its relation to the parent-poem as to generalize away the uniqueness of the earlier work.

Darío's 'personalized Counter-Sublime' derives from 'a movement towards' the vision of a specific form of the Godhead: 'los astros me han predicho la visión de la Diosa'. In reaction to the precursor's Sublime – 'Je pense plus longtemps peut-être éperdument' – Darío opens himself to the power of other(ness) not confined to a personal daydream of the absent breast but to 'a range of being beyond' that vision. His Counter-Sublime is at once more cosmic ('the stars') and more traditional ('the

Goddess'), although there remains a strong sense of the 'person-alized' in the privilege accorded to a poet–seer singled out by fate ('have foretold to me').

Darío 'generalizes away the uniqueness of the earlier work' by the fusion of the religious, the personal and the fatalistic, which *seems* to take his sonnet beyond the mere 'Beauty' of Symbolism, reinitiating the quest for 'the Ideal' early rejected by Mallarmé – 'after having found Nothingness, I found Beauty' (1959, 220). Yet can this be the case? I shall reserve my response to this question for my discussion of *kenosis*, pausing first to consider how *daemonization* operates in 'Yo persigo una forma'. The power which derives from Mallarmé's initial evocation of 'A ruin blessed by a thousand foams' certainly suffuses the equivalent construction in Darío's sonnet: 'Green palms adorn the white peristyle'. Yet Darío's sonnet goes further. Not only does the line provide a possibly impenetrable shrine for the Goddess of Darío's aspiration, but also the luxuriant foliage adorning and obscuring an *architectural* peristyle is mirrored, in verse, by the very adornment of Darío's own discursive evoking of not only (an external) content but also (an internal) form: namely, that of the *modernista* aesthetic so often equated with Symbolism, yet more accurately to be compared, in its concentration on the freezing of content and form in 'the immobile block of Art', with Théophile Gautier's Parnassianism. As in the case of 'pen-samiento', 'peristilo' here operates paronomastically, as a pun, by the fusion of two equivalent *presences*. The resultant conceit operates at a level more comparable with much earlier styles exploiting conceits and wit than with the Mallarméan technique of juxtaposing an imagined *presence* with a convoked *absence*.

It is by thus penetrating a personal 'peristyle' that Darío's poem appears to achieve, as the second quatrain ends, precisely the 'pursued form', the 'range of being just beyond that precursor': 'and in my soul the light rests as does the bird of the moon on a tranquil lake'. Such a moment of suspension, of repose, of quasi-mystic levitation before the would-be consummation and resolution of the imminent sestet, is typically conveyed not by the traditional possession of the mystic's soul by the dove of Holy Spirit, the Paraclete, but by the quintessentially *modernista* equiva-lent: namely, the indirectly evoked Swan, Ideal embodiment of spirituality and Art. It remains to be seen, however, whether the sonnet's tercets will sustain and fulfil the expectations raised in its quatrains, the possibility of fusing 'style' and 'form', of attaining the Ideal which Mallarmé's precursor quatrain specifically rejects (I retain the French in this instance to emphasize the point stylistically):

> Je n'y hululerai pas de vide nénie
> Si ce très blanc ébat au ras du sol dénie
> A tout site l'honneur du paysage faux.

Triumph derives here from a construction of negativities – negative verbal particles 'n'y/pas/né/-nie/dé/-nie' – which themselves provide the masking columns, the specifically Mallarméan *peristyle*, surrounding an enshrined *vide* ('void'). In this respect, I would argue, Mallarmé's poem provides its own Counter-Sublime, contains its own *daemonization*, whereas Darío's poem, up to this point, in a classic 'misprision', takes the precursor's temple to be the Sublime: in fact, it operates as a collapsed presence, 'a ruin'.

KENOSIS

> *Kenosis*, which is a braking-device similar to the defense-mechanisms our psyches employ against repetition-compulsions; *kenosis*, then, is a movement toward discontinuity with the precursor. The later poet, apparently emptying himself of his own afflatus, his imaginative godhood, seems to humble himself as though he ceased to be a poet, but this ebbing is so performed in relation to a precursor's poem-of-ebbing that the precursor is emptied out also, and so the later poem of deflation is not as absolute as it seems.

A re-initiation of the quest for the Ideal, a possible counter to the precursor's savouring of a 'learned' absence, as indicated already, is resolved not only in traditional sonnet manner, in the sestet, but also in the Bloomian 'revisionary ratio' of *kenosis*. The 'emptying of his own afflatus', the humbling of Darío's aspiration, takes the form of 'And I find only . . . ', counter-balance to 'I pursue . . . '. What *is* available, tauntingly, is 'the word'. Here, it is the word that flees, whereas in Mallarmé's poem it is the *Idea*, leaving the *Word* – in this case Paphos – to echo long after the book is closed, deprived of any context of presence, abandoned to mere resonant play, the frolic or 'revel' of guaranteed absence.

Yet the later poem does indeed contain 'a braking-device similar to the defense-mechanisms our psyches employ'. On the one hand there is an aspiration to the state of music habitually accorded to the Word by generations of post-Romantics and, ironically, not least by Mallarmé:

– Je sais, on veut à la Musique, limiter le mystère:
quand l'écrit y prétend.

(1959, 385)

[– I know, one wishes to limit the mystery to Music: when writing aspires to that.]

The 'melodic initiation' here serves as an anticipatory salve to yet another instance of defeat, the ultimate failure to marry 'style' with 'form' at the very end of *Prosas profanas*. Darío's poem clings on to Verlaine's imperative – 'music before all else' – just as his aesthetic will develop more in line with the latter's *Sagesse* than in the less obviously ethical (though infinitely more revolutionary) way of *Un coup de dés*.

Yet this later 'poem of deflation is not as absolute as it seems', nor can it be. For the 'defense-mechanism' shown above in the *aesthetic* context also operates at the *ethical* level. 'And I find only . . . /the boat of dream which floats in space', constitutes but a half-*kenosis*, fails to abandon the echo of suspension and potential illumination of the second quatrain discussed in relation to *daemonization*. Nostalgic for that lost state of receptive tranquillity, that readiness for a quasi-mystical transcendence, however, the dream-vision can evoke but a clichéd correlative of evasion – namely, the seaward as opposed to the mental – broached already in discussion of *tessera* and identified as indelibly Romantic.

In summary, therefore, while *kenosis* does indeed operate here as 'a movement toward discontinuity with the precursor', it is questionable whether the 'humbling' or 'emptying out' which occurs in the first tercet of Darío's sonnet expresses anything more than his reluctance, possibly inability, to accept Mallarmé's refusal to lament, with an empty wail ('nénie'), the loss of escapist transcendence through Art as a vehicle to 'the Ideal'.

ASKESIS

Askesis, or a movement of self-purgation which intends the attainment of a state of solitude. The later poet does not, as in *kenosis,* undergo a revisionary movement of emptying, but of curtailing; he yields up part of his own imaginative endowment, so as to separate himself from others, including the precursor, and he does this in his poem by so stationing it in regard to the parent poem as to make that poem undergo an *askesis* also; the precursor's endowment is also truncated.

The final tercet of Darío's sonnet involves both 'a movement of self-purgation' and 'the attainment of a state of solitude'. In the displacement of 'sobbing' from persona to nature, the poem exploits a pathetic fallacy associated not only archetypally with Romanticism but also, in this case, with a specifically *modernista* setting: the domesticity of Mallarmé's fireside meditation, is parallelled in a very different garden contemplation, that of a would-be 'Prince Charming' of the Sleeping Beauty. This state of solitude, therefore, 'yields up part of' Darío's 'own imaginative endowment', both by evoking the fairy-tale tradition and by diffusing personal emotion in a compliant, sympathetic Nature. The principal figure of this diffusion is one of Darío's most celebrated images: 'el cuello del gran cisne blanco que me interroga'. The line embodies the underlying doubt of a Romantic ethic in an iconography of Parnassian fixity. I would argue that the swan-image of frozen interrogation, virtually an analogue of *modernismo* itself, differs from Mallarmé's brand of Symbolism precisely in its reworking of his classic formulation 'to paint not the thing but the effect that it produces'. In short, Darío's poetry, his 'style', will ever 'paint the thing *and* the effect that it produces', giving rise to perpetual dissatisfaction in his quest for 'a form' – the ineffable.

Whether the second condition of *askesis* is fulfilled is problematical. Mallarmé's endowment, the heritage of Symbolism as many critics, and perhaps Darío, have inadequately understood it, is arguably 'truncated'. That is to say that a series of images – 'croisée'/'crossing', 'casement', 'miroir'/'mirror', 'vol'/'flight', 'cygne'/'swan' and 'azur'/'azure' has constituted the strong but misappropriated influence of Mallarmé upon his successors. In short, an *iconography* of the unattainable has masked and supplanted the *methodology* of convoking absence. Inevitably, the explanation is as theological as the term 'iconography' suggests. For *askesis,* it will be recalled, derives from 'the practice of pre-Socratic shamans'. I have argued already, in the section on *clinamen*, that Darío appeared initially unable to accept the non-theological trajectory of Mallarmé. The final tercet of 'Yo persigo una forma' confirms that fact. Yet this poem is not the only instance of a revisionary reading of Mallarmé on the part of Darío; and the echoes are telling:

> Ausencia de una religión; presencia virtual de todas, en su relación con el misterio, y las pompas litúrgicas, virtud de los signos, secreta fuerza de las palabras; el ensalmo musical; *lo hierático en movimiento* . . . he aquí que traza un signo nuevo, sobre el lago en silencio, el Cisne que comprende.
>
> (1955, 915, 920)

> [Absence of one religion; virtual presence of all, in its relation with mystery, and liturgical pomp, the virtue of signs, the secret force of words; the musical spell; *the hierarchical in movement* . . . all this traces a new sign, on the lake in silence, the Swan which comprehends.]

This final appraisal of Mallarmé by Darío, his obituary, brings me to the last of Bloom's revisionary ratios.

APOPHRADES

Apophrades, or the return of the dead. The later poet, in his own final phase, already burdened by an imaginative solitude that is almost solipsism, holds his own poem so open again to the precursor's work that at first we might believe the wheel has come full circle, and that we are back in the later poet's flooded apprenticeship, before his strength began to assert itself in the revisionary ratios of *clinamen* and the others. But the poem is now *held* open to the precursor, where once it *was* open, and the uncanny effect is that the new poem's achievement makes it seem to us, not as though the precursor were writing it, but as though the later poet himself had written the precursor's characteristic work.

It should now be obvious that the lesson of Darío's response to Mallarmé is that the 'burdened' later poet challengingly *misreads* the precursor. Darío chooses to read Mallarmé as *le Cygne* rather than *le signe*. In 'Yo persigo una forma', Darío 'holds open' his poem, from the very first quatrain, to the work of Mallarmé. The insufficiency of his own style prompts the pursuit of a major influence of 'the later poet's flooded apprenticeship, before his strength began to assert itself in the revisionary ratios of *clinamen* and the others'. Thus, initially, Darío's 'pansy-bud which seeks to be the rose' *was* open, in a humble, *kenosis-linked* way, to Mallarmé's 'I say: a flower'. In retrospect, according to the application of Bloom's ratios, Darío's poem is *held* open to 'the uncanny effect' of achieving 'otherness' ('l'autre'), momentarily, by its capacity to evoke Mallarmé's poem in a revisionary reading or 'misreading'.

Two transformations are at issue: first, the humble *flower* aspiring to the consummate beauty of the rose; second, the equally humble, embryonic thought opening itself daringly, but in ultimate failure, to Mallarmé's monumental achievement of 'l'absente de tous bouquets'/'the absent [idea] of all bouquets'. Darío's sonnet begins on the very note of 'I think . . . ' on which Mallarmé's sonnet ends. It is not prepared, however, to risk 'éperdument' (distractedly or 'with desperation', that is to say, both in joy and even unto madness) the implications of that aesthetic of consummation *not* achievable here ('ici'), nor in any physical passion ('where our love stirs the fire'). Though transcending Mallarméan domesticity (marriage?), Darío's flirtation with the mythical 'Goddess' and 'Sleeping Beauty' underlines his but *partial* rewriting of 'the precursor's characteristic work'. It merely displaces the love-object into versions of the Romantically unavailable; it fails to opt for the empty space left by the blazing non-consummation of 'the other love', the 'burnt breast' of an inexistent myth. If Darío's poem takes further its Mallarméan heritage, it merely re-inscribes an interrogative on the 'empty paper which whiteness defends'. Yet this is no condemnation, for Darío is not alone in his uneasiness with Mallarmé's invitation to silence.

In this chapter, it has not been my intention to generalize and extend the insights afforded by Bloomian analysis to the realm of literary history. My concern has been less the question of whether Darío is Parnassian or Symbolist than to show how poetic influence works *technically*. For this reason I have chosen to concentrate on the intricate play of Harold Bloom's ratios rather than on the psychoanalytic speculation in which they occur. I have not pursued Darío as a case-study of a poet living anxiously in the shadow of the 'strong' Mallarmé, let alone locked in Oedipal rivalry with a castrating precursor. Much less have I sought to psychoanalyse Mallarmé the father-figure himself in, say, his Kleinian preference for the 'good' but absent breast of a quintessentially literary mother-figure 'antique amazone', in rejection of the 'bad' but threateningly present ('fruits d'ici') breast. Rather has my own (anxious) reading sought, needed, to confront Rubén Darío – traditionally regarded as the classic ephebe – as 'the author-in-crisis, belated, wounded and mortal [for whom] there is always a prior plenitude of meaning to struggle against' (Wright 1984, 155); to confront, in turn, Darío's confrontation of Mallarmé, for whom such a plenitude can only be absence itself.

In order to problematize further not only Darío's misreading of Mallarmé but also the poetics of influence elaborated by Bloom, I again turn to the poetry of César Vallejo. In this case, building on the necessarily technical application of Bloom's ratios, I shall attempt to encompass several other important aspects of literary history and psychoanalysis. In the process Barbara Johnson's challenge to read Mallarmé's poetics as the 'construction of a systematic set of self-emptying, non-intuitive meanings' will be taken up and shown to be notably relevant to reading Vallejo.

First, the question of the 'self'. As Elizabeth Wright has objected:

there is something oddly self-validating about [Bloom's] practice. The crisis poem takes for granted a unique self, always there, however divided . . . Bloom writes as if his poet–poet confrontation were *sui generis*. The firm presupposition of a-historical single selves, with their past crystalized around them, makes Bloom's critical practice self-validating in a trivial way, for he thereby keeps out meanings that cannot be directly lodged upon these selves.

(1984, 155–6)

Bloom, of course, is far from alone in being locked, still, into a decidedly Romantic discourse of the self, and it is worth pausing, for a moment, to consider this legacy. M. H. Abrams's binary of the *mirror* and the *lamp*, though deploying images of reflection and projection, respectively, none-the-less situates the mind in but one, whole, or potentially unified space. The artistic process of the mind's contents and aspirations, indeed of its discontents and frustrations, is shown to involve a *framing*, a delimitation of total space, wherein the self both explores and is explored.

In retrospect, it becomes possible to assess the impact of such thinking not only on Darío but on Bloom too. Mallarmé's contemplation of the absent leads to a momentary loss of self in otherness, a *jouissance* (and I use the French term to underline the sublimated sexual activity) which permits the possible 'breaking out' from conceptual frames of time and space limitations, towards the contemplation of the mythical breast *in its absence*. 'Consummation' by possession is replaced by 'consummation' by fire, the element which destroys the delimiting shape and structures of an object of the poetic imagination clearly defined in words though not easily accessible via any framework of thought.

When Rubén Darío comes to confront the iconography of absence posed by Mallarmé, the epistemological problem of the relationship between words and ideas is immediately reflected only to be deflected. In pursuit of that 'totalizing' vision directly descended from the conflation poet = God (Bloom's 'prior plenitude of meaning') Darío's theologically orientated vision of the God(ess)head is literally 'framed', as I have already shown in a different context, within his own peri(phrastic) style. Consequently, since in this discourse the ethic is obscured by the aesthetic, the sonnet's trajectory is one of encapsulated doubt, the framing within the lake not of the open-ended 'signe'/'signifier' but of the closed symbol – a mere 'cygne'/'signified'. Whereas Mallarmé's sonnet exploited the creative–destructive element of fire to destroy delimiting and limiting linguistic closure, Darío's sonnet comes to rest on the becalming (stagnant?) element of water and the Swan Lake image, only to reinforce the 'framing' of linguistic interrogation.

As I address the breaking-up of the *modernista*, and the strong assertion of the modernist discourse, I again borrow and adapt from Michel Foucault's contribution to our understanding of the discursive practices which constitute, in this case, not history but 'literary' history. Rather aptly, Foucault's emphasis falls on that very epistemological challenge which, though ultimately daunting for Darío, is taken up more successfully by César Vallejo. In short, Vallejo is confronted, in his early poetry in particular, not only with the *general* epistemological problem of the 'rebellious, mean language' – or even with the psychological implications of the discourse of the other – but also with the culturally specific 'inheritance' of Darío's Hispano-American *modernismo*.

The 'archaeology' of Vallejo's knowledge in poem XXXVI of *Trilce*, 'Pugnamos ensartarnos por un ojo de aguja' (Vallejo 1991, 177–8), encompasses past, present and future *struggle*, again intensely physical as well as divinatory and eschatological:

Pugnamos ensartarnos por un ojo de aguja,
enfrentados, a las ganadas.
Amoniácase casi el cuarto ángulo del círculo.
¡Hembra se continúa el macho, a raíz
de probables senos, y precisamente
a raíz de cuanto no florece!

¿Por ahí estás, Venus de Milo?

Tú manqueas apenas, pululando
entrañada en los brazos plenarios
de la existencia,
de esta existencia que todaviiza
perenne imperfección.
Venus de Milo, cuyo cercenado, increado
brazo revuélvese y trata de encodarse
a través de verdeantes guijarros gagos,
ortivos nautilos, aunes que gatean
recién, vísperas inmortales.
Laceadora de inminencias, laceadora
del paréntesis.

Rehusad, y vosotros, a posar las plantas
en la seguridad dupla de la Armonía.
Rehusad la simetría a buen seguro.
¡Intervenid en el conflicto
de puntas que se disputan
en la más torionda de las justas
el salto por el ojo de la aguja!

Tal siento ahora al meñique
demás en la siniestra. Lo veo y creo
no debe serme, o por lo menos que está
en sitio donde no debe.
Y me inspira rabia y me azarea
y no hay cómo salir de él, sino haciendo
la cuenta de que hoy es jueves.

¡Ceded al nuevo impar
                    potente de orfandad!

[We strive to thread ourselves through a needle's eye,/face to
face, taking a chance./The fourth angle of the circle almost
ammonias itself./Female continues male, as a result/of probable
breasts, and precisely/as a result of what does not flower!/
Are you there, Venus de Milo?/You are scarcely maimed,
pullulating/entrailed in the plenary arms/of existence,/of
this existence which *yets*/perennial imperfection./ Venus de
Milo, whose amputated, uncreated/arm turns round and tries
to *enelbow* itself/across greening, stammering pebbles,/ dawn-
ing nautili, *yets* which cat-creep/recently, immortal eves./
Bow-tier of imminences, bow-tier/of parentheses./ Refuse, and
you, to place the soles/on the double security of Harmony./
Refuse symmetry with safety./ Intervene in the conflict/of
points which dispute/in the most on-heat of jousts/the jump
through the needle's eye!/So I feel now the little finger/too
much on the left hand. I see it and I believe/it ought [must] not
be me, or at least that it is/in a place where it ought not./And
it inspires rage and alarms me/and there is no way to get out
of it, but by making/the reckoning that today is Thursday./
Cede to the new odd number/potent with orphanhood!]

As a consequence of the pervasive, historically unavoidable
heritage of *modernismo* – and of the Judaeo-Christian intertext of
'the eye of the needle' – the opening verse re-writes (as it echoes)
'Yo persigo una forma'. The strong erotic, specifically coital,
image of full-frontal desire for conquest ('face to face, gambling')
re-enacts but sexualizes Darío's pursuit of the God(ess)head
rather as a confrontation of the maidenhead. That physical attraction is 'chemical' is a cliché explored in the powerful disruption
of geometry threatened by that (orgasmic) moment of 'reaction'
('the fourth angle of the circle ammonias itself') when the fusion
of male and female difference is abolished, not in the Mallarméan
echo of absent ('burnt') breast, but in the coming-together of
(burning?) nipples whereby the male's absent but potential
breasts are made verbally to flower.

This transformation, this virtualization of the inexistent,
overtly re-evokes the Darío precursor poem: 'Are you there,
Venus de Milo?'. The vocative 'Tú' ('you' singular), addressed at
once to both present lover and the 'enshrined' Goddess of an
inherited poetic discourse, calls upon no one person but a 'fused'
persona, now literally embraced not just in a single lover's arms

but in the clasp of existence itself. Yet this embrace is not 'framing', limiting, for it partakes of the imperfection, or the incompleteness, of time conveyed by the neologism 'yets' – a word, but hardly an idea.

A clear shift from second to third person, from vocative to description, initiates further virtualizations, in words, of 'impossible' ideas. Whether the Venus's arms were cut off or never even created, one of them is deemed to turn round and to attempt to *lean* (though 'encodarse' is another neologism which might call on *encodigarse*/'to encode' as much as on *acodarse*). Not that there can ever be a stable surface, a secure support: only greenish, stammering pebbles, sun-rise molluscs (nautili), creeping, cat-like 'aunes', another 'ungrammaticality' which forces time, momentarily, into a substantive (i.e. noun) frame, as if to encapsulate the very eve of immortalities. 'Imminence', then, is 'parenthesized' ('tied in a double bow') in a rather more Mallarméan than Rubén Darían feminine construction ('lace-adora . . . laceadora'). I pause briefly to challenge the reader, but only as a prelude to a gauntlet more explicitly thrown down by Vallejo's text in its sudden shift to the plural personal imperative 'Rehusad'. It will have been clear that, at various points of this book, I have sought to illustrate in critical practice the pervasive Derridan proposition that, in the play of presence and absence, we must necessarily conceive of the play before we can begin to conceive of presence or absence. It will have been no less evident that, so far, I have been at pains to stress that the most effective poetry – such as that of a Stéphane Mallarmé or a César Vallejo – has often already anticipated both the symptoms and the strategies of any critical theory. In positing the suggestion that Vallejo's play, in this poem, with *imminence* and *parenthesis* may be read as a prefiguration of Jacques Derrida's *sign of erasure*, I am all-too-conscious of the risk to be run. The sign of parenthesis ( ) might be viewed as a binary containing potential plenitude, albeit a quantity X as yet unknown. For the reader ('¿laceador/a?') eager to go beyond imminence to infinity (a move beyond teleology to theology), the closure of the lexical gaps of (X) will construct ∞. Yet if we were now to remove the parenthesis we first thought of – in mimicry of Reb Derrissa's graphic refusal ('¿rehusar?') to complete even the most non-figurative cipher of the hidden God – then we would be left with X as performative sign of erasure operating between parenthetical binaries once conceived of as present, now played with as absent. But enough of theory. Let (Vallejo's) poetry deconstruct for itself; or construct a poetics of 'perenne imperfección', a metaphysics *neither* of presence nor of absence, yet of *both*. For the reader is implicated now directly in 'Rehusad, y vosotros'. *We* are invited to 'refuse' the security (ever duplicitous) of Harmony as the *modernista* discourse breaks up, is rendered asymmetrical. By our intervention in the constricting frame of the jousting-lists of the rutting lovers' embrace, we might just (joust) break through, make the (conceptually) impossible leap 'through the needle's eye'.

The final section of *Trilce* XXXVI constitutes an interior monologue, though the first-*person* grammatical category is exploited to express dissatisfaction with the *space* or *frame* of a notional, limiting (post-coital?), solitary persona. The mirror-stage of self-perception, after the assaults on uni-vocality and the frame-breaking which have gone before, leaves uni-corporality as 'improper' perception ('it ought not be me'), an infuriating, shameful, *casting of the die*: and deliberately I re-echo the echo of 'Un coup de dés jamais n'abolira le hasard' to be found in 'azarea'. The paradoxical dependence on the 'institutionality' of the Mallarméan ethic, on the part of Vallejo, seeking a personal space or 'margin' in which to perform, has thrown up that knowledge (in this case anticipating not Derrida but Foucault) that the *poem* only 'becomes effective to the degree that it introduces discontinuity into our very being', as was argued in the last chapter with respect to literary history.

If *I* listen to that imperative, *I* must not have the final (closing) word. Rather I, and you, may hear Vallejo's poem in its parting injunction: its highlighting of differentiality rather than continuity in the history of institutions. Dare we cede to the uneven, the 'odd' *modernity*, of a poetic text struggling powerfully to shed the restricting paternity – or maternity – of the discourse of *modernismo*? Try! Cede to the potent oddness of orphanhood.

Vallejo's exploitation of the plural imperative raises – apart from (indeed, as part of) the other complexities of this poem – the question of *voice*. Who (what) speaks in the poem? Almost inexplicably, the proliferation of literary theories of the last two decades has thrown up much *narrative* but little poetic critical methodology to cope with, to explain, to situate, a literary discourse laden with multi-voicedness, citation, intertextuality and modes of defamiliarization. Lyric poetry has had to 'make do' with useful but rather limiting notions such as Riffaterre's ungrammaticality, or Todorov's poetics of discontinuity. For some reason, criticism has been content either to struggle to pull back lyric poetry, generically, to univocal (authorial) control, or to label, but not to accept, the more subversive implications of the non-controlled vocality of modern poetry by using such terms as 'Dada', 'Surrealism', 'post-modernism' and so on. Mikhail Bakhtin's notion of the dialogic imagination, so fruitfully applied to the novel, none the less bears (bares?) a blind-spot concerning poetry, the concession of a peculiarly unstructured, idealized autonomy to the originary, monologic voice of the poet. The notion of *heteroglossia*, however, seems to fit a poetic discourse of multi-voicedness, be it Guillaume Apollinaire's 'Zone', T. S. Eliot's *The Waste Land*, Fernando Pessoa's 'Tabacaria', or Vallejo's *Trilce* XXXVI. Though terms such as 'poème-conversation' have been applied to such poetry, all too rapidly 'voices' which seek to restore a so-called coherence or unity of viewpoint re-emerge; instance the role of Tiresias, in *The Waste Land*, whose transhistorical, multi-spatial, bisexual 'voicings' are re-assembled, admittedly at that voice's own instigation: 'These fragments I have shored against my ruin'. That presence will always seek to re-assert its own metaphysics is one of Derrida's most basic insights; that criticism has too often aided and abetted such restorative harmonies is no reason for the reader of Vallejo's poem to overlook, to fail to hear, glaring and resonant absences. For the poem states that such 'security' is 'double', duplicitous and different from itself. The poem commands the frame-breaking of *intervention*, against safe symmetries, such as those found in criticism's insistence on *self-presence*. Here I refer not to a theological model of self but to a psychological model of the *subject*, and it should be noted that I opt for a grammatical rather than an essential term in order to stress that, even for the purpose of academic presentation, the distinction between models of the self and models of meaning is but provisional and artificial. In both Darío's and Neruda's poetry – and implied in Bloom's Romantically derived poetics of influence – the process of self-reflection/projection within a (God-derived) 'Nature's vast frame', was identified as consistently narcissistic. In the process of equating 'self' with 'other', all signs become 'signified': that is, the signifying 'other' is framed, or enclosed, according to the dictates or desire of the reflector/projector. We have seen that such a model of construction of the self fixes identity in a *mirror-state*. And I play here with 'state'/'stasis'/'stability' as being notions consistent with the theologically orthodox tenet that man is made in God's own image and likeness. What is more, a theologically orientated or conditioned subject might well be content, feel whole, unified, at one, with his image and his Maker. In a post-theological, and a post-Saussurean, perspective, however – and certainly, within a Vallejo text not notably anxiety-ridden in its playful fragmentation of 'recognitions', its 'introduction of discontinuities', its 'effectiveness' (Foucault's terms) – such unity, such 'presence', may be insufficient, indeed, thrown into question. When Saussure suggests that in language there are only differences without positive terms, he affords the removal not only of the linguistic 'positive term' ('le signifié') but also of the positive certainty of a *term*inal, teleologically viable guarantor (God) of man's image. We are again confronted with the possibility of an image-construction, image-desire not satisfied with 'state'/'stasis'/'stability' but, rather, restless, unfulfilled, active, performative; subjects constructing identity on and in a *mirror-stage*. A further complication arises in so far as this 'performance' is by no means often, if ever, conducted consciously.

This is not the place for more than the briefest incursion into psychoanalysis. None the less, that is precisely the frame – perhaps a displaced theology – wherein we encounter subjects notoriously restless, unfulfilled, performative, even subjects seeking to construct a new identity, to break the frame, to engage with difference. And it is at this point, the point of (*Trilce* XXXVI's) engaging with difference, that the notion of the Symbolic Order intrudes:

> The absence of a gap . . . between a concept and its application is a proof of the concept's inadequacy. . . . The gap appears with the initiation . . . into the order of language, what Lacan calls 'the Symbolic Order'. The structures of language are marked with societal imperatives. . . . Society's injunction that desire must wait, that it must formulate in the constricting word whatever demand it may speak, is what effects the split between conscious and unconscious, the repression that is the tax exacted by the use of language.
>
> (Wright 1984, 109)

That 'desire must wait', always subject to 'the constricting word', takes up, but goes well beyond, Mallarmé's intuition of the need to cede the initiative to words, now echoed by Vallejo's text's final injunction. And, to demonstrate the implications of the inseparability of desire and language, I turn, once again, to French models, namely Mallarmé and Rimbaud. Unfortunately, Mallarmé's legacy has been rather one-sided; the earlier seeker of 'the Ideal' – with all the theocentric implications I have already discussed – is preferred to the more threatening author of 'after having found Nothingness, I found Beauty' (1959, 220). The 'most trenchantly agnostic' Mallarmé, whose 'powers of doubt played not only upon the time-honoured theologies and theodicies' of Western thought (Bowie 1978, 4), anticipates Lacan's intersection of the 'desire' (for Beauty) and the 'constricting word' (of non-referentiality, of the *non-signifié*). Most famously in the *sonnet en-x*, wherein the ineffable (since non-existent) word, but not the *idea*, 'ptyx', is not only spoken but – 'nul ptyx'/'no ptyx' – negated. An absent absence! In the case of Rimbaud, again, the powerfully anti-essentialist 'split' not only between conscious and unconscious, but between plural poetic voices, has been overlooked. JE EST UN AUTRE states plainly that grammatical subjectivity is ever other; never author. Vallejo's reading (which is misreading under erasure) of Mallarmé through Darío *may* be interpreted not as struggle but as play, a shift from the notion of poetic 'voicing' as subject (self)-centred orality to a non-subject (lack)-centred writing. A textual performance?

> Play is the disruption of presence . . . . Play is always play of absence and presence, but if it is to be thought radically, play must be conceived of before the alternative of presence and absence. Being must be conceived as presence or absence on the basis of play and not the other way round.
>
> (Derrida 1978, 292)

The epigraph of my Fore-word echoes in repetition but not as identity, is displaced *towards* the inexistent centre of fore-play.

WORKS CITED

Abrams, M. H. *The Mirror and the Lamp*. New York: Oxford University Press, 1953.

Bloom, Harold. *The Anxiety of Influence*. New York and London: Oxford University Press, 1973.

—— *A Map of Misreading*. New York, Toronto and Melbourne: Oxford University Press, 1975.

—— *Figures of Capable Imagination*. New York: Seabury, 1976.

Bowie, Malcolm. *Mallarmé and the Art of Being Difficult*. Cambridge: Cambridge University Press, 1978.

Compagnon, Antoine. *La Seconde main, ou Le travail de la citation*. Paris: Seuil, 1979.

Culler, Jonathan. *The Pursuit of Signs*. London: Routledge and Kegan Paul, 1981.

Darío, Rubén. *Obras completas*, IV. Madrid: Afrosidio Aguado, 1955.

—— *Prosas profanas y otros poemas*. Madrid: Castalia, 1983.

Derrida, Jacques. *Writing and Difference*, trans. Alan Bass. London: Routledge and Kegan Paul, 1978.

Foucault, Michel. *The Foucault Reader*, ed. Paul Rabinow. Harmondsworth: Penguin, 1984.

Hartley, Anthony (trans.) *Mallarmé: Poems*. Harmondsworth: Penguin, 1965.

Johnson, Barbara. *The Critical Difference*. Baltimore, Md: Johns Hopkins University Press, 1985.

Lentricchia, Frank. *After the New Criticism*. Chicago, Ill.: Chicago University Press, 1980.

Mallarmé, Stéphane. *Œuvres complètes*. Paris: Pléiade, 1945.

—— *Correspondance*, ed. H. Mondor and J. P. Richard, vol. I: *1862–71*. Paris: Gallimard, 1959.

Mondor, Henri. *Vie de Mallarmé*. Paris: Gallimard, 1941.

Riffaterre, Michael. *Semiotics of Poetry*. London: Methuen, 1978.

Todorov, Tzvetan. *Mikhail Bakhtin: The Dialogical Principle*, trans. Wlad Godzich. Minneapolis: Minnesota University Press, 1984.

Vallejo, César. *Trilce*. Madrid: Cátedra, 1991.

Verlaine, Paul. *Œuvres complètes*. Paris: Pléiade, 1968.

Wright, Elizabeth. *Psychoanalytical Criticism: Theory in Practice*. London: Methuen, 1984.

Chapter 5

Poetry, pedagogy and untranslatability

On *écriture* and *oralité* in two poems of César Vallejo's *Trilce*

> If a lion could speak, we could not understand him
> Ludwig Wittgenstein

Disruption of presence deriving from the structure of, and at, play for Derrida; the epistemological challenge of discontinuity for Foucault; such are the post-structuralist probings of the effectiveness of metaphysics and of history. As critics, we are thus constantly challenged to dismantle the easy continuities of successive eras, movements, '-isms', in order to reconceive the inherited wisdoms of our discipline. Might it be the case that Paul de Man, in 'Poetic Nothingness: On a Hermetic Sonnet by Mallarmé', had already intuited, in 1955, the dangers of univocality – but one form of continuity – in literary criticism?

> It must be stressed that all interpretations of Mallarmé are falsified because the discursive language of commentary is limiting and univocal, whereas the pluralism of possible levels of reading is requisite, the reflection provoked in the reader's mind being an integral part of the poem and constituting one of the forms its subjects take.
>
> (de Man 1988, 20)

Only after such a categorical statement of his critical reticence did de Man allow himself, in a preliminary discussion of 'Une dentelle s'abolit', the kind of background assertion later to be termed by Tzvetan Todorov *aetiological* criticism:

> As in so many instances, we may assume that Mallarmé took a quite personal and private perception as his point of departure. We know of his insomnia and the sort of hallucinated

contemplation that accompanied it. Several of his poems are written in that half-trance state that follows a sleepless night, impregnated with nervous fatigue and an entirely mental excitement; 'Je t'apporte l'enfant d'une nuit d'Idumée' (I bring you the child of an Idumaean night) is of course the classic example.

(ibid., 20–1)

Even the critically circumspect de Man, in approaching the Mallarmé text, betrays the tensions which always underlie, indeed constitute, explanatory exegesis. Reluctant to explain, let alone to explain away, the specificity of a complex poetic utterance, the critic has, none the less, constant recourse to a *vision* of the poem and of the moment(s) of its conception. The opening line of 'Don du poème' proves to be an irresistible temptation in bringing together, in de Man's words, 'the perfect correspondence between the idea of the object and the object itself' (ibid., 21).

In the last two chapters, I have argued that the insights and practices of such post-structuralist thinkers as Foucault, Derrida, White and Bloom, even in those cases where their engagement with texts does not directly bear on poetry criticism, still render problematical not only, as for de Man, correspondence between object and idea of object, but also that between any univocal critical commentary and the plural performativeness of poetry itself. The obviousness of such an assertion nevertheless stands at odds with the ever-predominant exegetic temptation for which the majority of poetry critics – albeit less self-consciously and apologetically than de Man – readily fall. And why shouldn't they? It is in this respect that post-structuralist insights have habitually been read as much as readings of readings as direct engagements with literary texts. In the engagement which follows, I am concerned to highlight the patterns into which our critical temptations also fall and to argue that such patternings and their implications might not be haphazard. There will be a strong note of pedagogy involved, both in what is commented on and in the mode or the tone of the commentary. The principal reason for this strain arises from my choice, first, of an insufficiently disseminated essay by Tzvetan Todorov on Arthur Rimbaud's *Illuminations* and, second, of a strategic borrowing from the arguably too academic debates of a rather narrow branch of modern philosophy in respect of problems of untranslatability.

My choice of texts is, for once, made the easier by a recent discovery and a not-so-recent unlearned lesson to which I shall return. Julio Ortega, a critic of singular sensitivity to the inter-play of written and oral devices and effects in the poetry of Vallejo, in the introduction to his 1991 edition of *Trilce*, strikes an impressively up-to-date critical note not just in his claims for the importance of Vallejo's collection but also in his justification of them:

> *Trilce* . . . is the most radical book of poetry written in the Castillian language. It is, first of all, the most difficult, and not only because it is a question of a writing for the most part hermetic, but also because the poem tends to delete its refer-ents as much as it fractures the representational function of language itself . . . . After the radicalism of *Trilce* poetry has other measures.
>
> (Ortega 1991, 9)

After distinguishing between the hermeticism of Symbolism or the Baroque and *Trilce*'s effect on representational discursive logic, Ortega continues:

> Naming for Vallejo is not sufficient for designating the object; the word puts the thing into difficulties . . . . Not a few critics, even the best, had fallen again into that exercise of domestic hermeneutics . . . as if the poems were immediate biographic documents, as if the I of the poet were the I of the author, and as if the poetry of Vallejo weren't language about the drama of naming and unnaming, of writing and unwriting . . . . So the poem says better that which does not have a name . . . . This is a new poetry working amidst great tensions with the wit and flexibility of a speech at once dramatic and ironic, tribal and mundane, oral and archaic, regional and technical, neologistic and agrammatical and remote and present . . . at times it stumbles, gets obscure and exasperated by its own stammering . . . in that synchretist activity orality is actuality, the pulse of presence.
>
> (ibid., 10–15)

I have quoted at length from Ortega because he captures better than any critic I know those qualities of Vallejo's writing which make his poetry not only peculiarly susceptible to the strategies of post-structuralist analyses but also strikingly symptomatic – or prefiguring – of the risks of post-structuralism's own (in Bloomian terms, belated) discursive tensions.

And now to my unlearned lesson. R. B. Tate, the Hispanic medievalist, advised me more than a decade ago never to publish anything in a *Festschrift*, 'because people don't read them'. I did (in his) and they didn't. Before attempting to match with the criticism underpinned by a tenet of untranslatability the radical challenge to hermeneutics posed here by Vallejo and later, but very differently by such as Susana Thénon, I therefore return to a case-study in post-structuralist analysis I first broached in 1983 – at a time when such critical practice was as rare, in criticism on Hispanic and Latin American literatures, as it is now:

> Quién hace tánta bulla, y ni deja
> testar las islas que van quedando.
>
> Un poco más de consideración
> en cuanto será tarde, temprano,
> y se aquilatará mejor
> el guano, la simple calabrina tesórea
> que brinda sin querer,
> en el insular corazón,
> salobre alcatraz, a cada hialóidea
> > grupada.
>
> Un poco más de consideración,
> y el mantillo líquido, seis de la tarde
> DE LOS MÁS SOBERBIOS BEMOLES.
>
> Y la península párase
> por la espalda, abozaleada, impertérrita
> en la línea mortal del equilibrio.

For Michael Riffaterre, the challenge to mimesis is never so complete that the reader has no chance at all to read the poem as a representation (1978, 16). But a representation of what? My purpose in tracing the representation of some of Vallejo's readers (critics) is not merely to catalogue their completions or mimetic recuperations; rather, it is a desire to distinguish between their representations and the nature of their critical (reading) activities. The context of that critical activity arises less from the text than from a reading self, 'The Interpreter's Self', as Walter Benn Michaels reminds us with notable simplicity: 'there are no text-derived canons of interpretation which prevent the self from doing what it wants, there is only our conviction that what the self wants has already been constituted by canons of interpretation' (1980, 199–200). As an aid to categorizing certain canons of interpretation and reader-response to *Trilce*, I have opted to begin by applying the four critical strategies identified as traditionally viable by Tzvetan Todorov in his analyses of Rimbaud's *Illuminations*: the Euhemerist, the aetiological, the esoteric and the paradigmatic. Todorov uses these categories, he writes, 'to place in context my own reaction to this text . . . summarize briefly the different attitudes it has inspired in the past, and explain why they appear unsatisfactory to me' (1982, 223). Despite the initially inhibiting effect of his categories' labels, they have consistently served to illustrate how criticism can situate, account for and learn to live with difficulty (and with reader 'perplexity', as he calls it), rather than to explain it away.

EUHEMERIST

Euhemerus was an ancient Greek writer who read Homer as a source of information . . . as a factual (and not imaginary) narrative; Euhemerist reading passes through the text without the slightest pause, in search for clues to some reality outside it . . . geographical indications occur, in order, it might seem, to slake the passions of an Euhemerist and allow identification of the places being spoken of.

(Todorov 1982, 223–7)

Eduardo Neale-Silva is the most overtly Euhemerist of *Trilce* I readers 'although conscious of limitations . . . offering an interpretative translation in the belief that it makes the component elements meaningful within a plausible construct . . . consonant . . . with the factual data contained in the poem and the probable intent of the poet' (1970, 2, 16). His 'consciousness of limitations' of the method is soon revealed to be but an apologetic caution readily cast to the wind:

Unquestionably, Vallejo was referring here to the unbelievable sight of thousands upon thousands of guano birds flocking together before dusk in the midst of a rare 'symphony' of raucous sounds and shrill noises. Robert Cushman Hardy, an authority on the ecology of the Peruvian littoral, agrees with

Vallejo on both the hour ('six o'clock in the evening') and the intensity of the 'racket' ('SUPERB B FLATS').

(Neale-Silva 1970, 13)

This authoritative pronouncement is, none the less, more readily categorizable, for my present purpose, than an instance of Neale-Silva's reservations at work:

It is difficult to believe that as discerning and conscientious a writer as Vallejo would have been satisfied with a simple scene of bird defecation or, for that matter, with the concept of universal elimination for the opening selection of his new book. He surely remembered the various prefaces with which Darío introduced his better known collection of verses to his readers.

(ibid., 13)

Todorov certainly offers no description of such an approach as Neale-Silva's here, beyond one characteristic of aetiological criticism: 'instead of referential transparency we find a transparency oriented towards the poet, whose text is not really considered as an expression but as a kind of symptom' (Todorov 1982, 225).

Rather than focusing on the more obvious complications of the biographical tendency, such as intentionalism and the 'supposed reading' approach, I would emphasize here the simple fact of the mixing, in many readings, of the categories which Todorov treats separately. Thus, it is common to find attitudes which slip from one to another of the interpretative methods, as any one reading fails to slake (the critical) passions. Into the space between Euhemerist and aetiological, for example, fall G. G. Wing's pseudo-biographical reading of *Trilce* I as being about 'homelessness and orphanhood' (1969, 268–84), and Jean Franco's more esoteric reading of the poem as 'the contradiction between the march of the species and the individual's attempt to read significance into his mortal life' (Franco 1976, 117–20).

AETIOLOGICAL

Rather than enquiring about the meaning of the text, the author asks what might have led Rimbaud to express himself as he did . . . At best it is a contribution to the physiology of literary creation . . . Was the author drugged?

(Todorov 1982, 225)

Was Vallejo defecating? Interrupted in the act by more accomplished *guano*-droppers than himself? No critic has (yet) gone that far, though G. G. Wing's Pegasus-flight of aetiological fancy is to add the detection of a 'comic' strain to André Coyné's view of *Trilce* I as 'a poem of defecation transposed to universal, cosmic terms' (1958, 82). 'Other specimens of aetiological criticism,' Todorov remarks, 'are those commentaries which say: if this text is strange, that is because it describes an operatic performance, or a painting, or an engraving' (1982, 225). Here, though again with slippage into another category, Neale-Silva offers:

> in the last stanza there is first a very graphic representation of the artist (the 'peninsula') rising up courageously to face life's trials; this is followed by another graphic suggestion of a barely discernible tightrope and a puny 'artist' reduced to a mere insinuation of a man. These masterly pictorial touches betray Vallejo's acquaintance with modern art; Miró, Braque, Derain, Matisse, Marcoussis, whom he was going to remember later on in one of his magazine articles.
>
> (Neale-Silva 1970, 15)

At the heart of this issue is the tendency of the critic to draw upon the author's experience and, in particular, his other writings. To this approach, most typically encountered in the recourse to an *ars poetica* for the explanation of a poem (for generations the standard approach to explication of texts), I shall return in considering the paradigmatic method. For the moment, however, let Todorov provide a reminder of how 'pictorial effect' might more effectively function: 'we speak not of the picture which Rimbaud allegedly saw, but the one which his text creates ... we speak, that is, of the pictorial effect, not of the pictorial pretext' (Todorov 1982, 225).

ESOTERIC

> Each element of the text – at least each problematic element – is replaced by another which is drawn from some variant of universal symbolism, from psycho-analysis to alchemy.
>
> (Todorov 1982, 225)

All too often, confronted with such forms of esoteric alchemy, poetry gapes at the transubstantiation of its own text. Re-working the repertoire of its own discourse and rephrasing Baudelaire, poetry itself accuses the esoteric critic: 'Je t'ai donné mon or et tu en as fait de la boue'. Vallejo's text achieves, repeatedly, a similar impact, ever dropping its 'guano'/'boue' in defilement of a gilded, or gelded, interpretative method:

'*Trilce I*' – *Interpretative Translation* (Neale-Silva 1970, 5)
Who is making all that (critical) fuss and will not even let the emerging islands (the poets) give their own testimony?

Give more thought to all that dwells outside of Time, and (thus) one will assay in its real value the (critical) dung, the simple, fetid and spurious treasure that salty pelicans (the critics) all too naturally drop on the insular heart of every new and amorphous (poetic) circle. Give more thought (to spiritual values): the misty mantle (is rising); it is six o'clock in the evening (AMIDST) THE MOST RESOUNDING FANFARE.

And the peninsula (of poets) does stand up behind the (critics') back, contained, unafraid, on the tightrope (of the literary scene).

The 'variant of universal symbolism' at play here is, in short, the reduction to a writing/reading 'performance'. Such interpretations as this, for Todorov, are never confirmable, or refutable either, which gives them minimal interest; in addition they translate (*sic*) the text bit by bit, with no attention to its articulation, and the final result, perfectly clear, provides no explanation for the initial obscurity: 'why should Rimbaud [Vallejo] have found it amusing to encode these rather ordinary thoughts?' (Todorov 1982, 226).

Verbal alchemy with reverse effect is but one sphere of activity by which the critic approximates to the Todorovian definition of the esoteric method. For there remains 'psychoanalysis': 'Vallejo must have felt like a solitary island surrounded by a sea of incomprehension. The symbol of the Island surrounded by an unfathomable ocean does, of course, bring to mind the Jungian concept of the collective unconscious. Whether or not it was in the poet's mind at the time he composed *Trilce* I is difficult to determine' (Neale-Silva 1970, 10). Lest Jung, however, be unfairly favoured, let the balance be restored, though with a more vigorous, more intelligent passage:

Jean Franco's remark that Vallejo 'gave priority to the raw material of experience which is always there, palpitating, so to speak, beneath the scaffolding of abstraction', goes far to explain why Vallejo preferred the pelican's guano to its heart's blood as a symbol. But there is another reason. Poetry in this post-Freudian age comes from the mind's 'guts', the sub-rational mind, not, as Musset believed for his own time, straight from the heart. The new symbol *works*.

(Shaw 1979–80, 168)

The force of D. L. Shaw's elaboration of the 'guano'/'corazón' juxtaposition derives from the interiority of an 'open contradiction' or 'lack of determinateness' which, stylistically, constitutes one of Todorov's own methodological categories of 'discontinuity' (Todorov 1982, 231–2). Yet, though Shaw analyses, in this instance, a symbol at work, it is he, above all, who indulges in an otherwise paradigmatic reading.

PARADIGMATIC

Its starting point is the postulate, explicit or implicit, that continuity is without significance, that the task of the critic consists in gathering together elements which are more or less distant in the text to show their similarity, or opposition, or relatedness; in short, that the paradigm is relevant, but not the syntagm.

(Todorov 1982, 226)

That Shaw's starting-point is paradigmatic is not at issue, for his concern with *symbol* is methodologically asserted: 'I should like to suggest that by addressing ourselves to the central symbol of the poem, the pelican, it is possible to arrive at a coherent explanation which to some degree reconciles elements accepted by Neale-Silva and Wing' (Shaw 1979–80, 168). Since all criticism must begin somewhere, it would not be fair to take exception even to his use of the unqualified term 'central'. What is problematical is the relationship between Todorov's rather overstated notion of 'the postulate that continuity is without significance' and Shaw's very clear and logically developed continuity of pelican symbolism. Here, 'more or less distant in the text' gains new dimensions. For Shaw's paradigm is not delimited by the text of *Trilce* I but by a vaster, or more fragmentarily available, text:

Vallejo's familiarity with modern French poetry is not a matter of dispute. A man who knew his Samain as Vallejo did, would certainly know his Baudelaire. To know Baudelaire is to know one of his most famous poems, 'L'Albatros'. In turn to know 'L'Albatros' is to know the other poem regularly thought of in relation to it, Musset's no less famous 'La Nuit de mai', especially lines 154–91 beginning: 'Lorsque le pélican, lassé d'un long voyage . . . '. When we recall Vallejo's strong interest in romanticism, attested by his thesis on the subject, there is every reason to believe that he was familiar with the French poem which, almost more than any other, expressed the romantic poet's view of his role in relation to his readers. . . . I should contend that *Trilce* I is in some sense a kind of parody of Musset's well-known poetic statement, designed to express a less pretentious, less rhetorical, more down-to-earth view of the poet's situation in the twentieth century.

(Shaw 1979–80, 168)

The paradigm of Shaw's analysis is not, of course, merely ornithological (though it is that, too) but literary-ornithological. In other words, his text is the (inter)text of that Romantic literature to which he, personally, has access. His position is theoretically close, though with no comparable pretension to sophisticated trope analyses, to that of Harold Bloom, and in this sense he is a literary historian employing a rhetoric of diachrony. The assumptions underlying Shaw's paradigmatic method are deeply rooted in at least one strain of contemporary poetry criticism, and Bloom's own statement of beliefs usefully supplements Shaw's analysis of *Trilce* I and helps to illustrate a paradigmatic method which operates even beyond Todorov's 'in the text' designation:

Poetic Influence – when it involves two strong, authentic poets – always proceeds by a misreading of the prior poet, an act of creative correction that is actually and necessarily a misinterpretation. The history of fruitful poetic influence . . . is a history of anxiety and self-saving caricature, of distortion, of perverse, wilful revisionism without which modern poetry as such could not exist.

(Bloom 1973, 30)

It is arguable that all this applies not only to the response of one poet to another but, perhaps above all, and ironically, to Bloom's (and Shaw's) response to the text. In analysing *Trilce* I,

Shaw opts for 'the central symbol' as point of entry. His subsequent method is entirely faithful to Bloom's diktat that 'images are ratios between what is uttered and what, somehow, is intended' (1975, 20). As such, his reading recreates the Bloomian 'psychic battlefield': '"a poetic text", as I interpret it, is not a gathering of signs on a page, but is a psychic battlefield upon which authentic forces struggle for the only victory worth winning, the divinating triumph over oblivion' (Bloom 1976, 2). Precedence is ever given to the psychic over the linguistic, and since, concomitantly, the pre-eminence of a subject (ego) is unquestioned, the struggle to survive is often expressed, not exaggeratedly but necessarily in Nietzschean terms (though here Shaw does insert a passing apologia for the detected disparity between the lofty sacrifice and the excremental register):

> Looked at like this the poem can be seen as concerned ultimately with the poet's view of himself and his art, expressed in serio-comic terms not as a pelican sacrificing its heart's blood, but as a pelican squeezing out of its gut *guano* (poetry) which may not be very attractive (and the image contains an element of modest self-mockery), but which none the less will fulfil one of the fundamental tasks of literature: that of fertilizing the reader's own experience.
>
> (Shaw 1979–80, 169)

A last word on the Bloomian/Shavian paradigm is its literariness: that is, its literary historicity as distinct from a broader, cultural historicity.

MIMESIS?

> The destruction of the mimesis, or its obverse, the creation of the semiosis, is thus exactly coextensive with the text: it *is* the text.
>
> (Riffaterre 1978, 19)

Co-extensiveness with the text is the syntagm, yet what of reading? Is it possible to read at all without penetrating 'the creation of the semiosis' and moving towards some construction of a mimesis? In the answer to this question lies the resolution of Riffaterre's two warring notions: namely, the incomplete (the 'not so complete') 'challenge to mimesis', and 'the destruction of the mimesis' which he equates, above, with the creation of the text. Instead of approaching *Trilce* I, therefore, as a poem about writing and reading, it is possible to pursue discussion of it as a performance, a dramatization of the linguistic (not just the psychic) 'battlefield' of referentiality. In order to do so, it is first of all necessary to accept the 'chance . . . to read the poem as a representation' (ibid., 16). The affirmation of this chance *à la* Riffaterre is but one throw of the die; this one will not abolish the chance of other readings, nor the (hap)hazard of this one. And the echo of Mallarmé, critically speaking, is apposite. Of the 'sonnet en -x', the 'battlefield' of a struggle between calculated non-referentiality ('ptyx') and a formal patterning which itself broaches the possibility of an analysable syntagm, Riffaterre observes: 'Even though it should be impossible to miss the meaning – an exercise in verbal exercise – we find at work here a nostalgia for referentiality that promises us no reader will ever get used to non-language' (ibid., 18).

The 'nostalgia for referentiality' is, it might be argued, an admission undeveloped by Riffaterre, perhaps even deliberately neglected, as threatening his theory of the 'text' as 'the creation of the semiosis'. For concomitant with such a nostalgia, surely, is at least the risk of re-creating and re-constructing a mimesis. Indeed, for Derrida, 'to enter language' at all 'means to risk being named, or recognized by name, to struggle against false names or identities' (1974, 62). It remains to be seen whether the nature of this 'struggle' is adequately approached in socio-linguistic rather than automatically psychic terms. What follows is a personal attempt to apply a post-structuralist critical practice and, strategically, to risk both naming and being named. To those who would argue that any reading constitutes but one more authoritarian discourse, I would concede that it does indeed offer a false name or identity to the primary text. It does so not only consciously but as a displacement of, a reaction against (in Bloomian terms), the established critical discourses of the type examined previously. Just as it takes the initiative against an establishment of the type discussed in my Fore-word and typified in Chapter 1, my overall method seeks to encourage others to take the initiative, in turn, against my own readings.

LIMENPERUGUANO

L'anagramme n'est pas à définir comme une dislocation réglée en mal de complétude, mais une multiplicité infixable. Indécidabilité radicale qui défait tous les codes.

(Lotringer 1975, 112)

[The anagram is not to be defined as a regulated dislocation, lacking completion, but an indeterminable multiplicity. A radical undecidability which undoes all the codes.]

My nostalgia for referentiality is for the whole of *Trilce* I. I am left, however, after many readings, with but a fragmentary frame of reference. That frame is not the syntagm but a partial anagram. Thus my critical 'representation' of the poem assumes a similar form: the threshold ('limen') of *Trilce*; linguistically localized (Trujillo-Peruvian) Castillian; culturally specific (again Peruvian) 'guano'.

limen

I is the poem's only title. Similarly, the other seventy-six poems in *Trilce* stand under numerals alone. *Trilce* I constitutes a threshold (*limen* but never *limeño*) of the creation of the semiosis of the whole collection, notoriously difficult, and the very title of which, *Trilce*, is itself a neologism. Of Mallarmé's neologism 'pytx', Riffaterre writes that it 'combines visibility, an almost obstrusive physical presence as a form, and an equally obtrusive absence as meaning' (1978, 18). I claim that *Trilce* I announces no less for the collection.

peru

Both cultural and linguistic specificity are at issue, inseparably. The more obvious cultural (mimesis-creating) specificity is neatly summarized by Neale-Silva as 'a Peruvian seascape: guano islands, pelicans, squawks, shrieks' (1970, 8). Linguistically, while the Peruvian flavour of the Spanish is peculiar in itself – signalled by the 'guano'/'alcatraz' associations – Vallejo's handling of his own language derives a further, deeper specificity from the power of dislocation. A series of neologisms (or near-neologisms) transforms the text into 'a detour or circuitous path around what it means', underlining Riffaterre's assertion that 'a constant component of poetic significance is that the poem's language looks as much like a ritual or a game (in many cases the poem is akin to a generalized pun), or pure artifice, as it does like a means of conveying sense' (1978, 164). Critically speaking, the poem's specificity shifts, through neologism, from cultural ('peruano') to linguistic ('peru/guano').

guano

Riffaterre suggests that 'the usual detour around the repressed matrix (minimal and literal), being made of separate, distinct ungrammaticalities looks like a series of inappropriate, twisted wordings, so that the poem may be regarded as a generalized, all-encompassing, all-contaminating catachresis [misuse of a trope]' (1978, 19). I read the matrix in *Trilce* I as *guano*, though present and hardly repressed. For the 'model', for Riffaterre 'the first or primary actualization' (ibid., 19) of the matrix, is:

y el mantillo líquido, seis de la tarde
DE LOS MÁS SOBERBIOS BEMOLES

The model 'generates the text by formal derivation affecting both syntax and morphology' (ibid., 166), so that the 'specific' *guano* – spatially Peruvian, temporally crepuscular, visually a liquid mantle, auditively (a misused trope?) OF THE MOST SUPERB B FLATS – is generalized, encompasses and contaminates in its textual, linguistic and non-specific form, the opening space, the moment, the scene (of writing/of reading) and the initial clamour of production. *Guano* is thus actualized as *Trilce* I, threshold of a looming, Riffaterre-like series of what *looks like* a series of twisted wordings of separate, distinct ungrammaticalities: in short, the poems of *Trilce* itself.

OVER THE THRESHOLD

Since reading is restricted, the reader's interpretation is a scanning of the sociolect's commonplaces, the practice of a lore of well-tested *exempla*, the recognition of forms and hallowed symbols through a scrambled transmission. . . . But the reader is reconverted to a proper reading when the structural equivalences become apparent all at once, in a blaze of revelation.

This revelation is always chancy, must always begin anew, since each rereading, or even the instinctive rechecking of a difficult passage, forces the reader to undergo again the experience or temptation of a decoding obedient to mimesis, hence to relive the block of distortion.

(Riffaterre 1978, 165–6)

A blaze of revelation dating from 1983 – and now purporting to operate as but one lore amongst the well-tested *exempla* of the symptoms and strategies of this book – is here transcribed. Spatial, temporal, visual and auditive functions have already been analysed performatively. Though structural equivalences, entirely within *Trilce* I, may indeed 'have become apparent all at once', I can but be aware, now as then, that crossing over the threshold of the poem towards a 'reader's interpretation', equally, is a step towards destruction of the semiosis and *con-struction* of a mimesis. At best, I can move towards referentiality along the corridor of those equivalences already established, though chary of Riffaterre's 'reconversion' to a 'proper reading'. The poem begins with an interrogative, the accented 'QUIÉN', posing a question of identity, and of utterance, in 'hace tánta bulla'; 'y ni deja testar' introduces a problem of reception, audi-ence, witness. So far, then, *identity, utterance* and *reception*. Yet the abstracted interrogative which might connote a throwing into question of the 'In principio erat verbum' is cut short. 'Un poco más de consideración' will not permit any primary questioning, let alone an ulterior ontology. Patience is required. Why? First, there is the temporal problem – 'en cuanto será tarde, temprano' – irremediably complex, insoluble as the oxymoron itself. For the function of ontological questioning is to occlude *time*, rush-ing back impatiently, unconsideringly and inconsiderately, to speculation on the origin of being: who? Saying what? To whom? And all too rapidly, impatiently, a '¿de dónde vengo?'/'whence come I?', would prompt an '¿a dónde voy?'/'whither go I?' and (Darío-like) teleological speculation on mortality.

Thus, *Trilce* I constitutes an initial (liminal) refusal of ontology. A more considered, balanced appraisal is offered: namely, another, different evaluation, in 'y se aquilatará mejor'. But what will? What has got value? What has got comparative worth? The answer, when juxtaposed with an ontology, is surprising, surprisingly simple: 'El guano, la simple calabrina tesórea'. 'El guano' is at once a simple and locally (Peruvian) specific matrix; yet, in its apposition, it finds a density richly suggestive referentially as well as verbally. The humblest subject, then, is rendered impenetrable, impenetrable perhaps as time. A 'generalized pun', an (incompletable) anagram? As the *simple* referentiality of *guano* is destroyed by the ritual of the poem's development, the word is dramatized, takes on spontaneity, celebration ('brinda sin querer'), breaks down barriers both emotional ('corazón') and geographical ('insular'). The idea of 'all-contaminating catachresis' is by no means confined, or confinable, to reference (semantically). It is *syntactically* affirmed, too, in the collision and possible fusion of 'el guano' with the potential but never necessary apposition 'salobre alcatraz' (which, equally, may stand in apposition to 'insular corazón'). Following the first possibility, *guano* raises a toast to each of the *guano* islands ('a cada hialóidea grupada') in the soaring flight of its own producer ('salobre alcatraz'). By contamination – contamination by a 'misused trope' – the poetic word as matrix, *guano*, toasts its own eventual setting, *Trilce* I. The *guano* setting acquires, in turn, as an apposition of its own, 'hialóidea grupada', island, but also impenetrably rich, fertile, *verbal* cluster, the poem. A cluster, a setting, of *words* (oral on anal) taking poetic priority (not belatedly) over ideas – in dialogical relation with Mallarmé's 'sonnet en -*x*' – which performs a similar toast to itself in its first line:

Ses purs ongles très haut dédiant leur onyx.

[Its pure nails very high dedicating their onyx.]

Yet with further patience, with further consideration (as if the first plea has not, already, evidenced enough assaying – 'aquilatará' – of the guano-treasure), an even greater verbal alchemy is to ensue. For the poem performs in its 'model', in its 'primary actualization', a this time *authentic* instance of the alchemist's boast: 'Tu m'as donné ta boue et j'en ai fait de l'or'. I have suggested already the *performative* function of:

y el mantillo líquido, seis de la tarde
DE LOS MÁS SOBERBIOS BEMOLES

Referentially, it proclaims itself as the utterance of the toast.

Even the peninsula is impressed: so impressed as to defy the laws of Nature ('párase'). In this act, the impenetrable oxymoron is penetrated; 'tarde, temprano', logically imminent dusk, is transcended by a Nature-stopping event. Thus, witness *is* borne; *place* witnesses an event, *time* is frozen, *auditively* all is hushed ('abozaleada'), and *visually* all is perceived to be in equilibrium. A poem has to have an end. But it does not, necessarily, as argued in the previous chapter, have a teleology. 'Muzzling' need not imply a mortal awe. The 'líneal mortal del equilibrio' is co-extensive only with the freezing of time on (and for) 'la península'. Juxtaposed with the mortality of a time-deprived nature in this poem are the earlier 'islas que van quedando', *referential* reminder of the extra-poetic, where such events as the poem celebrates are dramatic, perhaps, but undramatized, lacking (or pre-existing) the verbal alchemy, the performance which destroys mimesis. 'Impertérrita' proclaims that what has happened once, spontaneously, joyously, can happen again, that the event of *guano*, in *Trilce* I, undaunted, may defer, even suspend, first questioning, ontology. Rather than speculating on the meaning of being, the poem *is*, is a suspended, *un*mortal balance, a balancing *act*. Against those who have read Vallejo as a latter-day Romantic, crying out over his own sterility and the difficulty of poetic creation – the *page blanche* brigade as I would call them – I am saying that *Trilce* I fills a *page blanche* with a production of the lowest form of matter, shit, excrement, and performs an act, a rite of fertility greater than the constipated, Romanticized, no(n-mo)tion of the sterility of the creative process.

There does remain, however, as Julio Ortega was also to concede in revisiting the poem (1991, 43–7), Riffaterre's danger of 'reliving the block of distortion', 'the temptation of a decoding obedient to mimesis'. Yet Derrida can tell us why:

> The absolute Logos was an infinite creative subject in mediaeval theology: the intelligible face of the sign remains turned towards the word and the face of God . . . . The sign and divinity have the same time and place of birth. The age of the sign is essentially theological. Perhaps it will never end. Its historical *closure* is, however, outlined.
>
> (1976, 13–14)

Obedience to mimesis is never just a question of correspondence; rather, it is an affirmation of ideology, a theory of being. But does that ideology have to be Romantic? And why is it that, in the case of those interpretations of *Trilce* I examined, the most patently unfamiliar, self-assertively unfamiliarizable text is each time naturalized into a paraphrase, a recognizable form of literary-historical discourse?

The objective of this treatment of César Vallejo's poem, and of critical approaches to it, has been to serve as a foil to what I believe is still – and despite such a recent strategic invitation as Ortega's for us to define such poetry as 'a space of correspondences more physical than symbolic' (Ortega 1991, 47) – the dominant discourse both in and beyond the Hispanic field: namely, a criticism which works from a form which is not even the poem but a kind of blueprint, a 'sociolect's common place'; a criticism which constitutes 'the practice of a lore'. The nature of this discourse is not only decidedly Romantic, but also, as I argued in Chapter I, both theo- and anthropocentric, 'because we still live in what is essentially, though in derivative rather than direct manifestations, a Biblical culture and readily mistake our hereditary ways of organizing experience for the conditions of reality and the universal forms of thought' (Abrams 1971, 65–6).

It is also a discourse which betrays how, in criticism as in the teaching process which perpetuates and indulges that criticism, certain forms of power are inscribed. Catherine Belsey has reminded us 'that interpretation and criticism come not from individual subjectivity or "personal experience", but from existing discourses, which are always learned, and which (with whatever contradictions) are always in the interests of forms of power' (Belsey 1982, 58). In this chapter, the four existing discourses, as identified by Todorov and exemplified in existing studies of *Trilce* I, can no longer be treated, much less trusted, as innocent, subjective responses to the text. Rather, they are instances of the Romantic discourse and assertions of the Romantic *will*, reminders that:

> Romantic criticism makes literature live as a pseudopod of the author; and the more we have evidence how much our lives are played in obedience to prior rules, genetic, cultural, political, religious, even sartorial, the more it seems to insist that the most precious activities, such as poetry, are determined only by the individual will (an entity, like the soul, both indefinable and inviolable), and answerable only to the ends proposed by that will.
>
> (Spiller 1983, 39)

For while the Romantic discourse may have displaced theology from a God-centred to an ego-centred objective, the hermeneutical nature of the practice survives undaunted. The Euhemerist, the aetiological, the esoteric and the paradigmatic modes of this self-same practice are thus but instruments of reductive revelation. Respectively, these modes construct the Romantic discourse on fact and identity, motivation and intention, symbol and universal, model and archetype. What they each refuse, what the Romantic discourse refuses, is the *in principio erat verbum* – ever striving to supply an *apud Deum,* usually having recourse to that God's creation. In short, establishing, or taking for granted, *mimesis* by recourse to mimetic *proofs.* The theocentricity of the circular methodology is patent. Remove God and that method is but *ego*centric. Remove the text (*verbum*) and the Romantic discourse is simply *ex*centric.

Yet why such a nostalgia for *theo*centrism? The answer, I believe, is the ideological nature of what Riffaterre has called 'obedience to mimesis', and what Terry Eagleton identified as follows: 'this whole notion of language rested upon a naive mimeticism: the theory was that words are somehow healthiest when they approach the condition of things, and thus cease to be words at all. Language is alienated or degenerate unless it is plumped with the rank juices of real life' (1983, 37). How ironic that the 'plumping with the rank juices of real life', the noisy excretion which is *Trilce* I, none the less prompts the 'practical critic' to turn his/her back on the *guano,* 'healthiest when [approaching] the condition of things', and to do so for the ideological purpose of reasserting his/her power as hermeneut-interpreter and possessor of the Word. To decipher is to control, since the sacerdotal revelation, the transubstantiation, of even this base matter into *really* a theocentric discourse, re-establishes the critical voice as the voice of authority:

> because religion is for all kinds of reasons an extremely effective form of ideological control. Like all successful ideologies it works much less by specific concepts or formulated doctrines than by image, symbol, habit, ritual and mythology . . . . It is no wonder that the . . . 'ruling class' looked on the threatened dissolution of this ideological *discourse* with something less than equanimity.
>
> (Eagleton 1983, 23)

Julio Ortega has already made the connection with the economic importance in the history of Peru of the production of *guano* as fertilizer. Instead of pursuing the extended 'testimonial' association of 'el alcatraz'/'el hombre' to which he briefly refers, it is tempting to take up his other, undeveloped, remark concerning 'agonías . . . materias y miserias' (Ortega 1991, 47). For the performative force of the opening passage of what Ortega himself has claimed 'is the most radical book of poetry written in the Castillian language' (ibid., 9) opens *Trilce* with a shit no less accidentally than Neruda's *Veinte poemas* opened with a fuck. Any grandeur issuing from, or clinging on to, the performance is of a materiality which strenuously resists all defamiliarizations, strains against *ostranenie* and prefigures the politico-poetic discourse of both *Trilce* and *Poemas humanos*.

By naturalizing the Peruvian-specific opening excretion of *Trilce*, by turning its sign, via image, through symbol, into habit, ritual and an essentially Romantic mythology, the 'ruling class' class of criticism reveals 'something less than equanimity' before a 'threatened dissolution' (here, by a decomposing yet fertilizing *guano*) of their 'ideological discourse'. But the (explicit) undoing of the ruling critical class I prefer to leave to the poetry of the Argentine Susana Thénon, and to a later chapter.

This overtly pedagogical case-study attempts to show that a start may be made in suggesting to students of (Latin American) literature that the still predominantly but not exclusively Eurocentric and Romantic 'idea that Truth is One – unambiguous, self-consistent and knowable' is 'the intellectual equivalent of aggressiveness and a wish to dominate' (Crosman 1980, 162). If it is necessary to use the tools of post-structuralism to posit the extreme view that 'all reading is misreading' (Miller 1976, 98), it is only in order to expose traditional criticism's attempt 'to prove that a text is readable by exploiting it within certain reading techniques and reifying it within a particular ideological context (so that) it must be the task of the post-structuralist to make it, by "deconstruction", unreadable again' (Wenzel 1983, 64).

The use of literary theory never as a circumscribed field, never as an alternative to literary study, but built into one's critical and teaching practice, may ensure that one's own reading, each and every time, will be rendered, soon, unreadable, a deconstructed, displaced authority. It will come as no surprise that Vallejo's subsequent critico-poetical practice in *Trilce* rapidly transcribes – and thus undoes – the authority, even, of displacement.

TRANSCRIPT

From poetry (un-Platonically) to that distant Republic of Foucault's Philosophy. For the 'consoling play of recognitions' (Foucault 1984, 88) poses a question not far removed from that of conceptual differences and translatability which has, famously, exercised the minds of Wittgenstein, Quine and Kripke. Robert Kirk summarizes the extreme positions taken up with regard to the question thus:

> The main argument assumes that some exact translation between different languages is possible. However, there is a spectrum of different opinions on the degree of translatability that can be expected. One extreme view is that 'for any sentence of one natural language, there is at least one sentence in every other natural language that expresses the same proposition' (Katz). The other extreme view is that exact translation between different languages is impossible: traduttore, traditore?: conceptual differences are held to preclude exact translation altogether.
>
> (Kirk 1986, 212)

Surprising as it may seem to philosophers, César Vallejo came close to entering this supposedly modern debate himself. Less surprisingly, he did so via his ruminations on the untranslatability of poetry, in *El comercio*, as early as 30 July 1929:

> Todos sabemos que la poesía es intraducible. La poesía es tono, oración verbal de la vida. Es una obra construida de palabras. Traducida a otras palabras, sinónimas pero nunca idénticas, ya no es la misma. Una traducción es un nuevo poema, que apenas se parece al original. Cuando Vicente Huidobro sostiene que sus versos se prestan, a la perfección, a ser traducidos fielmente a todos los idiomas, dice un error . . . . Se olvida que la fuerza de un poema o de una tela arranca de la manera como en ella se disponen los materiales más simples y elementales de la obra. El material más elemental y simple del poema, es, en último análisis, la palabra y el color

de la pintura. El poema debe, pues, ser trabajado con simples palabras sueltas, allegadas y ordenadas según la gama creadora del poeta. Lo mismo ocurre en la arquitectura, en la música, en el cinema. Un edificio se construye con piedra, acero y madera pero no con objetos . . . . Pierre Reverdy vota también por la imposibilidad de traducir un poema. Habiéndole preguntado una vez si le gustaría ver los versos que me daba para 'Favorables', traducidos al español, me dijo que prefería que fuesen leídos en francés. Naturalmente. Como ya lo hemos dado a entender, lo que importa en un poema, como en la vida, es el tono con que se dice una cosa y muy secundariamente lo que se dice. Lo que se dice, es, en efecto, susceptible de pasar a otro idioma pero el tono con que eso se dice, no . . . sólo se conoce, en los idiomas extranjeros, las grandes ideas, los grandes movimientos animales, pero no se percibe [sic] los grandes números del alma, las oscuras nebulosas de la vida, que residen en un giro, en una 'tournure', en fin, en los imponderables del verbo.

(371–2)

[We all know that poetry is untranslatable. Poetry is tone, verbal oration of life. It is a work constructed of words. Translated into other words, synonymous but never identical, it is no longer the same. A translation is a new poem, which only resembles the original. When Vicente Huidobro maintains that his verses lend themselves, perfectly, to being translated faithfully into all other languages, he is mistaken. . . . It is forgotten that the force of a poem or of a canvas stems from the manner in which the most simple and elementary materials of the work are arranged in it. The most elementary and simple material of the poem, is, in the final analysis, the word and the colour of the painting. The poem must, then, be worked with simple free words, collected and ordered according to the creative range of the poet. The same happens in architecture, music, in the cinema. A building is constructed with stone, steel and wood but not with objects . . . . Pierre Reverdy also votes for the impossibility of translating a poem. Having once asked him if he would like to see the verses which he gave me for 'Favorables', translated into Spanish, he told me that he preferred that they should be read in French. Naturally. As we have already given to understand, what is important in a poem, as in life, is the tone in which a thing is said and, very secondary, what is said. What is said, is, in effect, liable to go into another language but not the tone in which it is said . . . all that is known, in foreign languages, are the great ideas, the great animal movements, but not perceptible are the great 'moments' of the soul, the obscure nebulosities of life which reside in a turn of phrase, in a 'tournure', in the end, in the imponderables of the word.]

It will be apparent to most critics of poetry that Vallejo's thinking in this passage might be read as a blueprint for any treatise on post-modern poetics. But such critics will already be used to poets' prefiguring of the insights of even the most challenging theorists of literature. For present purposes, it will suffice to draw attention to but three of the salient points of Vallejo's insight. First, as will be shown in detail in a later chapter on Borges and structuralism, there is a striking similarity between the 'se disponen' argument, here, and the narratology of Jean Ricardou to which, in Chapter 6, I have recourse in analysing detective fiction. Second, in an apparently throw-away anecdote, Vallejo reveals himself to be in the vanguard of aesthetico-theoretical debates of 1920s' Paris, overtly echoing Pierre Reverdy's celebrated – if contentiously genre-biased dictum: 'Le poète est maçon; il ajuste ses pierres. Le prosateur coule du béton'/'The poet is a mason; he adjusts his stones. The prose-writer pours the cement' (Reverdy 1948, 130–1). Third, and most importantly in the present context, Vallejo comes close, in the 'Como ya lo hemos dado a entender' sequence, to the Quinean/indeterminacy question as discussed by Kirk: 'The trouble is that no single language would do justice to two languages grounded in different forms of life' (Kirk 1986, 214). Or, put in another, more trenchant, more familiar, way – for poetry critics, and returning to Mallarmé – Vallejo proves himself to be the most assiduous of readers (in his aesthetics, his difficulty and, not least, his apostasy) of the primacy, for and in poetry, of *mots* over *idées*.

But there was plenty of time ('gentlemen, please') for such detail in Chapters 3 and 4. The issue I should like to touch on here is that of the ever more markedly emergent orality broached by 'Vusco volvvver'. For we do not have to wait for a post-idea (Oxford) discovery of *language games*. The (Latin) American in Paris – and previously in a Peruvian jailhouse – rocks the (drunken?) boat of philosophico-linguistic play-buoyancy, barely keeping (the reader) afloat in his renewed ('Invitation au . . .') voyage, not only in the wake of Mallarmé's consonants ('le sonnet en -x et -y') but also through the classic precursor of Rimbaud's 'Voyelles' (and well before Borges' *El Aleph* equivalent excursus of Chapter 10). *ALFA*:

> **Alfan alf**iles a **adh**erirse
> a las junturas, **al f**ondo, **a** los testuces,
> **al** sobrelecho de los numeradores a pie
> **Alf**iles y ca[u]dillos de lupinas parvas . . .
> Vienen entonces **alf**iles a **adh**erirse
> hasta en las puertas **falsas** y en los borradores.

['If a lion could speak, we could not understand him']

For this text, the reader is not even offered the rough-guideline English reluctantly used, in other cases, in the institutional need to trans-late (i.e. tardily) my chosen examples of modern Latin American literature. In the scandalous gap, but still symptomatically, I have preferred to let Wittgenstein speak for, but not as, the lion. As to the question of who will speak for César Vallejo, few critics have succeeded so valiantly, as I have already argued, as Julio Ortega. Both in his *La teoría poética de César Vallejo* (1986) and in his edition of *Trilce* (1991) he has drawn sensitively on, and gone subtly beyond, other brave commentators, in treading the tightrope of convincing interpretation. My strategy here is but supplementary to that balancing act. At several points in this book, I look closely at how language and the construction of subjectivity in writing are, in Vallejo's parlance and in the more recent sutures of Susana Thénon, forcibly threaded through the eye of the needle. In *Trilce* XXV, the stammering ambition of betting on *alfa* in fact ventures beyond Mallarmé, by 'rendering more *impure* the words of the tribe'. Even in the false accesses ('puertas falsas') to the first drafts ('borradores') of Vallejo's *archi-escritura*, the poem – like the first man – is moulded from clay ('alfar'). But, in the pottery of language, the broken shards of first syllables are scattered. When, in a first line, *adhe* is pieced together, the continuity link of *bece* is already (always) missing. By the last line, the transformed initial ciphers of intelligible reference, the *alfas*, have been subsumed, inverted, trans-but-too-lated, forged into *falsas* . . . (with excess, ex '-s'). For the chess-board grid on which a bishop (*alfil*) operates is limited, his oblique trajectory of omen (also *alfil*) is but one locus of potential enunciation. Another would be the loom on which the first threads of weaving ('cadillo') warp – and often come undone. But, for the moment, I shall use neither the pins (*alfil[er]es*) latent in *Trilce* XXV nor the needle ('aguja') of *Trilce* XXXVI to tack or sew meanings together. The task and the hazards of misreading have already been faced in various stratagems of post-structuralist risk-taking.

> What, then, is it to cross the ultimate border? What is it to pass the term of one's life? Is it possible? . . . The 'I enter', crossing the threshold, this 'I pass' puts us on the path, if I may say, of the *aporos* or of the *aporia*: the difficult or the impracticable, here the impossible, passage.
>
> Jacques Derrida

WORKS CITED

Abrams, M. H. *Natural Supernaturalism*. London: Oxford University Press, 1971.

Belsey, Catherine. 'A Space in the Syllabus'. *Literature, Teaching, Politics*, I (1982,1), 58–65.

Bloom, Harold. *The Anxiety of Influence*. New York and London: Oxford University Press, 1973.

—— *Kabbalah and Criticism*. New York: Seabury, 1975.

—— *Poetry and Repression*. New Haven, Conn.: Yale University Press, 1976.

Coyné, André. *César Vallejo y su obra poética*. Lima: Editorial Letras Peruanas, 1958.

Crosman, Robert. 'Do Readers Make Meaning?' in *The Reader in the Text: Essays on Audience and Interpretation*, ed. Susan R. Suleiman and Inge Crosman. Princeton, NJ: Princeton University Press, 1980, 149–64.

Culler, Jonathan. *The Pursuit of Signs*. London: Routledge and Kegan Paul, 1981.

de Man, Paul. *Critical Writings, 1953–1978*, ed. Lindsey Walters. Minneapolis: University of Minnesota Press, 1988.

Derrida, Jacques. *Glas*. Paris: Editions Galilée, 1974.

—— *Of Grammatology*, trans. G. C. Spivak. Baltimore, Md: Johns Hopkins University Press, 1976.

Eagleton, Terry. *Literary Theory: An Introduction*. Oxford: Basil Blackwell, 1983.

Foucault, Michel. *The Foucault Reader*, ed. Paul Rabinow. Harmondsworth: Penguin, 1986.

Franco, Jean. *César Vallejo*. Cambridge: Cambridge University Press, 1976.

Fry, Glyn, Powe, Nicola and Vernell, Paul. 'Politics, Teaching, Criticism'. *Literature, Teaching, Politics*, 1 (1982,1), 50–7.

Kirk, Robert. *Translation Determined*. Oxford: Oxford University Press, 1986.

Lotringer, Sylvère. 'Le Complexe de Saussure'. *Semiotexte*, 2 (1975), 112.

McGuirk, Bernard. 'Limenperuguano: Hermeneutics, Semiosis and the Defects of the Romantic Discourse: César Vallejo's "Trilce I"', in *Essays in Honour of R. B. Tate*, ed. Richard A. Cardwell, University of Nottingham Monographs in the Humanities. Nottingham: University of Nottingham, 1984, (pp. 71–82).

Michaels, Walter Benn. 'The Interpreter's Self', in *Reader-Response Criticism: From Formalism to Post-Structuralism*, ed. Jane P. Tompkins. Baltimore, Md: Johns Hopkins University Press, 1980 (pp. 199–200).

Miller, J. Hillis. 'Walter Pater: A Partial Portrait', *Daedalus*, 105 (Winter 1976), 98.

Neale-Silva, Eduardo. 'The Introductory Poem in Vallejo's *Trilce*', *Hispanic Review*, 38 (1970), 2–16.

Ortega, Julio (ed.). *César Vallejo. Trilce*, Madrid: Cátedra, 1991.

Reverdy, Pierre. *Le Livre de mon bord*. Paris: Mercure de France, 1948.

Riffaterre, Michael. *Semiotics of Poetry*. London: Methuen, 1978.

Shaw, D. L. '*Trilce* I Revisited', *Romance Notes*, 20 (Winter 1979–80), 167–71.

Spiller, Michael. 'The Grammarian's Resurrection?', *Bradford Occasional Papers*, 4 (1983), 37–51.

Todorov, Tzvetan. 'A Complication of the Text: The *Illuminations*', in *French Literary Theory Today: A Reader*, ed. Tzvetan Todorov. Cambridge: Cambridge University Press, 1982, (pp. 223–37).

Vallejo, César. 'Desde Europa', *El comercio*. (Lima), 30 July 1929.

—— *Trilce*. Madrid: Cátedra, 1991.

Wenzel, Peter. 'From Essays in Criticism to the Criticism of Essays: Major Directions in Modern Literary Theory and their Relevance for Evaluating Student Essays'. *Bradford Occasional Papers*, 4 (1983), 52–82.

Wing, G. G. '*Trilce* I: A Second Look'. *Revista hispánica moderna*, 35 (1969), 268–84.

Chapter 6

Beyond structural influence
Borges and the purloined detective: 'tecs, lies and video-hype

Genre/ linearity

> Often I see criticism as a form of story, as a variant of detective fiction. The critic as detective trying to decipher an enigma even though there isn't one.
>
> Ricardo Piglia

> Great works of literature have anticipated explicitly any deconstruction the critic can achieve.
>
> J. Hillis Miller

A post-modern symphony in scarlet and yellow, it opens with a message scrawled on a wall after a murder-cum-intended-entrapment of master detective by master criminal, whose first encounter takes place beyond a red door with a lozenge-shaped glass panel. A text dominated by the self-reflexive framing of its own setting and scenery, characters and names, dialogues and emplotment, self-announcing to the point of precluding any possible suspension of disbelief. The specialist in Latin American fiction might recognize – mistakenly – the outline strategies and structures of Jorge Luis Borges' fiction 'Death and the Compass'. The Hollywood buff ought to spot with ease the pastiche extravaganza of the cartoon framing in a cardboard city of the original comic-strip creation of Chester Gould, brought to the Silver Screen (Partners IV), in 1990, by Warren Beatty, in *Dick Tracy*. So what – despite the Argentine's celebrated assertion that a writer creates his own precursors – does Hollywood owe to Borges? Vying with 'tecs, lying with texts? But to the video-hype I shall return.

In 1992, the BBC, in a joint Karl H. Braun production with the Mexican company Ultrafilms, premièred the film *Death and the Compass*, which, at first glance, might be said to owe as much to

Warren Beatty and Hollywood special effects as it does to the short story by Borges which it at once follows and pastiches. It might further discomfit those many critics who have seen Borges' fictions as the last word in elitism to admit not only his much publicized influence on Latin American writers of the *boom* generation but also, increasingly, the impact of his texts on film-makers. Their treatments of his fictions have varied considerably in 'faithfulness' to stories such as 'The Intruder' (Jaime Chavarri), 'Emma Zunz' (Benoît Jacquot), 'The South' (Carlos Saura) and 'The Gospel According to St Mark' (Hector Olivera). In this case, the shuttling back and forth of the influence of film techniques on fiction, and of fiction techniques on film, is particularly effective in highlighting the structural relations which underpin both the Borges narrative and the screen version of it. Before engaging, however, with the video-'tecs, and in a first move beyond merely structural influence, I purloin the letter of the lore of the Borges 'original', an open and never shut case.

'Death and the Compass' is a text which has prompted un-ending commentary and explication. I stress the word *unending* since 'Death and the Compass' invites, has been granted and awaits still further explanations, solutions or *closures*. At the same time, it is an obvious example of a text which, despite its apparent detective-story traits, resists the final solution, 'the closing of the case'. It must be conceded that the choice of this text is a loaded one not just because of the film adaptation. In terms of reader-response, the initial French-inspired fervour since Borges' 'discovery' by Roger Caillois has been more than balanced by critical opprobrium and the charge, succinctly dismissed by D. L. Shaw, that Borges' work 'tends to deny or subvert exterior reality, is merely escapist and hence politically reactionary in its very essence' (Shaw 1976, 75–6). Where a reader is looking for a poetics of fiction, the text is construed as such; where a reader is looking for a specific production of meaning, the work is often seen as false. The distinction is that between structural and cultural read-ings. Borges, typically, fuelled the controversy. To structuralists he offered the bait, in 'Tlön, Uqbar, Orbis Tertius', that metaphysics is a branch of fantastic literature; to political polemicists he offered either the barb of the impossibility of penetrating the divine scheme of the universe or the admission 'I am an antagonist of *littérature engagée* because I think it stands on the hypothesis that a writer can't write what he wants to' (Di Giovanni 1973, 59).

If Piglia's assertion that the function of the critic is akin to that of the writer of detective stories is to be tested, we might pick up the issue of whether the critic can, indeed, 'write what he wants to'. I have already raised this question in my discussion of Pablo Neruda and of the critic's 'broad range of options for pleasure'. One of those options is the indulgence of a particular kind of intellectual pleasure, the mind-game whereby logic and literariness come together in, for Borges as for Piglia, a peculiar copula of genres traditionally differentiated as primary and secondary discourses. The Brazilian critic Eneida Maria de Souza, in a perceptive move, finds in Piglia a clear echo of François Lyotard, but in a way she relates specifically to Latin America:

> Piglia's literary proposal transforms a lesser genre into a machine that produces textual plots. The wish to copy the models of the great texts of world literature is undone, recreating literary tradition through the obliteration of the origin and by stealing ideas . . . there is plagiarizing, as in *The Universal History of Infamy* by Borges, of accounts of crimes and the stories of Billy the Kid. The deconstruction of great narratives occurs in cutting through the margins and entering by the back door. Piglia tells parapolice stories, giving them the ambivalent status of theory and fiction by making use of the tricks of the genre to denounce the myth of pure, innocent and authentic writing. *His position is useful for the rethinking today of the place of criticism and literature produced in the third world* [my italics]. The close tie of the essay form to the transformations and experiments of a changing society signals also the role of the author in the text of history, where he is required to think about not only what he has to say but about *how* to say it.
>
> (de Souza 1994, 20–1)

In this chapter, I shall deal presently with the reappropriation of a so-called 'Third World' *relato* (of Borges) by the text, hype and video-tape of a production more recognizably plagiarizing *Dick Tracy* than *Billy the Kid*. For the moment, however, I return to a more factual dimension of Borges' fascination with the detective mode and, especially, with Edgar Allan Poe. In a lecture given in 1978, he stated: 'Poe did not wish the detective story to be realistic, he wanted it to be intellectual, fantastic if you like, but a fantasy of intelligence, not merely of imagination; both things, of course, but above all, of intelligence' (Borges 1980, 69). Of another of his stories, 'Abenjacán the Bojarí', Borges tells us that it became a cross between a permissible detective story and a parody of one. The more he worked on it, the more hopeless the plot seemed and the stronger his need to parody. When, in the same lecture, he mentions 'Death and the Compass', he concludes: 'I shifted the detective story to a symbolic plane where I am not sure that it fits'. None the less, there are many of the rather peculiarly termed 'permissible elements' in this story, and they stem from a series of obvious echoes: of Poe's 'pure reasoner', Auguste Dupin, and of his 'time-eaten and grotesque mansion', or of Chesterton's 'the criminal is the creative artist; the detective only the critic' ('The Blue Cross') and of his straight-line labyrinth ('The Horseman of the Apocalypse'). On closer examination, however, the echoes prove misleading. The detective-genius Erik Lönnrot 'believed himself to be a pure reasoner, an Auguste Dupin' but, since he is in a tradition of Dupin-like detectives, is not a pure reasoner but an imitative (or impure) reasoner; Triste-le-Roy turns out to be anything but a mere 'abandoned country-house'; the artist/critic distinction is undermined in Lönnrot's complex relationship with Red Scharlach, the master-criminal; finally, the straight-line labyrinth operates but potentially, as an unfulfilled objective.

An alternative to the critical search for similarities with, or the plagiarizing of, Poe is to exploit the accessible archetype of the detective-story in order to show how 'Death and the Compass' may sustain the myriad meanings critics have ascribed to it whilst providing a commentary, too, on its own capacity to generate meanings without being decoded, deciphered or solved. In short, though evoking in its detective elements the genre most prone to 'decoding', Borges' text may be shown to participate in a system which refers to its own limitations, to what it is not. It may even (re-)pose Derrida's question: 'What happens when acts or performances (discourse or writing, analyses or description etc.) form part of the objects they designate? When they may be given as an example of the very thing about which they speak or write?' (Derrida 1980, 417). For, it might be argued, the text is not an *explanation* of a crime committed in a labyrinth, it *is* a crime committed in a labyrinth, an unsolvable text in the labyrinth of detective-fiction wherein the most heinous crime is that of remaining unsolved. An enigma as quintessentially unsolvable, perhaps, as the text it part-discloses: namely, the incomplete Tetragrammaton

YA–E: Yarmolinsky, Azevedo, –, Erik; where – is the *false* clue, the *non*-crime, the disguised Scharlach or Gryphius–Ginzberg, the unutterable, the undetectable. *YAVÉ* or *YAHVÉ* is the Spanish rendering of the Hebrew sacred name of God, or Jehovah. The insolubility of the anagram here, as in the previous chapter, prompts comparison with Saussure's anagrams, which Sylvère Lotringer, it is worth recalling, described as 'not to be defined as a regulated dislocation lacking completeness, but as an indeterminable multiplicity, a radical undecidability which undoes all codes' (Lotringer 1975, 112).

Thought-provoking as it may be to ponder Derrida's conundrum of a text's practice repeating what a text refers to, it is possible also to begin more humbly by reapplying a basic, not to say clichéd, Saussurean distinction. A first lesson on the relationship between the signifier and the signified is that the sign which lies between them and which gives rise to them is shown, in this story, to be agreed but arbitrary (in Saussurean terms), whereas, in the traditional, closed detective-story, the sign unites the signifier, ultimately, to one signified and to one alone. By no means accidentally here, the signified, far from a unified, closed oneness, assumes the form of the labyrinth of Triste-le-Roy: that is, a fatal but open or imperfect labyrinth. Imperfect, or unfinished, for Lönnrot, who claims it has 'three lines too many', and for Scharlach, who, for the next time he kills Lönnrot, promises him 'that labyrinth consisting of a single line which is invisible, and unceasing'. A reader, however, might surmise that he or she is already confronted with just such a linear, invisible and unending labyrinth (namely, the text of 'Death and the Compass' itself); furthermore (and this will be developed in discussion of characterization), that Lönnrot and Scharlach, 'tired' and 'saddened' by and 'hating' their status as prisoners of the organized, compass-point labyrinth of the text, stand in contrast to the freedom or open-endedness of the extra-textual function of the sign-reader of post-criticism.

Like structuralism, the story proposes no one, given meaning or any immutable content for a sign-system, be it labyrinth or language. Saussure's statement that in language there are only differences, without positive terms – because a positive term would depend on a unified concept of signifier and signified – might be said to prefigure Piglia's meditation on language system and detective story system. In 'Death and the Compass'

– although 'term' might imply both terminology and termination, a reminder that the story, like language, lacks just such a double-edged 'positive term' – are the final words 'hizo fuego' 'fired'. Semantically, as formally, this constitutes not so much a *closure* as a *consummation*.

At this point, it is instructive to see how specific structuralist practices consistently underpin the post-structuralist strategies which inform all the chapters in this book. Reiterating the words of Jonathan Culler, 'I am not proposing a structuralist *method* of interpretation: structuralism is not a new way of interpreting literary works, but an attempt to understand how it is that works do have meaning for us' (Culler 1975, 59). What follows treats the so-called *traditional* elements of literary analysis such as character, plot, genre and psychology, each in the light of the overt structural features of Borges' story and then the covert post-structural appropriations of them, subsequently.

First, character. Recalling Vladimir Propp's formalist analyses of fairy-tales, where, though the names and descriptions of characters change, the functions remain stable, it becomes apparent that what applies to the fairy-tale might be equally valid for the detective-story. Thus, the stock detective functions constitute, in the reader's expectation, the driving forces behind the syntagmatic movement of the narrative, rendering a certain sequential predictability. The text's use of, and breaking with, the convention in 'Death and the Compass', in the relationship between Erik Lönnrot and Red Scharlach, echoes A. J. Greimas' *actants*, or spheres of action based on binary oppositions. If characterization has been the aspect of 'Death and the Compass' most consistently broached, this fact may be attributable to the presence, in the opening paragraph, of undisguised generic codes and to the reader's stock response to detective-story archetypes. Though it is apparent that this opening paragraph contains, in embryo, many elements of the subsequent plot, it is consistently characterization rather than solubility that structures the text. Despite the setting-up of the classic binary opposition of brilliant, dilettante detective versus elegant, master-of-disguise criminal, a note of failure mars from the outset any expectation of omniscient, satisfactory solution. The first break, or gap, in the classic detective model prompts less the recognition of traditional characters of the genre than of a recognizable sphere of action wherein Lönnrot and Scharlach do not subscribe to the norms of expectation. Other, subsequent gaps such as Lönnrot's and Scharlach's shared redness, Scharlach's reaction at the moment of supposed *hubris*, 'a fatigued triumph, a hatred the size of the universe, a sadness not less than that hatred', Lönnrot's reaction to imminent death, 'he felt faintly cold and he felt, too, an impersonal – almost anonymous – sadness', and (as mentioned) a shared dissatisfaction with the labyrinth inhabited by both, all prompt the awareness that, as both Propp and Greimas suppose, the *actant* need not be a single character but may be, rather, an interdependent combination of characters with a common function. For this story subverts the syntagmatic binaries of criminal/artist, detective/critic and sender/receiver by rendering possible the interchangeability of each binary half. Lönnrot pursuer turns victim pursued, Scharlach pursued turns detective pursuer. Concomitantly, artist/communicator turns critic/communicatee and vice versa. Textually, and in terms too of *actants* or spheres of action, the point of convergence of Lönnrot and Scharlach is a fourth point, the existence of which is only permitted by a pre-existing triangle implicit in the role of TREviranus.

Some insight has been gained into how mimetic characterization is subverted, and a parallel soon becomes apparent with regard to plot. Here, it is appropriate to re-enact Tzvetan Todorov's 'The Typology of Detective Fiction'. He claims that the classic detective tale has two stories: *A*, the story of the crime; and *B*, the story of the investigation. For Todorov, *A* ends before *B* begins; the action of *A* is real but absent; the action of *B* is insignificant but present ('insignificant' here means that in *B* 'learning' takes precedence over 'acting'). The purpose of *B* is to mediate between the reader and the crime which was the action of *A*. In Todorov's words, 'we are concerned then in the whodunnit with two stories of which one is absent but real, the other present but insignificant' (Todorov 1977, 46). Borges subverts Todorov's classic norm. *A* is *accidentally* real, i.e. *A* does not end before *B* begins. *B*, the story of the investigation, *is* *A*, the story of the crime. *B* is not *in*significant but *all*-significant, inasmuch as it becomes *A*. The detective model is thus reversed. If a syntagmatic progression of three narratives, classically, is: (1) enigma, (2) pursuit, (3) solution, Borges' story at once follows the pattern whilst, at the same time, reversing it: (3) solution (Treviranus' 'error'), (2) pursuit (rabbinical explanation), (1) enigma (labyrinth). Vitally, Borges' text confirms a narrative pattern yet subverts a semantic expectation. In the process, the text renders ambivalent, opens, a foreclosed narrative pattern. Just as Saussure demonstrated that there was no relationship between the sign and the idea other than the agreed but arbitrary, Borges' text effectively disabuses the reader of any expectation of an agreed solution (a signified) deriving from a familiar generic formal pattern (a signifier).

After this linear reversal, the way is open for a patterning of a plot based not on a semantic passage from enigma to solution but rather on a geometric, formal enigma: that is, a projection of the equilateral triangle towards its potential as source of the rhombus. The departure from norm of the detective-story creator (Borges and/or Scharlach) gives pause for the reader to construe Lönnrot's final plea for a simpler, alternative, linear labyrinth as the natural desire of a frustrated detective-hero to be treated as such (that is, linearly and traditionally) by his disrespectful, ludic author(s).

After character, plot and genre, the question of psychology. Here too, the text promotes subversion, undermining reader propensity to classify as types even stock detective characters. Despite the parodying echoes of the brilliant amateur aided by the plodding professional, or of the classic Holmes–Watson duo pitting wit and virtue against the evil genius of a master-criminal, Moriarty, it is difficult to treat the characters only in terms of motivation and credibility, much less to consider them as sub-jectivities. Even Holmes and Watson cannot exist without each other, but only as intersubjectivities. And here the model of analysis is the Lacan–Derrida debate on Edgar Allan Poe's 'The Purloined Letter'. From this exceedingly complex area, it is rel-evant to select but two notions, Derrida's 'the pre-eminence of the signifier over the subject' (Derrida 1975, 41) and Lacan's 'I am not wherever I am the plaything of my thought' (Lacan 1966, 136).

The shifting roles of Lönnrot and Scharlach, whilst confined to the pattern of message-sender/message-receiver, reminiscent of the Minister and Dupin in Poe's story, none the less confirm the fluidity, even the chance elements, of relationships which consti-tute the convention. By constantly suggesting and affirming the interchangeability of Lönnrot and Scharlach, Borges takes further, overtly, what is only the implied relationship between the Minister and Dupin. Everything depends on there being no victor (recalling 'a sadness not less than that hatred' and 'an impersonal – almost anonymous – sadness'); on there being, after 'hizo fuego' (literally, 'he made fire', and thus 'he fired'), no reconstruction of a surviving self. Only the pre-eminent signifier, the sphere of action, survives. The identification or analysis of a stable, textual self (a psychology) is as impermissible a goal as the restoration, through psychoanalysis, of a stable ego. The text *consumes* the ego of Lönnrot and, in the same consummation, the ego of Scharlach. The actant which survives has no psycho-analysable being ('I am not') since it has no identity but as the 'plaything of thought'.

Thus, it is usually apparent, and by now certainly demonstrable, that the end of Scharlach coincides with the end of Lönnrot *not* because they are the same person (or interchangeable) but because Erik Lönnrot's death ends the intersubjectivity which defines the limits of Scharlach's existence. Scharlach's own reading of this intersubjectivity, this non-independence, is included in the text; his function is defined and limited by the relationships of the geometric action, a contrast with the linear, open-ended, extra-textual, labrynth-making function of the reader. Borges' ploy, or play, may be construed as a consistent if literal rendering of Lacan's 'Je ne suis pas là où je suis le jouet de ma pensée'. If a further post-Cartesian parody may be permitted – and mere reflection avoided – then we might say that our critical identity cards are issued by the Interpol(arity) established between the sphere of action of the readable (*ludens*) and the sheer refraction of the reader (*cogitans*).

Such an approach aims to support textual analysis with theory, and theory with text; to illustrate Borges' practice as an instance of Jean Ricardou's dictum 'composer ce n'est pas avoir l'idée d'une histoire, puis la disposer; c'est avoir l'idée d'un dispositif, puis en deduire une histoire' (Ricardou 1973, 39). Only the notorious difficulty of translating *dispositif* has prompted me to retain the original here. A possible, if problematical, version might be: 'to write is not to have the idea of a story, then to arrange it; rather, it is to have the idea of an arrangement, and then to deduce a story from it'. Echoing Ricardou, I might situate 'Death and the Compass' as a text dominated by its own *dispositifs*.

It is questionable whether it has ever been possible, let alone desirable, to separate structuralist from post-structuralist criticism. Far from applying to the short fiction of Borges those 'neat catalogues of structuralism' which Anny Brooksbank-Jones suspects of 'aspiring to critical mastery' (Jones 1987, 71) and, in the process, excluding a, for example, political reading, this approach, by exploiting a deliberately plural and open-ended series of structuralist strategies, ought to complement other readings. For not only may a classically structuralist demonstration of an actant theory of characterization at work prove to be an illuminating insight into the obsessive, Lönnrot/Scharlach-like patterns of post-criticism, as I shall presently suggest in my analysis of the BBC's *Death and the Compass*; it may also do so in the context of other, overlapping networks of social class, of money functions, gender relations, or of the vested political interests operating in the text, as my subsequent chapter on 'Emma Zunz' will show. To highlight, provisionally, the workings of a given structure should not diminish awareness of other networks of relations. In this sense, structuralism need not be regarded as ahistorical. I must always avoid the danger, in setting a text against itself and by juxtaposing quotations, either in pattern or in conflict, of merely pointing to paradigms or paradoxes. Structuralist practice may be seen, and used, as a multiple enabling device, as plural as the ideologies of its users. Is not the Barthes of *Mythologies* and *S/Z* engaged in an exposure of the structured nature of ideologies? Equally, Macherey, Kristeva and Derrida, in turn, have absorbed the lessons of structuralism to render more generalizable, more predictive the themes and implications underlying their respective critical praxes.

Bearing in mind that 'Derrida draws attention to the way that deconstruction inhabits even the structuralist model of language inspired by Saussure' (Tallack 1987, 161), it may seem an all-too-obvious deconstructive reversal to claim that that same structuralist model itself 'inhabits' deconstruction. Similarly, the undecidability, dissemination of meaning and intertextuality which pervade Borges' fictions are also in operation throughout the present volume. Derrida's notion of 'différance', as I suggested in my 'Fore-word: locating inequality', is structuralist 'différence' (relationality) *at work*. The politicizing of structuralist practice is precisely a matter of strategy and risk. The (free-)play of metaphors, of names and of numbers in a deconstructive reading of, say, 'Death and the Compass' or 'Emma Zunz' or 'The House of Asterion' need not, cannot, be just a further instance of structuralist *inter*play. Concomitantly, class as a differential concept, the frame as *mise en abyme*, shifting centres of focus in endless, overlapping networks of structural spheres of action, all inhabit both structuralist and post-structuralist readings, both textually and socially. Inseparably. All readings are inextricably enmeshed in the labyrinth, an argument to which I shall return in discussion of Carlos Fuentes' *Terra Nostra*.

The film which reads the Borges story, far from concealing its enmeshment in an intervening set of networks, derives considerable impact from the very foregrounding of the necessary multi-mediation involved in the translation from page to screen. 'Faithful' transposition is no longer conceivable, let alone sought. The only post-modern condition to be obeyed is that of pastiche, itself a genre which offers rich pickings to the criminally inclined producer–thief, the plagiarist–artist. Concomitantly, I think I choose, but am perhaps forced, to read *Death and the Compass* (1992) through and after *Dick Tracy* (1990).

The overlapping networks of the Borges and Beatty directorships have already been revealed in the first paragraph of this chapter. Subsequent to my analysis of character, plot, genre and psychology in the story, it will come as no surprise that the *dispositifs* of *Dick Tracy* (from which its minimalist *histoire* are to be deduced) are the cardboard scenery, the cartoon characters, the faceless (nick-)names, the borrowed harlequin colours and the Dick-dialogue of both the Borges blueprint and the many Hollywood intertexts. Taking these items one by one, and exemplifying, I might point to a switch of focus from 'tout est toujours déjà *écrit*' to 'tout est toujours déjà *dessiné*', in the reliance less on a post-structuralist than on the rather more pertinent post-modernist cliché. Thus, in the cartoon framings, Tracy's hat doesn't fall off, his yellow overcoat doesn't get dirty, the title of the daily paper is *Daily Paper*, the baddies are not so much ugly as gargoyles, the goodies are 'one in a million' like Tracy's gal, Tess Trueheart. Action can only occur, it would initially appear, against a background of the always already drawn. But what of Borges – the already written?

To detect 'Death and the Compass' beneath the dazzling surface of the film is neither easy nor, it goes without saying, necessary. But it is fun. In this instance, Barthes' reminder that to read is to struggle to name takes on a cinema-enthusiast's self-indulgence. Did you spot Dustin Hoffman behind the face of Mumbles? James Caan in Spaldoni? Al Pacino as Big Boy Caprice (contributing, incidentally, his own first name to the actant-source

'Capone')? And so on. From within the gang of Shoulders, Stooge, The Walnut, The Brow, Little Face, Itchy Siobhán, Piano Player, 88 Keys (Deep Throat?), Lips Manlis, perhaps only Lefty Moriarty takes you directly back-to-genre of a literary, as distinct from *Untouchables*, echo. But try listening to – as well as looking at – the Red/Scarlet-suited, -tied, -overcoated Big Boy Caprice (no less than Red Scharlach a reader/writer and, dare I say, a (mis)citer–siter of false clues: 'Fings ain't always what they seem'/'You gotta tell 'em everything. They crave leadership' (readership?)/'The way I see it, and Plato agrees with me, is that there is what is and then there is what we would like it to be'/'Law without order is as great a danger to the people as order without law – Jefferson'/'All's fair in love and business – Benjamin Franklin'/'A man without a plan is not a man – Nietzsche'. Shall we fall into the trap, the Caprice, of the Big Boy who would be super-criminal *qua* philosopher? Who apes Satan – 'I offer you the keys of the kingdom and you tell me you're the law. *I* am the law'? Or into the more tender trap of the God-like Tracy, who, to Madonna/Breathless Mahoney's 'What's your day off?' answers – beyond temptation – 'Sunday'; the same Tracy whose verbal confusion points to a loneliness no less isolating in the cardboard labyrinth than, in the word-maze original, was Erik Lönnrot's: 'The enemy of my enemy is my enemy.' By now, it might have become apparent that, for one reader at least, Beatty is creating a precursor. But I am concerned not so much with the name of the game as with the game of the name. 'How d'you like to pick your own name?', The Kid is asked. And, later, dressed – by DT – in an all-scarlet suit and cap by his all-yellow harlequin *alter pater*, coyly reveals his (actant-restricted) choice 'Dick Tracy Jnr . . . if it's alright with you'. Thereafter, The Kid, too, can dive *before* an explosion – and keep his hat on. This is my beloved son in whom I am well-policed?

From the opening credit of the film's title, *Dick Tracy*, in yellow on a scarlet backcloth, on which a yellow hat at once is placed, through the voicing of 'I want to leave a little message here', to the scrawling on the wall after the first crime of 'EAT LEAD TRACY', the film can be read as a dazzling inheritor-text of 'Death and the Compass' in a sense no less compelling, as a 'psychic battlefield', than any 'scene of instruction' imagined by Harold Bloom. The climactic *askesis*, the necessary corrective imposed on the Borges precursor-text by the purgative Hollywood intertextuality of 'happy endings for heroes', is set, inevitably, by a compass-point, by a framing, and by a 'new refutation of time' very much *à la* Borges. Thus, Big Boy Caprice sets the ruse to entrap Dick Tracy: 'OK, Freddie. Get down to the Southside ware-house'. The 'big pay-off' re-enacts the Triste-le-Roy confrontation–contemplation of Erik and Red: 'Those years are like a clock's. Every notch, tick, tock'. But with a difference. Refuted this time is the consummation – again, in two senses. No Face/Madonna (Ariadne?) comes to the rescue of *thes*(l)*eu*(th)'s *ephebe*, saving Tracy not for herself but for the 'true' heart of Tess. Not, however, before she has outwitted the master-criminal in a thoroughly postmodern proto-feminist genre reversal:

BREATHLESS: 'I brought you down with kidnapping – the only crime you *didn't* commit.'
CAPRICE: 'Whoever you are, I know we can make a deal.'
BREATHLESS: 'A deal? I'm making my deal with Tracy.'

Forlorn self-delusion, despite Breathless Mahoney's longing to find a time and a place to consummate her desire for union with her god: 'It's a big world. It must be Sunday somewhere.' In effect, her pleas to Tracy to extricate them all from the triangular labyrinth by eliminating Big Boy is the equivalent of Eric Lönnrot's wish, in a *previous* incarnation, for the similarly illusory single-line labyrinth of Zeno's paradox: 'Tracy. With Big Boy out of the way, we can own this town'. But Big Boy also fired ('hizo fuego'?), killing Breathless/No Face before, in turn, himself falling victim to the cogs of time and plunging down the clock-shaft.

It should now be apparent that, in line with my Hillis Miller epigraph claim, Borges' short story has anticipated more explicitly than the cinema-goer might have suspected any deconstruction of it that the Warren Beatty film might have achieved. No less is true of the Anglo-Mexican production of 1992. My basic claim is that the film appropriation of the intertext of 'Death and the Compass' cannot but read the story through strong precursor networks – networks which include the text of the original story, the detective genre itself, Hollywood's and other cinematic traditions' treatment of it and, principally, the myth which is Borges. In a later chapter, the relation between Borges the writer and Borges the blind citer will be examined. For the moment, I shall concentrate on how it becomes impossible for the film-maker to resist the temptation to *include*, in a way reminiscent of Jean-Pierre Richard's 1950s' phenomenological construction of a 'Baudelaire' or a 'Verlaine', the 'Borges' of both popular and, indeed, specialist consumption.

The differential labyrinth of images which is cinema might have been expected to respond to the rich play of colours and shapes, the harlequins and the geometries, of 'Death and the Compass'. The less obvious invitation thrown out by the narrative and readily taken up in the BBC film, however, is precisely the interplay of names and character functions – not necessarily restricted to the story's text. To suggest that the film attempts an *A to Z* of Borges' fictions would be both an exaggeration and a slight on Evelyn Fishburn's and Psiche Hughes' admirable *A Dictionary of Borges* (1990). But what is the name *Alonso Zunz*, hardly gratuitously given to the editor of the *Yiddische Zeitung*, but a quasi-Borgesian joke? The first, it turns out, of many. In this version, Red Scharlach, master of disguise, plays this AZ, a pseudo-walking dictionary of ersatz Jewish expertise constantly consulted by a Kojak-look alike Erik Lönnrot somewhat less inspired than the pure reasoner blueprint.

Appropriately, perhaps, in terms of the suspense genre, I prefer not to reveal my hand on the deciphering of Jewish name-codes until the chapter on 'Emma Zunz'. Here, I merely regard the play of names as an inevitable extension of the sphere of action whereby any new treatment of *one* Borges fiction comes to include nod-and-a-wink references to *all* of them.

The tightrope trodden by writer–director Alex Cox is that of amusing the *cognoscenti* without relaxing the tautness and humour of the narrative, as with *Dick Tracy's* 'swerve' away from its precursors. Alonso begins the process, describing his *Yiddische Zeitung* to Erik as 'small circulation, mainly for libraries', against the police-station intercom-reminder to detectives that 'the use of the torture-section is a privilege'. Updating for the post-feminist 1990s Borges' use of the Tetragrammaton, he confides: 'God is believed to be male, by the way'. And, in similar vein, but as much Washington- as New York-directed: 'The Hasidim . . . an extreme bunch'. Predictably, Daniel Simon Azevedo becomes a wide-boy politician, Treviranus (yellow-suit) the corrupt police commissioner, turning a blind eye to the (red-stockinged) whore-racket of Liverpool House, thinks aloud (for Cox?): 'I don't know what to think of it. Minotaur masks, carnival costumes. Is it always like this?'. Lönnrot (blue suit) turns thoroughly modern mystic-with-a-difference: namely, chess-playing philosophizer co-habiting with an in-and-out-of uniform NYPD-style sultry cynic:

HE: 'It doesn't do to get attached to things . . . if one gets attached to one's existence it's just as stupid as getting attached to non-existence.'
SHE: 'I'm not going to stop smoking.'
HE: 'I can accept that.'

An Idealist of the senses? Certainly one who responds to the end-game imperative 'Mate' quite literally, and (a joke for US consumption?) plays safe on religion, replying to Alonso's 'I'm an atheist' with 'You're a brave man, Zunz'.

Though the plot follows Borges *qua* text, it is to Borges *qua* postmodern myth that the jokes address themselves. Thus Lönnrot consults Mrs Spinoza, a seamstress from the 'colonia del Sur', who tells him explicitly that the murders point to the 'three vertices of an equilateral triangle – a symbol of completeness'. As the patchwork Jewish geometer decamps, so Treviranus camps – 'Have a nice day'. It is when the Cox film nears its climax that the hype of post-modernity spurts ahead of the Borges plot. Leaving behind the futurist city and its three-sector map (yellow, red, blue), Lönnrot is advised by Treviranus to take a fellow-detective, for protection, on his journey to Triste-le-Roy. He opts for Novalis (self-pitying Romantic mystic of *Hymnen an die Nacht* and principal inspirer of suicidal thoughts). On being told that Novalis is 'in the middle of a big bust at the airport', he is left only with the possibility of Blot (on his landscape? since, as I have argued, no detective can be a *pure* reasoner any more). But Blot has had an accident (with a fork-lift truck). So it seems Erik must go alone – but not before Treviranus' splendidly calculating irrelevance: 'A lot's riding on your handling of this case. See those foundations down there? In that very spot, in a few weeks, will stand the Civi-Scraper, one hundred and twenty-seven storeys tall. The entire city Police Department might be moving up there. Can you imagine? Our offices in the Penthouse Suite' – a pastiche of Lyotard-like mixing whereby the banal (for Lönnrot) but crucial (for Treviranus) civic politics dwarf and ridicule the noble sacrifice of the former's 'only lost causes are of interest to a gentleman' (a tall story). He might *echo* Holmes, but, as he traipses off to meet his alter-Sherlock Scharlach, Erik (the read) more resembles, in his garb of white mackintosh and soft hat, not so much a post-Bogart as a lost Clouseau.

In fact, Lönnrot is not allowed to travel alone, for post-modernity is no respecter of privacy. The 'story' is too good to be missed. Erik can't resist the *deus ex machina* offer made by Alonso Zunz, the cover story for *Mademoiselle Britannica* magazine, and an in-flight interview in hip journalese. After 'planes and trains – and a 'lift' from Borges' 'El Sur'/'The South' – Zunz still tails and tape-records him: 'You're stressed. You need a vacation'; 'I'm thinking about Egypt next year'. But before the Middle East can resolve Erik's crisis, the Hasidim 'who sometimes practice human sacrifice' intervene. AZ turns Red as Scharlach shoots five bullets into Lönnrot before, Cagney-like, delivering the inevitable 'You killed my brother' line, and the final explanation: 'I was delirious, imagining myself to be at the dead centre of all things, trapped like the Minotaur in some enormous maze'. And, to the final question, 'What was the Last Letter of the Name?', answers 'There was no name, there was no plot, it was all your invention'. Scharlach talking to Lönnrot – or Cox talking to Borges? It is the sixth and last bullet which mimics – but cannot reproduce – the Zeno trajectory of the desired single straight line – before the *never* 'final' credits. Six bullets – *Seven* deadly sins? But that's another story – another film.

Borges himself will have been seen as a purloiner of letters, notably in 'Death and the Compass'. Now, in turn, his letter-texts are purloined constantly. This chapter has first explored the intertextualities at work *in* Borges, then the intertextualities worked *on* Borges, but it has not only attempted to make one more reading of post-modernity through the lifting and adding. It has also laid the ground for further exploration, in Chapter 9, of how in Argentina itself there occurs, as part of a national identity in the (re-)making, a citing of 'Borges' as text as distinct from Borges' texts. In the light of both the Beatty and the Cox film responses to Borges, it becomes apparent that the claims for emptiness (of plot, characterization, psychology, ethics, and so on) of such as David Lynch, on post-modernity, can only be regarded as tongue-in-cheek commentary on post-reader-response criticism. What may reside in a text, a film, is ever a function of what the reader, the viewer, can (palimpsestically) superimpose. For the uninitiated, the Alex Cox *Death and the Compass* might evoke nothing of the Borges precursor-text but plenty of *Dick Tracy, Kojak* and *Miami Vice* – ironically, a parallel of Borges' own incorporation of elements from an Auguste Dupin and Sherlock Holmes tradition. In this process, his own use of cardboard 'non'-characters, shapes, colours, patterns, is highlighted and re-read. For the initiate(d), the story is not only read but also extended – sideways, through the accretion of names from other Borges texts, forwards, through the addition of the compulsory sexy girl-friend (Catherine, Katherine, Kathryn?) to join the by now TV-star Erik, and even backwards, in the revival of Borges' own lurid interest in violent death, knife-fights, criminality.

Cox's film, set in a state unnamed and in the future, but critically re-reading the past, far from allowing the empty peddling of a list of clichés, for Latin America, of crime, drugs and messianism, draws the viewer into a denser primitivism too often overlooked, or lost, by philosophically inclined readers of Borges. It broaches an atavism inseparable from his fictions' layered exploration of the psychic structures of his own Hispano-Italo-Germano-Judaeo-Anglo-derived violent hierarchies, dark archives in the archaeology of nation *qua* construct in *any* society. Lies, fictions, (video-)tape-recordings of the gloss(ia) of JLB, on whom Cox's film commits GBH. The body of the text is victim, divined cadaver not encompassed but pointed towards, and away from, again . . .

WORKS CITED

Borges, Jorge Luis. 'El cuento policial', in *Borges oral*. Barcelona: Bruguera, 1980 (pp. 69-88).

Chatman, Seymour (ed.). *Literary Style: A Symposium*. New York: Oxford University Press, 1977.

Culler, Jonathan. *Structuralist Poetics*. London: Routledge and Kegan Paul, 1975.

Derrida, Jacques. 'The Purveyor of Truth', *Yale French Studies*, 52 (1975), 41.

—— *La Carte postale*. Paris: Flammarion, 1980.

de Souza, E. M. *Tempo da pós-crítica: cadernos de pesquisa*. Belo Horizonte: NAPq, 1994.

Di Giovanni, Norman T. (ed.). *Borges on Writing*. New York: E. P. Dutton, 1973.

Fishburn, Evelyn and Hughes, Psiche. *A Dictionary of Borges*. London: Duckworth, 1990.

Jones, Ann. 'Feminism I: Sexual Politics. *In the Cage'*, in *Literary Theory at Work: Three Texts*, ed. Douglas Tallack. London: Batsford, 1987 (pp. 67–87).

Lacan, Jacques. 'The Insistence of the Letter in the Unconscious', *Yale French Studies*, 36–7 (1966) 136.

—— 'Seminar on the Purloined Letter', *Yale French Studies*, 48 (1972) 40.

Lotringer, Sylvère. 'Le Complexe de Saussure', *Semiotexte* 2 (1975), 112.

Ricardou, Jean. *Le Nouveau Roman*. Paris: Seuil, 1973.

Shaw, D. L. *Borges: Ficciones*, Critical Guides to Spanish Texts. London: Tamesis, 1976.

Tallack, Douglas (ed.). *Literary Theory at Work: Three Texts*. London: Batsford, 1987.

Todorov, Tzvetan. *The Poetics of Prose*. Ithaca, NY: Cornell University Press, 1977.

Chapter 7

On the semi(er)otics of alterity
Beyond Lacanian limits: Julio Cortázar's 'The Other Heaven'

> The time is out of joint.
> *Hamlet*

> Ego = ghost . . . . Wherever there is Ego, *es spukt*, 'it spooks'.
> Jacques Derrida

In *Specters of Marx*, Derrida returns relentlessly to the discursive disjunctions of time and of the self. The context of his meditation, historically speaking, was a conference, held in 1993, on 'Whither Marxism? Global Crises in International Perspective'. From the narrower perspective of this book, however, I am struck by the closeness of Derrida's obsession to a similarly spectral text of Julio Cortázar, 'El otro cielo'/'The Other Heaven' from *Todos los fuegos el fuego/All Fires the Fire*, of 1966. The text is set in a political economy of crises which, throwing story time and narrator identity out of joint, provides a (doubled) base for a super-structure/superego haunted by the spectres of other readings. As is often the case, Derrida's writing, too, is spooked by other authors, precursor-*confidants* with whom he plays (and reads) along:

> There is the temptation to add here an aporetic postscript to Freud's remark that linked in a same comparative history three of the traumas inflicted on human narcissism when it is thus de-centred: the *psychological* . . . the *biological* . . . the *cosmological* . . . . Our aporia would here stem from the fact that there is no longer any name or teleology for determining the Marxist *coup* and its subject. Freud thought he knew, for his part, what man and his narcissism were.
> (Derrida 1994, 97–8)

So what kind of reading, and with what relevance to Cortázar, can emerge from a post-structuralism so haunted by a Marx–Freud hegemony? The reading which follows might not answer such a question. It will, however, suggest that Cortázar's text had already anticipated Derrida's conclusion:

> In proposing this title, *Specters of Marx*, I was initially thinking of all the forms of a certain haunting obsession that seems to me to organize the *dominant* influence on discourse today. At a time when a new world disorder is attempting to install its neo-capitalism and neo-liberalism, no disavowal has managed to rid itself of all of Marx's ghosts. Hegemony still organizes the repression and thus the confirmation of a haunting. Haunting belongs to the structure of every hegemony.
>
> (ibid., 37)

When it comes to literary hegemonies – or intertextualities – the legacies exploited by Cortázar are multiple. His use of the double is pervasive, never more caricaturedly so than in *Todos los fuegos el fuego*. For every Jekyll there is a Hyde. In every Stevenson there hides a Borges. In every Cortázar, a spook. In every *fuego, juego*. Always at play is the deferral of the hegemony. And reading, too, must play along:

> there is no such thing as an expert who interprets. Therapy is a co-operative effort to create understandings which are of value. We don't discover in therapy that we conform to Freud's view and wanted to make love to our mother; we grapple for more personal meanings, the sense we have made and are making of our lives. Therapy is a forum for understanding and changing, but not through interpretation being handed down.
>
> (Orbach 1994, 48)

The era of critical theories has hardly diminished what Julio Cortázar, one of the archetypal practitioners of the *nueva novela*, perceived as overdue: namely, the development of the *critic-accomplice*, alternative *par excellence* to the 'expert who interprets'. Though the gap between so-called primary and secondary textuality has been diminished occasionally by *critical* novelists in the intervening years, there has been an enduring resistance to an equivalent writing-practice of *creative* critics. When Roland Barthes wrote *S/Z*, he did not tell the reader what *Sarrasine* is about, much less did he act as guide to Balzacian realism. Rather, did he write in parallel both to Balzac's text and to our reading of it, providing a bridge, more accurately a series of bridges, by which access becomes not only possible but the more pleasurable. In the process, Barthes' work is parasitic on Balzac's, but necessarily parasitic on the reader, too. In living off the reader, however, Barthes brings about the realization in the reader that he or she has life to offer – and this is where the connection with Julio Cortázar arises. In his conception of the *lector cómplice*, Cortázar demands just the opposite of a reader who can tell what the text is about.

On the contrary, he anticipates a reader who, like Jorge Luis Borges' Minotaur, 'grapples' (perhaps in vain) 'for more personal meanings, the sense we have made and are making of our lives'. In this respect, Cortázar constructs a post-structuralist reader – a strong and, at the same time, wholly vulnerable monster, one whose blindness of insight carelessly exposes it to the bravado-borne cutting edge of the boastful Theseus-cum-liberating-human(ist). A mighty (referential) sword cuts through the maze of meanings to re-impose a fatal order upon a chaos in which, scandalously absent from responsible readership, the 'unnatural' critical voice declares: 'jamás he retenido la diferencia entre una letra y otra. Cierta impaciencia generosa no ha consentido que yo aprendiera a leer' / 'I have never retained the difference between one letter and another. A certain generous impatience has not permitted that I learn to read' (Borges 1972, 68). Fatally divided between the (*underwriterly*) bullish vigour of Stock Exchange, i.e. traceably modish literary values, and a gentler (*readerly*) escapism in intertextual echoes of River Plate–Parisian *l'autre(a)mondisme*, I shall feed parasitically on the split narrator of that *other heaven* – that ideal fiction *à la* Borges – who unrelentingly struggles with labyrinthine ideological, psychological and ever non-fictional by-ways. Cortázar as new Minotaur inhabits (without expertise) the House of Asterion inherited from his most obvious precursor, not blindly but with the failing eyesight of that most accomplished accomplice, the non-expert. For once his struggle with the early post-structuralist era is engaged, his writing will reflect a shift from any unified conception of meaning, or of the nature of reality. It thus becomes impossible to say what such writing 'is about'. At best the critic might show how it works and in what ways Cortázar's fiction exploits, for example, the priority of diegesis over mimesis.

One possible point of entry into 'El otro cielo' might be the rather obvious statement that we are confronted, in this text, not merely with a story of parallel events (parallel both in time and space) occurring in a Paris of 1870 and a Buenos Aires of 1945. The question is: how do the interwoven textual parallels interact, and in what way(s), if any, does the text exceed its dual spatio-temporal organization? In order to penetrate the surface story or stories to examine the elements of composition, I return to Jean Ricardou's *nouveau romancier* handling of the *dispositif*. In the case of 'El otro cielo', the composition is 'arranged' on *two* cities (Buenos Aires and Paris); *two* 'novias' or lovers (Irma and Josiane); *two* jobs (in the 'Bolsa' and in the 'Bourse'); *two* labyrinths (the 'Pasaje Güemes' and the 'Galerie Vivienne'); and *two* years (1945 and 1870). The unitary or unifying link or axis between these binary elements is the single or, more exactly, undifferentiated narrator.

Two epigraphs help situate 'El otro cielo', intertextually, against the (notoriously erotic) *Chants de Maldoror* – an obvious trans-Atlantic precursor of Cortázar's story. The quotations from Lautréamont are as follows: 'Ces yeux ne t'appartiennent pas . . . où les as-tu pris?' / 'These eyes do not belong to you . . . where did you get them?' (Cortázar 1979, 135), which prompts the double focalization of the short story; 'Où sont-ils passés les becs de gaz? Que sont elles devenues, les vendeuses d'amour?' / 'Where have the gas-lamps gone? What has become of them, the sellers of love?' (ibid., 147), which inspires and evokes the Paris night-setting of criminal sexuality exploited, in the text, by Cortázar. In short, the intertexts provide the background, not only literary but also socio-cultural, of an urban setting on the eve of political catastrophe: namely, that of the Prussian invasion of Paris in 1870.

Composing the short story against this background of double intertextuality (poetico-erotic and socio-political), Cortázar exploits *le dispositif* (or 'the arrangement' of his tale) with a classic demonstration of the high-structuralist characterization theory analysed in the previous chapter. The 'characters' of the spatio-temporal double plot can be conceived of in no way as *actors* in a dramatic act or acts but, rather, as *dispositifs* themselves, arranged within the sphere of action of the story: namely, as *actants*. In this way, Cortázar, like Borges before him, underlines schematically and almost parodically the anti-natural(ist), not to say the 'defamiliarized', dimension of the process of characterization. In so doing, as Jonathan Culler puts it, he places 'an emphasis on the interpersonal and conventional systems that traverse the individual, that turn him/her into a space in which forces and events come together, more than into an individual essence, [an emphasis which] leads to a rejection of the predominant conception of character in the novel' (Culler 1975, 230).

The basically structuralist-derived analysis of *actant* theory is, as in the case of detective fiction, complicated and rendered problematic by the question of name(s). For all the 'characters' – save the narrator – have names. At this point, analysis can shift to a more strictly post-structuralist phase, again exploiting Barthes' suggestion that to read is to struggle to name, and pursuing the way in which an unnamed narrator struggles towards an identity, leaving open the question of whether, in the text of 'El otro cielo', this struggle takes the form of an incomplete search:

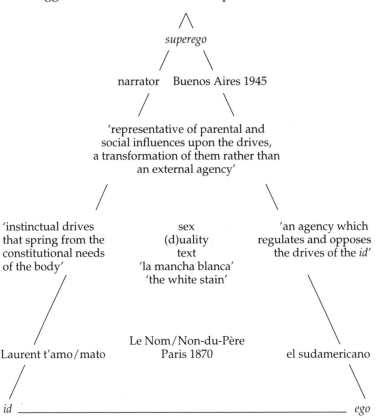

Beginning with an adolescent, even infantile, narrator in an amorphous state, yet ever more prepared by his mother for the 'stable' fate of adult maturity, marriage, the text none the less initiates the narration at a moment of outright resistance against such a normalizing maternal influence. My diagram is based on the Lacanian structuring of the psyche, simplified, and supplemented by short-hand definitions of Wright (1984, 10–11, 107–22). The opening words of 'El otro cielo' are as follows:

> Me ocurría a veces que todo se dejaba andar, se ablandaba y cedía terreno, aceptando sin resistencia que se pudiera ir así de una cosa a otra. Digo que me ocurría, aunque una estúpida esperanza quisiera creer que acaso ha de ocurrirme todavía.
>
> (Cortázar 1979, 135)

> [It happened to me at times that everything would let go, soften and I would give ground, accepting without resistance that it was possible to go like that from one thing to another. I say that it happened to me, though a stupid hope would like to think that it is perhaps still to happen to me.]

Such a fluid, soft, unresisting shift from one state to another is close, textually, to Lacan's basic metaphor of the egg's breaking to disclose the *(h)om(m)elette* (or little man), spreading out and wandering, in this case, through a series of quasi-amorphous labyrinths: namely, the fused or coagulated Pasaje Güemes (in Buenos Aires) and Galerie Vivienne (in Paris), ultimately in search of a new, formed, rounded identity – and a proper name. But he breaks out of his shell *not* to a rhythm dictated by his mother (or her eventual substitute, his 'novia'); for the narrator's narcissism holds him back at the mirror-stage (*le stade du miroir*), – a mirror made up, for him, by and from his pseudo-erotic reading(s) of *Les Chants*. He thus wanders through the passages/galleries of his native habitat – and through those of his precursor/father-figure, Lautréamont – with his hands in his adolescent pockets, fingering a packet of caramels and 'el sobrecito del preservativo comprado con falsa desenvoltura en una farmacia atendida solamente por hombres y que no tenía la menor oportunidad de utilizar con tan poco dinero y tanta infancia en la cara'/'the little pack with the condom bought with false casualness in a chemist's where only men served and which he hadn't the slightest chance of using with so little money and with such a baby face' (ibid., 137). None the less, and in Lacanian terms, the infant indulges in an imaginary identification with his own reflection in the mirror, an image not always faithful or consistent – as inconsistent, as gooey, indeed, as the *(h)om(m)elette* himself.

In this instance, the process of self-identification – with a borrowed/inherited father-figure whose words (i.e. the French epigraphs) are ever more illusory and unrepeatable – remains as incomplete as Harold Bloom would have us expect. Thus the mirror-image fragments: at the level of the *id*, the impulsive drives of the body struggle to complete and imitate the Name-of-the-Father, the beloved Lautréamont implied by the fragmented anagram (*Laurent t'amo*). The strangled act-of-love played out in the text *appears* to be twofold:

male/violent/sexual/criminal/Parisian prostitution
versus
female/docile/castrating/respectable/Buenos Aires marriage

In short, at the level of the *ego*, a South Americanness (through the *madre/novia* 'agency') struggles to regulate and oppose the drives of the *id*. This 'South Americanness', however, is much more than a maternal agent. For the narrator-as-writer (South American writer) must go to Paris to gain literary maturity, just as the adolescent believes that he must penetrate the labyrinth of the brothel district ('où sont les vendeuses d'amour') to pass from immaturity (*d'hommelette*) to an idealized place (*où l'homme se complète*). So, the dynamic struggle between *id* and *ego* is both sexual and textual, whereby the Parisian figures of the criminal (Laurent) and the inseparable 'regulating and opposing agency' ('el sudamericano') represent the absent father (long since dead) of the narrator. As such they constitute 'a transformation of the paternal and social influences upon the drives' of the narrator, illusorily and all too briefly unleashed, in the company of Josiane, literary whore *à la* Toulouse Lautrec, whose friend Kiki was already talking of the parties being planned in 'a *moulin* on La Butte' and who, moreover, lives in 'lo más alto', 'los altos de la galería'/'the high point', 'the heights of the gallery' of the sex/textuality of a narrator momentarily displaced from the Buenos Aires of an imminent marriage described by Irma, the 'novia', as part of a bureaucratic normality.

In order to go beyond a sexuality at once empty (of experience) and full (of guilt) – the nameless 'white stain' applicable to both adolescent masturbation and to the white-shirted criminal guillotined in Paris – the narrator must go through the textuality of the construction of his own *superego*. The textuality of 'El otro cielo', it might be argued, conforms consistently with the Lacanian model. The initial state of the narrator would be the mirror-stage, the 'delight' derived as much from a packet of caramels as from the nutrition of his mother, for whom 'no hay mejor actividad social que el sofá de la sala donde ocurre eso que llaman la conversación, el café y el anisado'/'there's no better social activity than the lounge sofa where there takes place what they call conversation, coffee and anis-liqueur' (ibid., 170). The tone here is one of resistance to the bitter-sweet ('café'/ 'anisado') comfort of the maternal breast; yet that resistance still derives from a narrator deprived of entry to, or initiation in, a linguistic structure termed by Lacan the Symbolic Order. Organized according to rules imposed by another figure, in turn equally dominant, the figure of the father, the Symbolic Order is structured, in this case, according to the vicarious rule of the 'paternal' Lautréamont. In this way, the 'Name-of-the-Father' replaces the 'Desire-for-the-Mother' at precisely that moment when the paternal element (absent in the mother) of the phallus, is transformed into the symbol of Patriarchal Law. It ought not to be forgotten, however, that the Lautréamont father-figure is not a person but a *text* – a 'written' phallus, handled voyeuristically by the adolescent. *Les Chants de Maldoror* constitute not only a textual instance of Lacanian phallologo-centrism but, for this narrator, also that one-handed literature called erotica. Those trans-Atlantic see(k)ers *voyants/voyeurs* familiar with Lautréamont's 'Éloge à la masturbation' might glimpse an intertext here with Cortázar's own handling of the theme: 'por lo menos algo se sabía de Laurent: la fuerza que le permitía estrangular a sus víctimas de una sola mano'/'at least something was known about Laurent: the strength which allowed him to strangle his victims with just one hand' (ibid., 143). The transference which takes place via a reading of Lautréamont concentrates their strength not in the hands of the narrator, a member of the male sex, but rather in the *putative* arms (and lap) of Josiane, alternative to the pre-maternal embrace of Irma. In this respect, 'El otro cielo' might be said to resemble *Les Chants de Maldoror* as 'une épopée de la masturbation' (Philippe 1971, 65-6).

Inevitably, the process of self-identification with the father

(Lautréamont) not only imbues the narrator with the illusion of equal masculine status but also, and in the same act, inserts him in a sexual rivalry which leads to the Oedipus complex. Either the narrator or the fragmented father-figure of Laurent/ 'el sudamericano' is condemned to the castrating (fatal) blade (guillotine). Although I have toyed with a Lacanian structural model, it must be said that the danger of such a game is that of inevitable hermeneutic reductivism. My intention has been to construct one possible reading of the 'text in which we are' before embarking immediately upon a tactic of deconstructing that same reading of 'El otro cielo.'

Of the many available cutting instruments used by Derrida, I wish only to exploit here two basic interventions. First, I shall recall his warning against the 'totalizing' capacity of any hermeneutics: 'the movement of any archaeology, like that of any eschatology, is an accomplice of this reduction of the structurality and always attempts to conceive of structure on the basis of a full presence which is beyond play' (1978b, 285). Just as Derrida, in the same essay, stresses that the tactics of Lévi-Strauss, or the discourse of his method, are a *bricolage* as opposed to *engineering* of all hermeneutical analyses, so I, in turn, would stress that the Lacanian discourse I have used has been, must be, *bricoleur*. For even if one were to succumb to the temptation of a 'totalizing' psychoanalytical interpretation of 'El otro cielo', it would still be necessary to heed a second Derrida warning: 'one cannot determine the centre and exhaust totalization because the sign which replaces the centre, which supplements it, taking the centre's place in its absence – this sign is added, occurs as a surplus, as a supplement' (ibid., 285). In short, the dynamics of any reading of 'El otro cielo' will always depend on the momentary 'event' (Derrida uses the term 'événement') of such a structuring as mine here. The process of supplementation will always de-centre the discourse of the method employed. In this way, I am forced to situate the 'event' which follows as but momentary – as nothing more than my (present) pretext.

My present pretext is the writing of this chapter – no other. As the Derrida spectre which spooks this book asserts, '*We must begin wherever we are* . . . . It is impossible to justify absolutely a point of departure. *Wherever* we are: in a text where we think we are' (1976, 162). And the text in which I think we are, this time, I have situated already in a multiple intertextuality. I now add a co-text to 'El otro cielo', that of *Irma la Douce*, Alexandre Breffort's comic opera and, later, the Billy Wilder film (1963), in which there is also but one narrator yet *two* Jack Lemmons; the film which also sends its narrator on a trans-Atlantic journey of punishment (to Devil's Island) before a 'resolution' in marriage with Irma (a now 'sweet' Shirley Maclaine), about to give birth at the altar steps. But the text with which I wish to end is the sub-text of the *economics* of 'El otro cielo.' The only 'essence' – self-attributed 'essence', to be more exact – of the unnamed narrator is the one so unashamedly admitted (despite the declared desire to 'olvidarme de mis ocupaciones'/'forget my occupations', 'soy corredor de bolsa'/'I'm a Stock Exchange runner'). What I am driving at here is the sub-text of 'la plena lucha bursátil'/'the full stock market struggle' with which the story ends. Despite the efforts of the narrator to forget his occupations (not, interestingly enough, his preoccupations), the text transforms his literal function of *corredor de bolsa* (a Stock Exchange lackey) into a very different kind of *corredor*: namely, a *corredor/trasfaldero* – or skirt-chaser. In the process (and in Derridan terms), the narrator's economic metaphor is deferred; and differs from the 'pasaje(s) de corredores' of his own emergent (though already always pre-textualized) sexuality, rather than from the literal passages and corridors of the Stock Exchange. It may be recalled that, in 'Speculations – on Freud', the corridors of power of any exchange of childhood for maturity are constructed, for Derrida, as here for Cortázar, from many doubles:

> with reference to fetishism, the double bind (the double has an erection/the double bandages/the doubles have erections; *le, la, les* double(s) bande(s)(ent) and the economic problem of masochism . . . how and with what does the so-called child indebt himself in a game that is supposed to be without debts? . . . The superego is the heir of the Oedipus complex and represents the ethical standards of mankind.
>
> (1978a, 79-81)

On the free-play of foreplay and on the double binding or bandaging of, and bandying with, Latin American masculist sexuality I have written (at length) with reference to Gabriel García Márquez's *Crónica de una muerte anunciada/Chronicle of a Death Foretold* (McGuirk 1987, 169-89). In that novel as in this short story, I would again argue, 'at play, perhaps, is the "neurotic unpleasure" of death which, dwelt upon, returned to again and again, becomes, is, the "pleasure that cannot be felt as such". Thus, through *writing*, the *difference* operates; in the overlay of apparent opposites – pleasure, unpleasure – there is a residue, a remainder' (ibid., 187). In 'El otro cielo', too, the residue, the remainder, is inseparably sexual, economic, political and eschatological. Yet how does this text negotiate the difference between (within) the private erotology and a public thanatography?

According to the Lacanian model, the *superego* is imposed precisely at the moment of transition from pleasure principle to reality principle. In this case, then, what is the reality principle? The text concludes with the dropping of the first atomic bomb on Hiroshima – an Asiatic reality effect which intrudes upon, and re-unites, the European and American spatio-temporal levels of the story. As a result, past (1870) and present (1945) realities and fantasies merge into a new, unified, undifferentiated *presence*: namely, that of transnational economic realities:

> una larga batalla para salvar los valores más comprometidos y encontrar un rumbo aconsejable en ese mundo donde cada día era una nueva derrota naci y una enconada, inútil reacción de la dictadura contra lo irreparable.
>
> (Cortázar 1979, 158)

> [a long battle to save the most threatened stocks and to find an advisable route in this world where each day brought a new Nazi defeat and a bitter, futile reaction on the part of the dictatorship to the inevitable.]

It is no coincidence that another 'plena dictadura militar'/'full military dictatorship' – an Argentine version – is coming to a close here. It would appear that the moment has passed for any or all nationalisms, whether German, Japanese, Argentine – or the now half-forgotten French nationalism of a bygone 1870. Yet, while elections are being prepared for, the text plays with the illusory nature of the triumph of democracy:

> Y entre una cosa y otra me quedo en casa tomando mate, escuchando a Irma que espera para diciembre, y me pregunto sin demasiado entusiasmo si cuando lleguen las elecciones votaré por Perón o por Tamborini, si votaré en blanco o sencillamente me quedaré en casa tomando mate y mirando a Irma y a las plantas del patio.
>
> (ibid.)

[And between one thing and another I stay at home taking *mate*, listening to Irma who's expecting in December, and I ask myself without too much enthusiasm if when the elections come round I'll vote for Perón or for Tamborini, if I'll cast a blank or simply stay at home taking *mate* and watching Irma and the patio plants.]

If imminent democracy is presented here as a possible solution to the multi-, or trans-, national invasion unleashed by that explosion of nationalism called Hiroshima, it is by no means a final solution. (There can never be a final solution as long as the supplement is in operation.) What happens is nothing other than the continuing process of *différance*: deferred, ultimately, to 'un voto en blanco', (nostalgically) reminiscent of that 'mancha blanca' of an uncoagulated, an *un-set* psyche ('un psique sin *n*ombre', 'sin *h*ombre'). The only specifically Argentine responsibility – the only specifically Argentine reality principle – accepted by the 'corredor de Bolsa' is that of sipping *mate*, or that of listening (interminably) to Irma ('la dulce') with whom he shares the ordered continuation of the race/the nation. In short, a full maturity is ever restricted by the rules of the Stock Exchange. It is, irretrievably, financial rather than economic, and is very far from being a mature political economy.

The repeated metaphor of 'lo blanco' (be it blank vote or white stain) remains inseparable from its multiple contexts: namely, politics, crime and sexuality. And this discussion of 'El otro cielo' plays with the double situation of a double 'gran terror.' If, at first sight, the 'great terror' is seen to be built on the Paris-based activities of the Lautréamont-derived criminal 'Laurent' (a 'false' name, for the true name of the 'gran terror' was not French but Prussian), what cannot be forgotten is the historical *fact* of *La Débâcle*/'grande terreur', the Prussian invasion of Paris, or an instance 1870-style of 'plena dictadura'. The general sense of relief and rejoicing felt by the public who witness the execution by guillotine of a poisoner – 'la policía no había sido capaz de descubrir a Laurent. Se consolaban guillotinando a otros'/'the police had been unable to find Laurent. They consoled themselves by guillotining others' (ibid., 148) – can be identified with the (albeit brief) euphoria of the Paris Commune. In textual terms, this takes the form of a *prolepsis* of momentary, but inseparably, political and sexual liberation:

un rapto de la mancha blanca por las dos figuras que hasta ese momento habían parecido formar parte de la máquina, un gesto de arrancar de los hombros un abrigo ya innecesario, un movimiento presuroso hacia adelante, un clamor ahogado que podía ser de cualquiera, de Josiane convulsa contra mí, de la mancha blanca que parecía deslizarse bajo el armazón donde algo se desencadenaba con un chasquido y una conmoción casi simultáneos. Creí que Josiane iba a desmayarse, todo el peso de su cuerpo resbalaba a lo largo del mío como debía estar resbalando el otro cuerpo hacia la nada.

(ibid., 152–3)

[a grabbing of the white blur by the two figures who until that moment had seemed to form part of the machine, a gesture of pulling off the shoulders a now unnecessary coat, a hurried forward movement, a stifled cry that could be anyone's, of Josiane convulsed against me, of the white blur which seemed to slip under the frame where something was unchained with an almost simultaneous rattle and a commotion. I thought that Josiane was going to faint, the whole weight of her body slipped across mine as the other body must have been slipping towards nothingness.]

Any political reading of this sexual moment also affords a possible feminist reading. For Josiane (previously the putative object of the client's sexual whim) and the narrator (previously the practitioner of a one-handed reading which leads him down the past of solitary pleasure to a traditionally supposed 'criminal' sexuality) here come together in a physical climax. As distinct from achieving merely another 'éloge à la masturbation' *à la* Lautréamont, a mere textual repetition compulsion, the narrative momentarily embodies a triumph over a politico-sexual double dictatorship, over the double crime of military and *machista* repression. However briefly, 't'amo' turns to 'mato' in the anagram relation of narrator to Laurent. Eros–Thanatos operates as a chiasmus – sudden death provokes orgasm: orgasm permits a killing-off (of the spooky Isidore Ducasse).

From this moment on, the narrator finds it hard to return 'al barrio de las galerías [que] ya no era como antes el término de un deseo'/'to the district of the galleries [which] was no longer as before the termination of a desire'] (ibid., 154). Having glimpsed (even if only proleptically) a full text-/sex-uality, the narrator will, however, remain incapable of crossing the barricade of the Paris Commune, where he might indeed have experienced a full satisfaction of desire. And it is in the interval between Hiroshima and democratic elections that he loses his chance to repeat in Buenos Aires the 'événements' of Paris. Opting for a very different *plénitude*, that of the 'plena lucha bursátil', the narrator confronts only a double closure: an end to his readings, and the withdrawal he won't admit: 'Nunca he querido admitir que la guirnalda estuviera definitivamente cerrada y que no volvería a encontrarme con Josiane en los pasajes o boulevares'/'I've never wanted to admit that the garland was definitively closed, and that I wouldn't return to meet Josiane in the passages or boulevards' (ibid., 158). In the act (or in the non-act), he even loses his capacity to go on creating 'manchas blancas', being left with the banal alternative of 'un voto en blanco': the *sexually* immature adolescent is replaced by the *politically* immature adult.

The sub-text is nothing other, in capitalist terms, than the *bottom line*. The narrator's incapacity to reach a full political maturity remains attached to a similar sexual incapacity on the Lacanian model. Perhaps the narrator of 'El otro cielo' falls into that trap so tellingly described by Hugo of Saint-Victor in the twelfth century: the man who finds his own country sweet is but an immature beginner; the man for whom every country is like his own is a strong man already; but only that man for whom the whole world is foreign has achieved perfection. The narrator of 'El otro cielo' falls into the trap of finding too sweet his own (mother) land, seduced in a domestic world of bitter-sweet complicity towards a false, a deferred and over-differentiated 'nationality', as false, as differentiated and as deferred as the traditionalist sexuality of a prototype 'esposo burgués argentino'. He is espoused and handcuffed, then, to 'los valores más importantes' (ibid., 158) of 'las esposas porteñas'; and to those of the Stock Exchange, of capitalism – bourgeois values only illusorily internationalizing yet as irreparably nationalizing (and insipid) as *mate*.

PS – GHOST-SCRIPT

What exactly is the difference from one century to the next? Is it the difference between a past world – for which the specter represented a coming threat – and a present world, today, where the specter would represent a threat that some would like to believe is past and whose return it would be necessary again, once again in the future, to conjure away?

Why in both cases is the specter felt to be a threat? What is the time and what is the history of a specter? Is there a present of the specter? Are its comings and goings ordered according to the linear succession of a before and an after, between a present-past, a present-present, and a present-future, between a 'real time' and a 'deferred time'?

If there is something like spectrality, there are reasons to doubt this reassuring order of presents and, especially, the border between the present, the actual or present reality of the present, and everything that can be opposed to it: absence, non-presence, non-effectivity, inactuality, virtuality, or even the simulacrum in general, and so forth. There is first of all the doubtful contemporaneity of the present to itself. Before knowing whether one can differentiate between the specter of the past and the specter of the future, of the past present and the future present, one must perhaps ask oneself whether this opposition, be it a dialectical opposition, has not always been a closed field and a common axiomatic for the antagonism between Marxism and the cohort or the alliance of its adversaries.

(Derrida 1994, 39–40)

PPS – SPECTRES OF FREUD

My friend Graciela is a product of Buenos Aires. As a freelance set designer, she has trouble making ends meet and is usually behind with the rent. But when a big contract came through last month, she stopped denying herself certain staples. The first person she called was her psychoanalyst. 'You feel so alone and incomplete without therapy, so cut off from yourself.' This city of elegant cafés and broad avenues looks and sounds like a Woody Allen film dubbed into Spanish. Psychobabble is its second language; if middle-class *angst* were a cash crop, Argentina would be a wealthy nation. The trappings are everywhere. In the city's shady plazas, *porteños* – the citizens of Buenos Aires – let off steam through the gentle movements of t'ai chi. Fluency in arcane Eastern therapies is *de rigueur*. Agony aunts clog the air-waves and the newspaper classifieds are jammed with ads from home-based Freudians. There are 30,000 psychoanalysts here and, not surprisingly, the Spanish verb *trasnochar* ('to stay up very late or all night') gets a good workout. At four in the morning, cold-sober and leaning over empty cups of coffee, hard-core *trasnochadores* earnestly chew over the problems of the soul, the conversation laden with the words 'my analyst thinks'.

Nor is the next generation immune. Like priests in another era, some analysts treat three generations of the same family. During his election campaign, President Carlos Menem knew which buttons to push in the *porteño* psyche. His slogan was: 'For the hunger of the poor children, for the sadness of the rich children, follow me!' Why all the navel-gazing? For 15 years, Raquel López Llames has been analysing *porteños* in an apartment three floors below mine. Her patients look like the faithful at confession: solemn but self-satisfied. She blames history for the obsession with analysis: the middle class, she says, is still reeling from the dark days of the dictatorship. In the late Seventies, the military 'disappeared' more than 9,000 people. In the Eighties, the country tried to come to terms with its ugly past by prosecuting the junta and its torturers, but a series of military uprisings frightened civilian leaders. In December 1990, Menem granted an amnesty to all military officers.

On top of those uneasy memories, frustration is a way of life in Buenos Aires. Simple tasks, such as paying a gas bill, are horrendously complicated. A dearth of professional jobs and cheap accommodation forces many young people to live with their parents well into their twenties. That pits the new Argentina against the old. 'For all its modern pretensions, our middle class is still very rigid and traditional', says López. 'Inevitably, young people collide with the Catholic hang-ups.' There is also an intellectual snobbery attached to analysis. In the two decades before the return of democracy in 1983, analysis came back on the back of high culture. It was in group therapy that banned books were exchanged and forbidden films screened. Today, analysis is considered a vital piece of cultural armour. Many *porteños* are analysis junkies. López spends half her life on the phone dispensing everyday tips, such as what to wear to a job interview or what kind of cake to bake for an ailing aunt. Sometimes, though, the obsession backfires. Last week, a magazine interviewed an analyst who is himself seeking professional help after seducing a married patient. Graciela and López are appalled. Offstage, you can hear Woody Allen chuckling.

(Honoré 1994)

It would be absolutely impossible for me to live if I couldn't play: everything that doesn't represent work, obligation and moral necessity

Julio Cortázar

WORKS CITED

Barthes, Roland. *S/Z*. Paris: Seuil, 1970.

Borges, Jorge Luis. *El Aleph*. Buenos Aires: Emecé, 1972.

Cortázar, Julio. 'El otro cielo', in *Todos los fuegos el fuego*. Barcelona: Edhasa, 1979 (pp. 135–58).

Culler, Jonathan. *Structuralist Poetics*. London: Routledge and Kegan Paul, 1975.

Derrida, Jacques. *Of Grammatology*. Baltimore, Md: Johns Hopkins University Press, 1976.

—— 'Speculations – on Freud', trans. Ian McLeod. *Oxford Literary Review*, 3, 2 (1978a), 78–97.

—— *Writing and Difference*, trans. Alan Bass. London: Routledge and Kegan Paul, 1978b.

—— *Specters of Marx*, trans. Peggy Kamuf. New York and London: Routledge, 1994.

Honoré, Carl. 'Guilt-Ridden Argentines Hooked on their Hang-ups', *Observer*, 6 March 1994, 21.

McGuirk, Bernard. 'Free-play of Fore-play: The Fiction of Non-Consummation. Speculations on *Chronicle of a Death Foretold*', in *Gabriel García Márquez: New Readings*, ed. by Bernard McGuirk and Richard Cardwell. Cambridge: Cambridge University Press, 1987 (pp. 169–89).

Orbach, Susie. 'Freudian Slip into Ignorance', *Guardian Weekend*, 5 February 1994, 48.

Philippe, Michel. *Lecture de Lautréamont*. Paris: Armand Colin, 1971.

Ricardou, Jean. *Le Nouveau roman*. Paris: Seuil, 1973.

Wright, Elizabeth. *Psychoanalytical Criticism: Theory in Practice*. London: Methuen, 1984.

Chapter 8

Mirror × scissors
Reflections on cuts from Carlos Fuentes' *Terra Nostra*

> What proof did I have, except what I had carried from the coasts of
> Spain in the pocket of my doublet . . . my mirror, and my scissors?
>
> *Terra Nostra*

What proof can there be? What guarantee 'contra los espejismos
de esta tierra'/'against the mirages of this land'? (Fuentes 1975,
479). By what act of possession can *Terra* be deemed *Nostra*?
Above all, how can an encounter be separated from (violent)
possession? And how are these questions to be represented?

Symptomatic of the strategic risks taken in this book is
reversibility. The play of presence and absence, of representation
and erasure, of mimesis and distortion, will be ever mobile, never
stable. The double(t) bondage of my deconstructive apparel will
have always operated as both strait-jacket and (in)vestment. So I
begin this encounter with Carlos Fuentes' novel by juxtaposing
two conflicting interpretations of the scope of textuality. First, an
archetypally Judaic, erasive, view of Scripture, of *écriture*:

> Le livre est, peut-être, la perte de tout lieu;
> le non-lieu du lieu du lieu perdu.
> Un non-lieu comme une non-origine, un non-présent,
> un non-savoir, un vide, un blanc.
>
> (Jabès 1978, 71)

[The book is, perhaps, the loss of all place;/the non-place of
the place of the lost place./A non-place as a non-origin, a non-
present,/a non-knowledge, a void, a blank.]

Second, a contrastively assertive Graeco-Roman assumption
of both existential dualism and the viability of discursive

representation: 'This is Magical Realism with a vengeance; the vengeance of Latin American culture against its Spanish paternity, the culmination of almost a century of literary parricide' (Martin 1989, 258). Thus does Gerald Martin describe *Terra Nostra*, adding that 'Mexican culture has often reacted to him as an outsider . . . a man for whom Mexico is above all an idea' (ibid., 258). Despite the double lure – namely, the implausibility of a (literary) text's capacity for standing, speaking, writing for 'Latin American culture', and the tease of Fuentes' novel so doing when, purportedly, 'Mexican culture has often rejected him' – Martin nevertheless touches upon a most problematical confrontation. Perceptively, he selects the following passage to provide him with a powerful argument regarding the imposition of civilization by Old World upon New:

Sentí, Señor, que enloquecía: la brújula de mi mente había perdido su norte, mis identidades se desparramaban y multiplicaban más allá de todo contacto con mi mínima razón humana, yo era un prisionero de la magia más tenebrosa, la que en piedra figuraban en este panteón todos los dioses y diosas que no pude vencer en esta tierra, que con sus espantosas muecas se burlaban de mi unidad y me imponían su proliferación monstruosa, destruían las razones de la unidad que yo debía portar como ofrenda a este mundo, sí, pero también la unidad simple en la que aquella unidad total se mantendría: la mía, la de mi persona. Miré los rostros de los ídolos: no entendían de qué hablaba.

¿Qué prueba tendría, sino la que conmigo mismo portaba, desde las costas de España, en la bolsa de mi jubón? Contra los espejismos de esta tierra, contra la vara mortal del dios desollado, contra el límpido reflejo en la cabeza de la grulla, contra el nombre mismo del espejo de humo, contra las incomprensibles imágenes de los veinte días de mi otro destino, el destino olvidado porque aún no se cumplía, o quizás el destino cumplido porque ya lo había olvidado, opuse mi propio espejillo, el que usamos Pedro y yo en la nave que aquí nos trajo cuando hicimos oficio de barbero, el que le mostré al desolado anciano de las memorias en el aposento del templo; mi espejo, y mis tijeras.

(Fuentes 1975, 478–9)

[I felt, sire, as if I were going mad: the compass of my mind had lost its directional needle, my identities were spilling over and multiplying beyond all contact with minimal human reason, I was a prisoner of the most tenebrous magic, the magic represented in stone in this pantheon of all the gods and goddesses I could not conquer in this land, who with fearful grimaces mocked my oneness and imposed upon me their monstrous proliferation, destroying the arguments of unity I had meant to carry as an offering to this world, yes, but also the simple unity in which that unity was to be maintained: my own, the unity of my person. I looked upon the faces of the idols: they did not understand what I was saying.

What proof did I have, except what I had carried from the coasts of Spain in the pocket of my doublet? Against the mirages of this land, against the fatal staff of the flayed god, against the limpid reflection in the head of the crane, against the very name of Smoking Mirror, against the incomprehensible images of the twenty days of my destiny, the destiny forgotten because it was still to be fulfilled, or perhaps the destiny fulfilled because it was already forgotten, I had opposed my own small mirror, the one Pedro and I had used on the ship that brought us here when we performed the office of barber, the mirror I had shown to the distressed ancient of memories in the temple chamber: my mirror, and my scissors.]
(Peden 1978, 544–5)

Having cited this long extract to some effect, Martin appears to broach the relation which gives the title to this chapter: 'Mirror and scissors involve imaging and cutting, imposing civilization upon barbarism, a key symbol in Fuentes's work, not unconnected to blindness' (Martin 1989, 262). He then wanders momentarily from his argument to belabour Fuentes for 'incorporat[ing] structuralist criticism into the body of his novel' and 'reveal[ing] here that his thinking is somewhat surprisingly coarse' (ibid., 263).

It is another critic, Jo Labanyi, however, who takes up and develops Martin's inchoate and, I shall argue, 'blind' insight. In a seminal meditation, 'Dos mundos a través del espejo: *Terra Nostra* de Carlos Fuentes', Labanyi extrapolates from the opposition of American Smoking Mirror/European small mirror to echo Michel Foucault's argument that Renaissance culture is based on similarities:

todas las cosas se reflejan y se repiten en un universo simétrico y cerrado. Mundo y lenguaje se identifican, porque todo es un signo capaz de ser interpretado como reflejo de todo lo demás; por tanto todo es escritura.

(Labanyi 1993, 310)

[all things reflect each other and repeat each other in a symmetrical and closed universe. World and language are identifiable with each other, because everything is a sign capable of being interpreted as a reflection of everything else; therefore everything is writing.]

Martin – inevitably, albeit implicitly, refuting the extreme textualization of, say, Jabès' 'lieu/non-lieu' stance on representability – (provocatively?) misreads the activity of the 'todo es escritura' brigade, 'post-structuralist antidotes', he says, to the 'preconceptions' of equally to-be-avoided 'Anglo-Saxon commonsense', in a laudable declared aim to 'rehistoricize' (Martin 1989, 359). Labanyi is more patient, pausing to reflect, in fact, on what she paraphrases, in Spanish, as follows: 'Gerald Martin observes that the mirror and the scissors carried by the pilgrim to the New World symbolize cinematic projection and montage. The journey to the New World constitutes a spectacular cinematographic sequence' (1993, 311). Her reflection, then, takes the form of applying Foucault's notion that, at the end of the sixteenth century,

a new cultural space is opened in which things are defined by the way in which they relate to each other: or, rather, by the difference between them. In this dispersed and mobile order, things circulate incessantly and the only constant is the relation between them. Language no longer forms part of the world, but relates to it in the act of representing it. This new classical culture is ruled not by repetition but by difference, not by interpretation but by representation.

(ibid., 310)

Although Labanyi might be said to be as prone here as I was in Chapter 3 to exaggerating Foucault's stance on difference by giving too positive a weight to what the latter regards as the negative onset of an over-neat dividing-up of discrete and clear-cut identities, her key point is undoubtedly both effective and pertinent to my argument. Velázquez, she reminds us, is, for Foucault, a key exponent of the representation of representation.

Splendidly evoking, in miniature, Foucault's critique of 'Las meninas', Labanyi captures the relation of work to world: 'the work opens up with the external world an unstable and deceitful relation, through the subjects of the invisible canvas being situated in the place where we the spectators find ourselves' (ibid., 310). Her decisive insight here concerns Fuentes' transformation of Velázquez, the narrator Julián ('painter and miniaturist' himself in the novel's opening list of *dramatis personae*), into a figure whose 'preeminencia narrativa concede un lugar primordial a lo visual, como también lo hace la presencia del ciego aragonés Ludovico, versión ficticia de Luis Buñuel'/'narrative pre-eminence concedes a primordial place to the visual, as does the presence of the blind Aragonese Ludovico, fictitious version of Luis Buñuel' (ibid., 310–11).

In brief, Labanyi, having tantalizingly played but in passing with the deaf cutter of the eye, Buñuel, concentrates her critical power, memorably, on 'Philip II and his court [*corte*]':

> And the mirror, just as in *Las meninas*, is occupied by the mobile image which converts its apparent presence into absence. The section entitled 'Las miradas' dramatizes explicitly the play of looks which is Velázquez's picture. Here the space of the invisible canvas is occupied by the bed of Philip II (another 'place of the King'), where the pilgrim, with Celestina and Ludovico, narrates his adventures in the New World in the representation of an empty space, an absence.

> (ibid., 311)

I have taken pains to reproduce in detail the lines of Martin's and Labanyi's opening-up of the problematical representation of New World in and by the Old for two reasons: first, in acknowledgement of the importance and originality of their insights; second, in pursuance of the striking blindness of insight which at once allows both to cite the Fuentes mirror/scissors relation yet to overlook, to refuse to see, the (perhaps scandalous) absented term of the textual binary. Dazzled by mirrors? By mimesis? No. That would be unfair. Rather, seduced by reflection theory away from a trenchantly different *corte*.

In the case of Gerald Martin, as I have suggested, the option is unapologetic, even self-conscious:

> One must now come clean . . . . Extrapolating from Derrida, one might say that there is nothing outside the labyrinth:

paraphrasing Foucault, one could add that there is no other reality but the reality we are in ... nevertheless, to coin a slogan for survival, even post-Modern relativity is only relative ... this book has not wished to dissolve the traces of history, with its successively and endlessly superimposed events and perceptions ('the totality of all effective statements': Foucault), into the ultimately univocal perspective of contemporary, and no doubt transitory, deconstructionist analysis. Personal scepticism apart, to have done so would have confused the issue and concealed the fact that the labyrinth, like the metaphors mentioned above, has its own entirely concrete basis in a continent at once unitary and diverse, where identity is never given, and where history and culture themselves have always seemed to be a question of opting between different, already existing choices and alternative forking paths. For Latin Americans the problem was not a deluded assumption of metaphysical 'presence', but a situational inability to achieve such blissful illusions in the first place: ... the defeatism which lies just below the surface of most deconstructionist criticism would be doubly debilitating in a context where there have always already been more than enough reasons for discouragement or despair.

(Martin 1989, 360)

Indisputably, Gerald Martin's declared critical position is as honest as it is forthright. Notwithstanding his problematical attributing to 'Latin Americans' of an Adamite, not to say, prelapsarian metaphysical status, I am more concerned here with his commitment to combating that 'hegemony of Derridan post-structuralism closely shadowed by the influence of Foucault and Lacan' whilst aligning himself to 'the left in the midst of its acute disarray, [which] has recuperated the dialogical Bakhtin – whose work is particularly helpful in the light of Latin America's bi-cultural societies – and made out as best it could, in the face of a massive shift to French influence in the academies' (ibid., 317). Echoes abound, then, of Fredric Jameson and, in particular, of Perry Anderson, whom Martin justifiably regards as 'essential reading in the debate on Modernism' (ibid., 205). No less crucial, it must be stressed, however, is Terry Eagleton's by now classic rejection of Anderson's 'summary treatment of Jacques Derrida'. However seriously the reader takes (and, indeed, should take) Martin's re-historicizing intent, it is none the less my view that he (wilfully?) repeats the 'seriously one-sided approach to his topic' of Perry Anderson to which I briefly referred in Chapter 1 and on which it is now opportune to elaborate. Eagleton warned, four years before the publication of *Journeys through the Labyrinth*, of that particular trap:

> Language, as Anderson interprets Derrida's view of it, is a 'system of floating signifiers pure and simple, with no determinable relation to any extra-linguistic referents at all' [Anderson, *In the Tracks of Historical Materialism*, 1984, 46]. This is indeed the ridiculous case touted by many of Derrida's less canny acolytes on both sides of the Atlantic, but Derrida himself has specifically defended the place of authorial intentionality in discourse, acknowledged the determinate forces of productive matrix and historical conditions in the construction of meaning, and firmly denied that he is a pluralist. The statement that 'there is nothing outside the text' is not to be taken, absurdly, to suggest that, for example, Jacques Derrida does not exist, but to deconstruct empiricist or metaphysical oppositions between discourse and some 'brute' reality beyond it. Derrida has insisted in recent years that deconstruction is a political rather than textual operation – that it is by touching solid structures, 'material' institutions, and not merely discourses or significant representations, that deconstruction distinguishes itself from analysis or 'criticism'. . . . Anderson's polemic quite fails to distinguish between 'left' and 'right' deconstruction – between those for whom the theory merely offers an opportunity for hermetic textualism and self-indulgent word-play, and those who have discerned in it (not least within the women's movement) political possibilities.
>
> (Eagleton 1985, 5)

In the determination to confront the *brutality* of much Latin American reality, Gerald Martin falls precisely into the lure of a discourse too mimetic of *brute* reality, too mirroring ever to achieve a cutting edge. It is thus inevitably that he draws back from his own potentially (and politically) incisive encounter with Carlos Fuentes' pairing of mirror/scissors – though he no doubt knows as much, for he revealingly echoes Borges' formalist forking-paths textuality at the very moment he broaches a *continental* identity, history and culture. Martin both knows and acknowledges that the continent is 'at once unitary and diverse', only baulking at the dreaded capacity of the 'deconstructionist's' analysis to be other than universal. Again, an original if unusual criticism. Yet what of Fuentes himself? Does he similarly fail to exploit the connotations of his own cutting device?

> Nos miraron. Los miramos. Lo primero que cambiamos fueron miradas. Y de ese trueque nació mi veloz, silente pregunta: – ¿Nos descubren ellos . . . o les descubrimos nosotros? . . . y de un instinto hondísimo, milagrosamente recobrado en ese instante, desenterrado por el simple caso de que primero habíamos cambiado miradas y luego no habíamos podido cambiar palabras, y de las miradas trocadas nació un asombro original y gemelo, pero de las palabras sin respuesta sólo nacía la violencia . . . . Arranqué las tijeras fajadas en mis calzas y las levanté . . . y todas las lanzas volaron con un solo movimiento hacia un blanco único: el corazón de Pedro. El terror me paralizó con el brazo en alto y las tijeras en el puño . . . . Alargué mi mano. Abrí mi puño. Ofrecí las tijeras. El jefe sonrió. Las tomó. Las hizo brillar contra el sol. No sabía manejarlas. Las manipuló con torpeza. Cortóse la carne de un dedo. Arrojó las tijeras a la arena. Miró con azoro su sangre. Me miró con azoro a mí. Recogío con gran cuidado las tijeras, como temiendo que tuviesen vida propia . . . . El jefe apretó las tijeras con una mano. Con la otra pasóme el bultillo. La sopesé entre mis palmas abiertas. La rugosa y tiesa tela abrióse sola. Mis manos sostenían un brillante tesoro de pepitas doradas. El regalo de mis tijeras había sido correspondido. Miré hacia el cadáver de Pedro, con mis manos llenas de oro.
>
> (Fuentes 1975, 384–6)

> [They looked at us. We looked at them. And from that first exchange was born my fleeting, silent question: 'Have they discovered us . . . or did we discover them?' . . . and at that instant, born from some miraculously recovered instinct, came an idea born of the exchange – the simple fact that we had exchanged looks and then been unable to exchange words, and from the mutual looks had been born an original and duplicated amazement, but only violence had come from the unanswered words . . . . I pulled my scissors from my breeches and raised them to strike . . . as one, their weapons flew

towards a single target: Pedro's heart. I was paralyzed with fright, my scissors still in my upraised fist: . . . I held out my hand; I opened it. I offered the chieftain the scissors. He smiled. He accepted them. He flashed them in the sun. He did not know what they were. He manipulated them clumsily. He nicked a finger. He threw the scissors upon the sand. Uneasy, he looked at the blood. Uneasy, he looked at me. With great caution, he picked up the scissors, as if fearing they had a life of their own . . . . The chief clutched the scissors in one hand. With the other he handed me the small parcel . . . . My gift had been reciprocated. My hands filled with gold, I looked at Pedro's body.]

(Peden 1978, 440–1)

In this extract from 'The Exchange', seventh sequence of 'The New World' section of *Terra Nostra*, it might seem that Fuentes is parodying Marcel Mauss's lapidary project to catch the fleeting moment when a society and its members take emotional stock of themselves and their situation as regards others (*Essai sur le don*, 1925). The confrontation of Old and New, of self and other does, indeed, perform according to a rhythm Eduardo González has described thus:

> In *The Gift*, Mauss rebuilt an instance of social being which was significant in that it seemed to be total and, in spite of its aberrant display of excess and waste, practical. He saw the act of gift-exchange, or total presentation, as that juncture in time and space where structure and event intercept each other. As an object of story-telling, the group *becomes*, it begins at such a moment: social reality originates as *kairos*, as an occasion over-ruled by its own disclosures.

(González 1987, 17)

True, to the extent of echoing Mauss, Fuentes is again 'incorporating structuralist criticism into the body of his novel' (Martin 1989, 263). But his thinking here, *pace* Martin, cannot justly be described as 'coarse' – however surprising. A checklist of the elements of my chosen extracts' construction might read: instinct/idea/exchange/looks/words/original/duplicate/amazement/violence – all before the narrative proper of the *incident* itself begins. Is, then, a case of *kairos*, 'an occasion over-ruled by its own disclosures', to ensue? The narrated event certainly conforms to Mauss's 'aberrant display of excess and

waste' both in its violence and in its brutal juxtaposition of failed
pre-economic human communication with the immediacy of
the materialist pact between base metal (scissors) and gold.
Paradoxically, it is precisely here that Fuentes underwrites the
encounter of two worlds with the discourse of base and superstructure. What is more, the confrontation of *manufactured* metal
goods and the invaluable *raw* material is a prefiguration of
economic relations to come, underpinning materialist inequality
and dependency theories. All this, were Martin to have wished,
might have been read as Marxist. But that is not my point.

Eagleton has suggested that the ready association of deconstructive reading with the Right is 'too sweeping an excoriation'
(Eagleton 1985, 5). I claim no less for its reversal. Merely to invert
the terms and to deconstruct for the Left would be too facile a turn
of the screw (or the Yale lock?), as blind a counter-reaction as
opting for mirror over scissors. For to opt for mirror is to opt for
the self in replication. And, in my view, *Terra Nostra* consistently
refuses at least that self-indulgence. The sequence 'Night of
Reflections', from which Gerald Martin takes his cue, continues
as follows:

Contra los espejismos de esta tierra ... contra el nombre
mismo del espejo de humo ... opuse mi propio espejillo, mi
espejo ... y mis tijeras. Ambas cosas saqué de mi jubón,
echado allí, como una fiera, ante la fiera enigma, mi doble, el
Espejo Humeante ... maté con mi espejo; ahora el espejo me
está matando a mí .... La imagen del doble echado frente a
mí, traspasándome con su mirada de vidrio negro; él me
otorgó el tiempo de mi premonición y yo le mataría con mis
tijeras; las levanté, las clavé en su rostro, rasgué ese rostro que
era el mío, rebané su mirada con mis frágiles aceros gemelos.
(Fuentes 1975, 479)

[Against the mirages of this land ... against the very name of
Smoking Mirror ... I had opposed my own small mirror, my
mirror ... and my scissors. I removed both from my doublet,
stretched out there like a wild beast facing an enemy beast, my
double, Smoking Mirror ... I had killed with my mirror; now
the mirror is killing me .... The image of the double lay before
me, transfixing me with his eyes of black glass; he had granted
me the time of my premonition and I would kill him with my
scissors; I raised them, and drove them into his face, ripping

the face that was my face, I sliced his gaze with my fragile twin steel blades.]

(Peden 1978, 546)

And this is a moment in which deconstruction may be seen as a 'political rather than textual operation'. Fuentes' text 'touches solid structures, "material" institutions' in precisely that sense of the hand that wields the scissors. For what is lacerated, sliced, cut (or deconstructed) is 'the face that was my face' of perpetuated subjectivity, that very countenance which, in the encounter with other, registers not mere difference but *différance*, difference not between but within, whereby the violence done to all other (by mimetics or dissection) is, inseparably, a violence done to all self. Whence the 'fragility' of the *twin* blades?

I have dwelled perhaps too long on Thanatos. Fuentes' text is more balanced. For the famous closing sequence of *Terra Nostra* performs Eros, too:

Llevas a Celestina al lecho. Ella y tú se recorren lentamente, con besos, con caricias, todo lo besa ella, tú lo besas todo . . . entras muy lentamente . . . piensas en otra cosa, no te quieres venir aún, la quieres esperar, los dos juntos, otra cosa, viviste una vez en la rue de Bièvre . . . allí vivió un día Dante, allí escribió, empezó a escribir, París . . . el Infierno, te repites en silencio los versos, para no venirte todavía, nondum, aún no, la mitad del camino de nuestras vidas, una selva oscura, perdimos el camino, selva salvaje, áspera y dura, el recuerdo del terror, no, no es eso lo que quisieras recordar, más adelante, aún no, un canto, nondum, el canto, el canto veinticinco, eso es, ed eran due in uno, ed uno in due, grita la muchacha, dices el verso en voz alta, due in uno, ed uno in due, grita la muchacha, grita, cierra los ojos, miras su rostro crispado por el orgasmo, sus muslos temblorosos, su sexo cargado de tempestades, ahora sí, ya, te vienes con ella, riegas de plata y veneno y humo y ámbar su negra, rosada, perlada, indente vagina, ed eran due in uno, ed uno in due . . . Dios mío, tu brazo es el de la muchacha, tu cuerpo es el de la muchacha, el cuerpo de ella es el tuyo: buscas, enloquecido, instantáneamente, otro cuerpo en la cama, esto no lo has soñado, has amado a una mujer en tu lecho del cuarto del Hotel du Pont Royal, la muchacha ya no está, sí está, no está, hay un solo cuerpo, lo miras, te miras . . . es la misma que acabas de

poseer, es la misma que volverás a poseer, hablas, te amo, me
amo, tu voz y la de la muchacha se escuchan al mismo tiempo,
son una sola voz, déjame amarte otra vez . . . te amas, me amo,
te fecundo, me fecundas, me fecundo a mí mismo, misma, ten-
dremos un hijo, después una hija, se amarán, se fecundarán,
tendrán hijos, y esos hijos los suyos, y los nietos bisnietos,
hueso de mis huesos, carne de mi carne, y vendrán a ser los
dos una sola carne, parirás con dolor a los hijos, por ti será
bendita la tierra, te dará espigas y frutos, con la sonrisa en el
rostro comerás el pan, hasta que vuelvas a la tierra, pues de
ella has sido tomado, ya que polvo eres, y al polvo volverás,
sin pecado, con placer.

No sonaron doce campanadas en las iglesias de París; pero
dejó de nevar, y al día siguiente brilló un frío sol.

(Fuentes 1975, 781–3)

[You lead Celestina to the bed. You kiss one another, slowly,
caress one another, she kisses your whole body, you kiss her
whole body . . . very slowly, you enter . . . you do not want to
come yet, think of something else, you want to wait for her,
both together, something else, you lived once along the rue de
Bièvre . . . Dante lived there once, he wrote there, he began to
write, Paris . . . the Inferno, you repeat the verses in silence,
don't come yet, *nondum*, not yet, midway along the journey of
our lives, a dark wood, we lose our way, wilderness, harsh
and cruel, the recollection of terror, that isn't what you want
to remember, more recent, not yet, a canto, *nondum*, the canto,
the twenty-fifth canto, that's it, *ed eran due in uno, ed uno in due*,
the girl cries out, you say the verse aloud, *due in uno, uno in
due*, she screams, closes her eyes, you look upon her face
convulsed by the orgasm, her trembling thighs, her tempest-
ridden sex, now, yes, now you come, with her, you flood her
black, rosy, pearly *vagina indente* with silver and venom and
smoke and amber, *ed eran due in uno, ed uno in due* . . . my God,
your arm is the girl's arm, your body is the girl's body, her
body is yours; crazed, in that instant you look for the other
body in the bed, you have not dreamed this, you have just
made love to a woman in your bed in your room in the Hôtel
du Pont-Royal, the girl is no longer here, yes, she is here, no,
she is not, there is but one body, you look at it, you see yourself . . . it is the same, the one you have just possessed, it is
the one you will possess again, you speak, I love you, I love

myself, your voice and the girl's speak at the same time, they are a single voice, let me make love to you again, I want to make love again . . . you make love to yourself, I make love to myself, I fertilize you, you fertilize me, I fertilize myself, my male and female selves, we shall have a son, then a daughter, they will make love, they will fertilize one another, they will have sons and daughters, and those sons and daughters will have sons and daughters, and the grandsons and grand-daughters, great-grandsons and great-granddaughters, bone of my bones, flesh of my flesh, and the two shall be one flesh, and in joy thou shalt bring forth children, and blessed is the ground for thy sake, thorns and fruit shall it bring forth to thee, and in the smile of thy face shalt thou eat bread, till thou return unto the ground, for out of it wast thou taken: for dust thou art, and unto dust shalt thou return – without sin, and with pleasure.

Twelve o'clock did not toll in the church towers of Paris, but the snow ceased, and the following day a cold sun shone.]

(Peden 1978, 890–1)

Fear not. I offer no analysis. Merely re-echoes of the intertexts, the shuttle effects, between the (ironic) analepses – 'Todos los buenos latino-americanos vienen a morir a París'/'all good Latin-Americans come to die in Paris' (Fuentes 1975, 765) – are you there, Julio, Laurent?; and the (parodic) paralepses – *cette autre écriture bisexuelle?*; and the (*converso*) prolepses of the *midrashic* discourses to which I shall return in Chapter 10. Merely a reminder of repetition and difference, of the mirror which is both, of the scissors that cut across Thanatos in Eros and vice versa. A re-minder, too, intertextually, of Fuentes' palimpsestic re-narration of the César Vallejo (ad)venture, pursued in Chapter 4:

Pugnamos ensartarnos por un ojo de aguja,
enfrentados, a las ganadas.
Amoniácase casi el cuarto ángulo del círculo.
¡Hembra se continúa el macho, a raíz
de probables senos, y precisamente
a raíz de cuanto no florece!

[We strive to thread ourselves through a needle's eye/face to face, taking a chance./ The fourth angle of the circle almost *ammonias* itself./Female continues male, as a result/of probable breasts, and precisely/as a result of what does not flower!]

In the *Terra Nostra* encounter of male Self with male Other, the 'image of the double' was consumed in violence. In the encounter of male Self with female Other, the double image of lovers is consummated in ecstatic oblivion of difference, not in but *towards* androgyny, where every cut, every fold, every penetration seeks to delay that essential loss of *due in uno, uno in due* through the desperate canto of *nondum*. Has Derrida convinced us that the metaphysics of presence is necessarily the spur to the conceiving of absence? Not yet . . .

And what of Jo Labanyi? Did she, too, opt for the mimetic (mirror) perspective by picking up, rather than cutting through, Gerald Martin's unpicked thread of Fuentes' fabric? Perhaps not. For in favouring a Foucauldian perspective on the representation of representation, she has taken one step back from both mirror and canvas. A next step might have been to re-read differently the 'separation from the public by the drawn curtains' (Labanyi 1993, 311). Though led into this labyrinth, from the start, by the guiding thread of Labanyi's brilliant reading, I now place my hand on the scissors of a different agency (as if it were still necessary to remind anyone that deconstructions cannot occur spontaneously). 'This staging', she argues, 'converts the encounter of Europe with the New World into the representation of an empty space, an absence' (ibid., 311). Both in her own palimpsest on Martin and in her teasing suggestion that we might read Ludovico, 'the blind Aragonese', as a fictitious version of Buñuel, Labanyi already takes us beyond the possibility of reading without cuts, to that of reading cinematographically, as she says. Were she to be consistent with her own initial claim, 'The journey to the New World constitutes a spectacular cinematographic sequence' (ibid., 311), then she might disavow the very possibility of 'a representation of an empty space, an absence'. But not yet.

Nondum. 'Ante la multitud reunida, el Señor sentía, más que las presencias, ciertas ausencias; y al querer darles un nombre, las llamó Celestina y Ludovico' (Fuentes 1975, 349) / 'Regarding the crowd before him, El Señor was more aware of certain absences than of the assembled presences, and as he wished to identify those absences, he named them Celestina and Ludovico' (Peden 1978, 398). Not yet, not ever, is absence, that space without name, conceivable. Even for El Señor, the epistemological imperative prevails: 'Il faut nommer' (Rimbaud); 'Lire c'est lutter pour nommer' (Barthes); for the Name is Hallowed:

¡Oh mi señor! no saltes de tan alto,
que me moriré en verlo; baja, poco
a poco por el escala; no vengas con
tanta presura.

(Rojas 1965, 158)

[Oh, my lord, do not jump from so high,/for I shall die if I see
it; come down little/by little by the ladder; do not come/with
such haste.]

Melibea's *nondum*? Deferral . . . .

Not yet is the 'totality' of a Renaissance vision possible, *pace*
Foucault, *pace* Labanyi. Throughout *Terra Nostra* any view of the
New World's reflecting, representationally, the mirrored Old, in
difference, is undercut. Renaissance continuities (or Foucault's
later projection of them) are littered with medieval disrup-
tions; be it the Dantean echo of Infernal destruction (violence,
Thanatos) or of Purgatorial delay (not yet pleasure), not yet the
full, though promised, *jouissance* of Paradise – the vision, the representation of the face of God the Other; or be it the Celestinan
promise of earthly rapture (rape?), Garden of Delight, Eros
possessed, loss of Self in Other, the abolition of difference in
collided, fusing mirrors. The Foucauldian notion of double
representation is too harmonious to capture the encounter of the
two worlds without coming to constitute another *kairos*, another
instance of an occasion overruled by its own disclosures.
Disclosures ✂ dis-apertures, (non-)openings ✂ (non-)closings,
cross-cuts, scissorings.

Yet Foucault's (or Labanyi's) reflection on Worlds – Old
Infernos, New Paradises – is not undone by the co-existence of
mirror and scissors: and, as I suggested in Chapter 3, 'this is
because knowledge is not made for understanding; it is made for
cutting' (Foucault 1986, 88). It is never a question of either/or. The
mirror (just as the metaphysics of presence) must exist in order for
its suppressed other to be conceived. The scissors function as the
sign of erasure ✂ which (pre-)figures the scandalous 'absent'
term, not as nothingness (Labanyi's 'representation of a vacuum,
an absence') but as the discontinuity of shattered, flashing, reflecting fragments, smithereens. As the encounter of Old and New
Worlds occurs, representation consists of the clash, the smash of
mirrors colliding. Separateness is no longer (re-)presentable:

piensas en tu viejo Erasmo y su elogio de una locura que
relativiza los pretendidos absolutos del mundo anterior y del
mundo inmediato: al Medievo, le arrebata Erasmo la certeza
de las verdades inmutables y de los dogmas impuestos . . . . La
locura erasmiana es una puesta en jaque del hombre por el
hombre mismo, de la razón por la razón misma, y no por el
pecado o el demonio. Pero también es la conciencia crítica
de una razón y un ego que no quieren ser engañados por
nadie, ni siquiera por sí mismos. Piensas con tristeza que
el erasmismo pudo ser la piedra de tu propia cultura
hispanoamericana. Pero el erasmismo pasado por la criba
española se derrotó a sí mismo. Suprimió la distancia irónica
entre el hombre y el mundo.

(Fuentes 1975, 774)

[you think of your aged Erasmus and his praise of a madness
that relativizes the pretended absolutes of the former world
and the present world: Erasmus wrested from the Middle
Ages the certainty of immutable truths and imposed dogmas
. . . Erasmian madness is the checkmate of man by man himself, of reason by reason itself, not by sin or the Devil. But it is
also the critical consciousness of a reason and an ego that do
not wish to be deceived by anyone, not even by themselves.
You ponder with sadness the fact that Erasmism could have
been the touchstone of your own Spanish American culture.
But Erasmism sifted through Spain defeated itself. It suppressed the ironic distance between man and the world.]

(Peden 1978, 882)

EPIGRAPH

Paradoxically, Gerald Martin, who opts for the chapter-heading
'Conclusion: Out of the Labyrinth' to end, in suggestively
polemical manner, and whose stated objective is to 're-historicize'
the very concept of the labyrinth, does not exploit the most overt
precursor text: namely, Borges' 'La Casa de Asterión':

El sol de la mañana reverberó en la espada de bronce. Ya no
quedaba ni un vestigio de sangre.

– Lo creerás, Ariadna? – dijo Teseo. – El minotauro apenas se
defendió.

(Borges 1972, 71)

[The morning sun reverberated from the bronze sword. There was no longer even a vestige of blood./'Will you believe it, Ariadne?' said Theseus. 'The Minotaur scarcely defended himself.']

And if Ludovico were not (only) the Buñuel, 'blind Aragonese', that he is represented as being?

Tardíamente el viejo Pierre Menard propuso que se dotara a bestias, hombres y naciones de un surtido de espejos capaz de reproducir infinitamente sus figuras y las ajenas, sus territorios y los ajenos, a fin de apaciguar para siempre las imperativas ilusiones de una destructiva ambición de poseer, aunque el dominio nos asegurase la pérdida tanto de lo conquistado como de lo que ya era nuestro. Sólo a un ciego pudo ocurrírsele semejante fantasía. Es cierto que, además, era filólogo.

(Fuentes 1975, 765)

[Later in life an aged Pierre Menard proposed that all beasts, men and nations be apportioned a supply of mirrors that would reproduce infinitely their and other figures and their and other territories, for the purpose of appeasing for all time the imperative illusions of a destructive ambition for possession, although dominion only assures us the loss of what is already ours. Only to a blind man could such a fantasy occur. And of course he was, in addition, a philologist.]

(Peden 1978, 871)

Fuentes has inscribed a *Ludic Vico* without name in his text: 'Vico's insight is that poetry is born of our ignorance of causes . . . and again Vico is the best of guides' (Bloom 1976, 27). Borges' text (no less than Fuentes') reflects on the cutting instrument of Theseus, threatening potential repetition, or further mirroring of the *agonic* labyrinth just broken, threaded but cut through. With no insight, and much blindness, Theseus fails to grasp the enlightened folly of Asterión, whose territories are but a dominion of 'infinite doors' though no exit, 'infinite pools' of reflection. Trapped, as 'all beasts, men and nations' in infinite self and other representation. '¿Será un toro o un hombre? ¿Será tal vez un toro con cara de hombre? ¿O será como yo?'/'Will he be bull or man? Will he perhaps be a bull with the face of a man? Or will he be like me?'. The Minotaur desires release from

that monstrous *mirror* shuttle of Archos ↔ Telos, Self ↔ Other;
desires, requires, the *cut*.

> Natura il fece, e poi ruppa la stampa.
> [Nature made him, and then broke the mould.]
>> Ludovico Ariosto, *Orlando Furioso*, X.84

WORKS CITED

Anderson, Perry. *In the Tracks of Historical Materialism*. Chicago: Chicago University Press, 1984.

Bloom, Harold. *Poetry and Repression*. New Haven, Conn.: Yale University Press, 1976.

Borges, Jorge Luis. *El Aleph*. Buenos Aires: Emecé, 1972.

Eagleton, Terry. 'Marxism, Structuralism and Post-Structuralism', *Diacritics* (Winter 1985), 2–12.

Foucault, Michel. *The Foucault Reader*. Harmondsworth: Penguin, 1986.

Fuentes, Carlos. *Terra Nostra*. Tabasco, Mexico: Editorial Joaquín Mortiz, 1975.

González, Eduardo. *Gabriel García Márquez: New Readings*, ed. Bernard McGuirk and Richard Cardwell. Cambridge: Cambridge University Press, 1987 (pp. 17–32).

Jabès, Edmond. *Le Soupçon dans le désert: Le Livre des ressemblances II*. Paris: Gallimard, 1978.

Labanyi, Jo. 'Dos mundos a través del espejo: *Terra Nostra* de Carlos Fuentes', in *Actas del Primer Congreso Anglo-Hispano, Tomo II: Literatura*, ed. Alan Deyermond and Ralph Penny. Madrid: Castalia, 1993 (pp. 309–16).

Martin, Gerald. *Journeys Through the Labyrinth: Latin American Fiction in the Twentieth Century*. London: Verso, 1989.

Mauss, Marcel. *The Gift: Forms and Functions of Exchange in Archaic Societies*. New York: Norton, 1967.

Peden, Margaret Sayers (trans.). Fuentes, Carlos. *Terra Nostra*. Harmondsworth: Penguin, 1978.

Rojas, Fernando de. *La Celestina*, trans. Ian Cunnison. Buenos Aires: Losada, 1965.

Vallejo, Cesar. *Trilce*. Madrid: Cátedra, 1991.

Chapter 9

Subjectivity, history, ideology
Relocating the Self: 'Borges and I'

Objects do not go into their concepts without leaving a remainder.

Theodor Adorno

According to one of the Indian schools of philosophy, the ego is merely an onlooker who has identified himself with the man he is continually looking at.

Jorge Luis Borges

Trapped in infinite self and other representation, the instances of Latin American literature on which I have meditated in this book may not differ from, though they will always defer differently, Adorno's proposal that 'one of the motives of dialectics is to cope with . . . the difference that shows how inadequate the *ratio* is to thought' (Adorno 1973, 85). For *ratio* and thought I shall shortly read 'Borges and I'. As a pre-text, I recall how often the *ratio* which is 'Borges' continually emerges from the thought of the texts of so many subsequent Latin American writers, as if, to pastiche (fragmentarily) Carlos Fuentes' insight, they had been 'apportioned a supply of mirrors that would reproduce infinitely . . . only . . . a blind man . . . a philologist'. The use of a 'Borges' as intertext is, needless to say, a ploy anticipated by Borges:

Borges y yo

Al otro, a Borges, es a quien le ocurren las cosas. Yo camino por Buenos Aires y me demoro, acaso ya mecánicamente, para mirar el arco de un zaguán y la puerta cancel; de Borges tengo noticias por el correo y veo su nombre en una terna de profesores o en un diccionario biográfico. Me gustan los relojes de arena, los mapas, la tipografía del siglo XVIII, las etimologías, el sabor del café y la prosa de Stevenson; el otro comparte esas preferencias, pero de un modo vanidoso que las convierte en atributos de un actor. Sería exagerado afirmar que nuestra relación es hostil; yo vivo, yo me dejo vivir, para que Borges pueda tramar su literatura y esa literatura me justifica. Nada me cuesta confesar que ha logrado ciertas páginas válidas, pero esas páginas no me pueden salvar, quizá porque lo bueno ya no es de nadie, ni siquiera del otro, sino del lenguaje o de la tradición. Por lo demás, yo estoy destinado a perderme, definitivamente, y sólo algun instante de mí podrá sobrevivir en el otro. Poco a poco voy cediéndole todo, aunque me consta su perversa costumbre de falsear y magnificar. Spinoza entendió que todas las cosas quieren perseverar en su ser; la piedra eternamente quiere ser piedra y el tigre un tigre. Yo he de quedar en Borges, no en mí (si es que alguien soy), pero me reconozco menos en sus libros que en muchos otros o que en el laborioso rasgueo de una guitarra. Hace años yo traté de librarme de él y pasé de las mitologías del arrabal a los juegos con el tiempo y con lo infinito, pero esos juegos son de Borges ahora y tendré que idear otras cosas. Así mi vida es una fuga y todo lo pierdo y todo es del olvido, o del otro.

No sé cuál de los dos escribe esta página.

(Borges 1980, 69–70)

Borges and I

[The other one, the one called Borges, is the one things happen to. I walk through the streets of Buenos Aires and stop for a moment, perhaps mechanically now, to look at the arch of an entrance hall and the grillwork on a gate; I know of Borges from the mail and see his name on a list of professors or in a biographical dictionary. I like hourglasses, maps, eighteenth-century typography, etymologies, the taste of coffee and the prose of Stevenson; he shares these preferences, but in a vain way that turns them into the attributes of an actor. It would be an exaggeration to say that ours is a hostile relationship; I live, let myself go on living, so that Borges may contrive his literature, and this literature justifies me. It is no effort for me to confess that he has achieved some valid pages, but those pages cannot save me, perhaps because what is good belongs to no one, not even to him but rather to language and to tradition. Besides I am destined to perish, definitively, and only some instant of myself can survive in him. Little by little, I am giving over everything to him though I am quite aware of his perverse custom of falsifying and magnifying things. Spinoza knew that all things long to persist in their being: the stone eternally wants to be a stone, and the tiger a tiger. I shall remain in Borges, not in myself (if it is true that I am someone), but I recognise myself less in his books than in many others or in the laborious strumming of a guitar. Years ago I tried to free myself from him and went from the mythologies of the suburbs to games with time and infinity, but those games belong to Borges now and I shall have to imagine other things. Thus my life is a flight and I lose everything and everything belongs to oblivion, or to him.

I do not know which of us has written this page.

> (Translation [adapted by the removal of two
> definite articles] Yates–Irby 1971, 282–3)

The context of this discussion is also twofold. First, there is my long-standing fascination with what might be termed the 'querelle Borges'. 'Discovered' by the French (particularly Roger Caillois) but, on occasion, repudiated in Latin America, a 'politicized' Borges has been and still is – after his death in 1986 – very much villain or hero of institutions and institutionality, of 'identity' and 'nationality'. Notoriously, when asked to comment on his consistent failure to be awarded the Nobel Prize for Literature, he is said, perhaps apocryphally, to have responded with only the slightest hint of malice towards his denigrators: it was generally well known that he was an admirer of tradition, and it had now become a tradition not to offer 'Borges' the Nobel Prize. Second, there will be my attempt to come to terms with 'Borges and I' in terms of the theoretical debate concerning literary subjectivity. The sporadic emergence of instances of 'Borges' in the preceding chapters, and my treatment of them, might be viewed as part of a post-structuralist commonplace of intertextuality. The publication, in 1988, of Paul Smith's *Discerning the Subject*, in my view, constituted a *post*-post-structuralist perspective:

> In recent years the modes and manners of thinking which we know as 'post-structuralism' have consistently concentrated on the 'subject' in order to question its traditionally privileged epistemological status. In particular, there has been a sustained effort to question the role of the 'subject' as the intending and knowing manipulator of the object, or as the conscious and coherent originator of meanings and actions.
>
> (Smith 1988, xxviii)

In brief, Smith regards post-structuralist treatments of the subject as further attempts, in a long tradition, to 'cern' – both to inherit and enclose – subjectivity. Thus he is able to describe his project as:

> an attempt to *dis-cern* the 'subject', and to argue that the human agent *exceeds* the 'subject' as it is constructed in and by most poststructuralist theory as well as by those discourses against which poststructuralist theory claims to pose itself . . . begin[ning] with the questions raised within contemporary Marxist and post-Marxist thought about the place of the 'subject' in ideology.
>
> (ibid., xxx)

The extract from Smith's book which I have chosen to juxtapose with, in order to analyse, Borges' text is taken from his chapter on autobiography. Here, Smith himself is concerned with three late Barthes' works which he regards as 'autobiographical': *Roland Barthes par lui-même* (1975); *Fragments d'un discours amoureux* (1977); *La Chambre claire* (1980). He prefaces his short study with the comment that 'Barthes' writings run many risks' and, with no small coincidence as regards the standard political criticisms levelled against Borges, points out that Barthes' 'writing is often regarded as flirting with a kind of anarchic or romantic individualism' (ibid., xxxi–ii):

> An autobiographical narrative, a writing of the story of the self, is like any other discursive arrangement in that it is subjected to a necessary organization in terms of *discours* and *récit*. From the distinction between these two elements it can be suggested that there can be no 'subject' of the story, the *récit* (that is, no 'subject' unproblematically or cohesively a product of the life of the autobiographer). The 'subject', after all, appears only when the *récit* is uttered, enunciated from the place of language. In other words, the *récit* can only be represented in the discourse's organizing parameters. Any specific mode of organizing is, of course, pressured by the historical, the ideological: the subject/individual is cerned by being offered particular modes of organization or for particular historical and ideological purposes. The 'subject' of the *discours*, the 'I' that speaks, is immediately not available as the 'subject' of the *récit* but is rather the organizing 'subject', different from the putative or desired 'subject' of the *récit*. This split

corresponds to what structural linguists describe as a division in any utterance between the 'subject of the enunciation' and the 'subject of the enounced'. 'I' does not talk about or correspond to 'I': rather 'I' talks about 'me'. Inscribed, thus, in the formal structures of utterance is the 'enunciatory abyss' that Barthes is intent on opening up, where the 'I' that speaks constitutes the enunciatory subjectivity and the 'me' that is absent constitutes the 'subject of the enounced'. Such a non-self-possession in the speaking 'subject' is familiar insofar as it is constitutive of the very gap which is inscribed at the roots of our tradition and which it has been the continual task of the epistemologist to anneal. From Augustine's 'I am not what I was', through to logical positivism and on into the pop psychology of the last few decades, for example, the consistent ideological effort of epistemological procedures has been to 'rescue' the subject of the enunciation from its distance from the enounced. However, it is clear enough that, when Augustine writes 'I am not what I was', for example, not only are the two different 'I's' in fact admitted to be separated or discernible, but that also a third 'I' emerges – the 'I' that would be prefigured or desired by the moral or ideological operation of trying to maintain the coherence (the wholeness) and the propriety (the wholesomeness) of the ideological subject (in the case of Augustine, the proper 'subject' of Christianity). This third 'I' – if I can crudely call it that way – is the one which is elided in de Man's pessimistic account of the specularized motions of epistemology. For de Man, there is 'subject' and there is object, and never the twain shall meet, since the 'subject of the enunciation' can never stand in the place of any other except by the illusion of the mirror. What de Man symptomatically ignores (symptomatically, I mean, in that it is a signal to the moral and political blindness of his brand of deconstruction) is the third 'I' that is the intended moral effect of a closing down of the enunciatory gap. That third 'I' is the cerned and complete individual which will be called upon to hold in place the circuit of guarantees obtaining between 'subject' and knowledge. It is in fact the ideological 'subject'.

(ibid., 104–5)

It should be obvious from the above passage that Smith owes a debt to the work of Philippe Lejeune's basically structuralist division of the difference between the subject of *discours* and the subject of *récit*. Wishing to move beyond the merely structural differentiation of narrative states, he sensibly points beyond the organization of *récit* within *discours* to the *organizing* subjectivity historically or ideologically defined. In a sense, Smith's trajectory here is a reversal of structuralism's shift of attention from 'originator' to text. The *récit* discloses a 'me that is told'; the *discours* discloses an 'I that is telling', and that 'I' is situatable in history – a history which includes, however, a number of attempts to bridge the gap between the supposedly separate 'me ' and 'I'. At this point, the claim for 'a third I' emerges. And the key words in Smith's description of such an 'I' are 'prefigured or desired by the moral and ideological operation'. Although Smith opts – via his attack on de Man's 'moral and political blindness' to the possibility of closing down the enunciatory gap – for the notion of 'guarantor' of knowledge, with the consequent emphasis on safety, it might have been equally possible to develop the argument for 'a third I' along a trajectory of desire, where the emphasis might thus have been on risk. Yet Smith makes no attempt to conceal that his own strategy is Marxist rather than Nietzschean. For the moment, however, I wish to consider just how he has progressed in his argument towards the need to argue for a 'third term', however defined, in the first place. Any unitary convention, such as Lejeune's 'autobiographical contract', has been rejected. Lejeune's formula accepts 'the affirmation in the text of the identity between the names of the author, narrator and protagonist, referring in the last resort to the *name* of the author on the cover . . . manifesting an intention to "honour the signature"' (Lejeune 1982, 202). Such an 'extended' signature, however, loses the presence of self – Being – in the differential character of the language system and the arbitrariness of signs of a Saussurean or standard structuralist objection. Which is where Smith came in, opening his account of the autobiographical subject by problematizing the (structuralist-derived) binary of the *discours/récit* difference. What we have now witnessed then, via the example from Paul Smith, is virtually a blueprint of the literary theoretical developments of the last quarter-century: unitary presence rejected in favour of a third term. This will come as no surprise to the Hegelians (for whom, amongst others, I have appended not a concluding synthesis, merely a supplementary 'Post-postscript'); but, for the moment, back to literature and to

Borges. To what extent, if at all, does the text 'Borges and I' reflect or express some of the issues I have raised from the Paul Smith extract?

The title 'Borges y yo' might indeed convey, either for the traditionalist biographical critic or even for the signatory to Lejeune's contract, the unitary presence of an extended subject-signature. Its form, nevertheless, signals the implicit binary of proper name versus grammatical first-person subject. (A similar division, of course, is at play in the opening phrase, 'Al otro'.) Instead of 'the self-referential gesture itself as the central and determining event in the transaction of autobiographical reference' (Eakin 1986, 4), Lejeune's claim, Borges' text projects initially the 'life in time' of that 'me told' in the *récit* to whom 'things happen'. The reduction of the functions of the 'I' of *discours* to the 'mechanical' looking – and seeing and telling and knowing – none the less operates directly, whereas only indirectly, i.e. through the mail, on a list, in a dictionary, is the 'me' divulged. In parallel fashion, 'Me gustan los relojes de arena, los mapas, la tipografía del siglo XVIII, las etimologías, el sabor del café y la prosa de Stevenson'/'I like hourglasses, maps, eighteenth-century typography, etymologies, the taste of coffee and the prose of Stevenson' might be said, echoing Barthes, to express *jouissance*, whereas 'el otro comparte esas preferencias, pero de un modo vanidoso que las convierte en atributos de un actor'/'he shares these preferences but in a vain way that turns them into the attributes of an actor' relegates like to preference, the *plaisir* of indirect, dependent gratification.

Here lurks the shadow of originary subject, of plenitude, behind the mask (per-sona) of actor ('empty' sign). Yet the terms of any hierarchy between *récit* and *discours* are immediately reversed: 'yo vivo, yo me dejo vivir, para que Borges pueda tramar su literatura y esa literatura me justifica'/'I live, let myself go on living, so that Borges may contrive his literature, and that literature justifies me'. Here, dependency is inverted, the 'I' suddenly switched to within the parameters of 'me'. What is more, the vehicle of reversal is 'literature', promoting, in the 'bridging operation' between 'I' and 'me', a heightened role for textuality. Not, however, a textuality without subject – for the key word here is 'belongs' – rather a textuality without proprietary rights: 'lo bueno ya no es de nadie, ni siquiera del otro, sino del lenguaje o de la tradición'/'what is good belongs to no one, not even to him but rather to language and tradition'. Here we are close not only to Derrida's notoriously misquoted, mistranslated and misunderstood formulation 'il n'y a pas de hors-texte' but also to an uncommonly intelligent reading of it, given the word – and place – of 'tradition'; for the Borges text is careful not to exclude history from textuality.

If there appears to be an inexorable shift towards a preoccupation with the role of an ethics in post-structuralist discursiveness – and in my own treatment of such a move in this book – then, before I address more directly, in the remaining chapters, 'the meaning of the *copula* in this proposition "Jewgreek is Greekjew"' which I raised in my 'Locating Inequality', I again 'meet [not] extremes', but Borges in Derrida (in 'Borges'). Accidental or not, my mention of Derrida here relates to a point in Borges' text immediately prior to its own citing (or mis-citing) of one of Derrida's principal philosophical precursors in the dialectics of negativity: namely, Baruch Spinoza. For Spinoza – Borges style – 'todas las cosas quieren perseverar en su ser'/'all things long to persist in their being'. For Spinoza – *à la* Derrida – 'all determination is negation, i.e. what a thing *is* depends upon its limits, and these limits depend upon what a thing is *not*. Thus negativity can no longer be simply subordinated to positivity' (Harland 1987, 153).

Reversal, then, abounds: 'Yo he de quedar en Borges, no en mí'/'I shall remain in Borges, not in myself' inserts the telling 'I' into the told 'me'; one is within the other as much as the positive, for Spinoza, is within the negative . . . or vice versa. Beyond the narrow bounds of subjectivity, too (namely, in the culturally specific references to Argentine tradition, time and place), reversals apply. General and specific ('books' and 'guitar') give way to specific and general ('suburbs' and 'games with time and infinity'). At play is an ever-onwards compulsion ('I shall have to'), a 'flight', an undecided, at least unresolved, 'loss' of 'I' in either oblivion or otherness . . . equipoised before the coda: 'No sé cuál de los dos escribe esta página'/'I do not know which of us has written this page'. Coda or supplement? Trace of 'I' in 'Other'?

The reference 'I' makes to external reality, and the extent to which external reality stuffs to bursting, to mortality, the 'I' that sees and feels and speaks and writes, is a relation that Borges explores in the incapacity of Funes to survive the completion of his own putative name ... *funesto*. And the but approximating of the *funereal* term in both 'Funes el memorioso'/'Funes the Memorious' and 'Borges y yo' again brings the Borges ethic close to Derrida's meditation on Husserl in *Speech and Phenomena*:

> the relationship with *my* death (my disappearance in general) thus lurks in this determination of being as presence, ideality, the absolute possibility of repetition. The possibility of the sign is this relationship with death .... The appearing of the *I* to itself in the *I am* is thus originally a relation with its own possible disappearance. Thus *I am* originally means *I am mortal. I am immortal* is an impossible proposition.
>
> (Derrida 1973, 54)

Borges, in fiction(s), gets to the point more quickly. His arch-empiricist, Funes, dies of an *excess* of life's details, of taking in too much, of surplus supplementarity ... of 'una congestión pulmonar'/'pulmonary congestion'. But it should by now be apparent that I am less concerned to make specific comparisons between Borges and Spinoza, Spinoza and Derrida, or Derrida and Borges than to question both unitary subjectivity and an unsatisfactory binarism in which the so-called 'enunciatory abyss' is situated. The structuration of subjectivity does not merely differentiate between 'I' and 'I' (or 'I' and 'me') but consists in the interpellation of voices and positions (grammars and ideologies) which provisionally separate and conjoin these instances of writing. But also instances of *reference*. Listen, again, to Paul Smith: 'I think it worth re-iterating here that the era of what is commonly called post-structuralism has perhaps brought with it a tendency to problematize so much the "subject's" relation to experience that it has become difficult to keep sight of the political necessity of being able not only to theorize but also to *refer* to that experience' (Smith 1988, 159). In my 'Post-postscript' on Latin America and the 'third term', I shall wish to pursue the general question of the interpellation of theorizing and reference, as posed by texts of Augusto Monterroso and João Guimarães Rosa. With immediate and particular reference to the parallel treatment of Roland Barthes, Smith has recourse to that 'ideologized' aspect of Freudian theory which is most readily historicized – 'Freud's focus on the bourgeois individual and its unconscious constitution ... the repression, exactly, of conflict and contradiction in the life of the "individual"' (ibid., 60). Such a repression conspires 'to assign to the subject/individual a "false consciousness" of social and personal relations' (ibid., 60). Leaving aside the obvious suggestion that the Borges text highlights and exploits, as distinct from repressing, such 'conflict and contradiction in the life of the individual', I wish rather to play along with Smith's tactic regarding Barthes. The repression detected there emerges from a late Barthes lecture given at the Collège de France: 'Barthes described his discourse as like the "comings and goings of a child playing beside his mother, leaving her, returning to bring her a pebble, a piece of string, and thereby tracking a locus of play around a calm center"' (ibid., 112). It is but a short step forwards (and backwards if we, too, are to be put under the spell of *fort/da*) to Smith's conclusion that Barthes' writing points increasingly not only to the mother but to despair, 'a collapse into the familiarly comforting and fixed image of the "subject"'. For Smith, 'with that collapse the oppositional moments and impulses of structuralism finally die out' (ibid., 116).

Shall I now pursue a parallel 'analysis' of Borges, confined in an all too nineteenth-century bourgeois transplant to the Argentine: namely, the predominantly English library of his father? Is the primal scene, in this case, to be a repeated reversal of Mallarmé's 'J'ai lu tous les livres / Et la chair est triste, hélas!'? Although I have, indeed, outlined in the Borges text a trajectory of compulsive loss, this is not, in my view, tantamount to 'collapse'. Rather does a like momentum invite further reflection on such a dialectics as Theodor Adorno's: 'the subject is spent and impoverished in its categorical performance . . . . It must cut itself loose from itself' (Adorno 1973, 139). If such a (slanted) quotation from Adorno makes him sound suspiciously like Derrida (not to mention Borges), then that may be because the enterprises of post-structuralism and post-Marxism are not, by any means, necessarily at odds, as Terry Eagleton's review of Perry Anderson's *In the Tracks of Historical Materialism* and, by now, my own *Symptoms, risks and strategies* might have indicated.

Far from following a line of critics who might grasp the opportunity to situate Borges' consciousness (false or otherwise) in the anal stage of text-collecting in the shadow of a book-collecting father – a male version of Paul Smith's narrative of the Barthes 'collapse into a familiarly comforting and fixed image of [a] "subject"'– I prefer to advance a reading of Borges' text(s) which might rescue him (momentarily) from any Anderson-style 'rightist' image of 'hermetic textualism and self-indulgent word-play'. I prefer to set 'Borges and I' not just alongside Theodor Adorno's negative dialectics as read by Paul Smith: 'objectively, dialectics means to break the compulsion to achieve identity, and to break it by means of the energy stored up in that compulsion and congealed in its objectifications' (Smith 1988, 59). This preference I shall transfer to another Borges text, and one which will betray a strategy of compulsion both to achieve and, at once, to flee from identity in the riskiest of effects; for such will be the symptoms and the strategies of my particular appropriations of 'Emma Zunz'. It will pose the (some would say improbable) challenge of reading Borges' fictions as performing *beyond* what Malcolm Bowie claimed for Mallarmé, as I did for Vallejo, in earlier chapters; namely, the *political* application of those 'powers of doubt played not only upon the most time-honoured theologies and theodicies of Europe' (Bowie 1978, 4) but also upon the most sinisterly layered ideological repressions at play in Latin America . . . or its shuttle-space *par excellence*, Buenos Aires.

> My death is structurally necessary
> to the pronouncing of the *I*.
> Jacques Derrida

WORKS CITED

Adorno, Theodor. *Negative Dialectics*. New York: Seabury Press, 1973.

Barthes, Roland. *La Chambre claire*. Paris: Gallimard Seuil, 1980.

Borges, Jorge Luis. *El hacedor*. Madrid: Alianza, 1980.

Bowie, Malcolm. *Mallarmé and the Art of Being Difficult*. Cambridge: Cambridge University Press, 1978.

Derrida, Jacques. *Speech and Phenomena, and Other Essays on Husserl's Theory of Signs*, trans. David B. Allison. Evanston, Ill.: North Western University Press, 1973.

Eagleton, Terry. 'Marxism, Structuralism and Post-Structuralism'. *Diacritics* (Winter 1985), 2–12.

Eakin, Paul John. 'Philippe Lejeune and the Study of Autobiography', *Romance Studies*, 8 (Summer 1986), 1–14.

Harland, Richard. *Superstructuralism*. London: Methuen, 1987.

Lejeune, Philippe. 'The Autobiographical Contract', in *French Literary Theory Today*, ed. Tzvetan Todorov. Cambridge: Cambridge University Press, 1982 (pp. 192–222).

Smith, Paul. *Discerning the Subject*. Minneapolis: University of Minnesota Press, 1988.

Yates, Donald A. and Irby, James E. (trans.). Borges, Jorge Luis. *Labyrinths*. Harmondsworth: Penguin, 1971.

Chapter 10

Z/Z

On *midrash* and *écriture féminine* in Jorge Luis Borges' 'Emma Zunz'

An echo. The most obvious of many echoes. Any resonance in this analysis of Borges' story 'Emma Zunz' will be, must be, however, incomplete; merely a reminiscence of *S/Z*. *S/Z* is arguably Roland Barthes' most conclusive assault on re-presentation – yet, of course, I shall be asking 'What does "Emma Zunz" represent?' and, still more, 'How does it represent?'. The answer to the question 'What?' must be ever plural, an ever-deferred correspondence with the 'real worlds', the 'realities' out of which it is constructed. The answer to the question 'How?' will reveal the story's cultural, narrative, semantic and psychological structures as the interplay of conventional signifying strategies. As in the case of *S/Z* and 'Sarrasine', my 'Z/Z' can only situate 'Emma Zunz' as a text deferring the very reality towards which it gestures.

For Barthes, the particular discursive strategies of any narrative are the 'traces' or 'codes' which traverse it. These codes or 'cultural voices' belong to no one in particular, function as impersonal structuring principles, and are constantly re-initiated and re-vitalized by creative reading practices. For this reason, then, my 'Z/Z' can release, provisionally, but some of the 'cultural voices' that echo from within 'Emma Zunz', voices social, semic, semitic and sexual . . . and countless other voices, too.

POLITICAL GESTURES: CONSCIOUS AND UNCONSCIOUS

Before examining modes of deferral (or textual gestures), the Argentine context of a beleaguered Jewish enclave in a predominantly Catholic Buenos Aires culture of the 1920s may be taken into account. Setting aside the known, and well-documented, facts of Borges' life-long opposition to an ever-present undercurrent of anti-Semitism in Argentina, the socio-cultural specificity of a *Jewish* drama played out within the broader structures of an industrializing, capitalist society is unmistakable. A Borges text, notoriously 'formalist' and so often considered unsuitable for ideological analysis, does betray many inviting gaps for the reader to fill. For whatever motivates Emma, the locus of her action is the factory from where her cashier father is driven by the villainous textile manager-cum-owner, whom she entraps and kills in the machinations of a threatened strike, though declaring herself, as usual, against all violence. In a sense, therefore, Emma uses the strike both as a pretext and as a *pre*-text for violence; for the personal act of violence she commits both conceals and inscribes roles and motivations well beyond the desire for vengeance of 'worker Zunz'. The text may indeed begin and end with *capital*, may proceed from a successful embezzlement to an alibi of exploitation of worker by boss, via torn bank-notes, and miserly calculation . . . but, as text, 'Emma Zunz', while gesturing to the 'real world' by affirming an economic base, at the same time ever defers that reality by denying the closure of its 'bottom line'.

An ideological reading of the Borges text, however, may pass beyond the merely 'gestural'. It is not sufficient to show the ways in which the text initially points to a 'real world' before ultimately 'going transcendental', in Christopher Norris' sense, thereby inviting, in the complexity of its tropes and metaphors, permanently deconstructive reading (Norris 1985, 10). Which is not to say, however, that it is easy to obey, when reading Borges, Fredric Jameson's imperative 'Always historicize!'. Indeed Jameson himself appears to concede the difficulty of access to such as Borges' 'reflexive meaning' (albeit via problematical assumptions about organicism and class solidarity), when he describes 'the classical anxiety of intellectuals at their "free-floating" status and their lack of organic links with one or other of the fundamental social classes: this reflexive meaning is explicit in Sartre, but implicit in writers like Conrad or Borges' (Jameson 1981, 258). The key word, here, is 'implicit', and the access of which Jameson might approve would ideologically be a Machereyan 'symptomatic reading': 'we always eventually find, at the edge of the text, the language of ideology, momentarily hidden, but eloquent by its very absence [as in] the work of Borges,where the *myth of reading* has to be interpreted rather than taken literally, and where the problem of writing is posed independently, well before the problem of reading' (Macherey 1987, 60, 140).

What Macherey may be referring to as 'the *myth of reading*' can be exemplified, in 'Emma Zunz', as the text's resistance to historical engagement. Despite the specificity of a 1920s' Buenos Aires setting, and the meticulously chronological narration of events of 14 and 15 January 1922, the introduction of a thoroughly unreliable narrator, at the moment of Emma's initial decisive action, leads rapidly to textual *de*-historicization in the phrase 'during that time outside of time'. In the process, the reader is invited to 'mythologize', to read and come to terms with *un*reality:

> Referir con alguna realidad los hechos de esa tarde sería difícil y quizá improcedente. Un atributo de lo infernal es la irrealidad, un atributo que parece mitigar sus terrores y que los agrava tal vez. ¿Cómo hacer verosímil una acción en la que casi no creyó quien la ejecutaba, cómo recuperar ese breve caos que hoy la memoria de Emma Zunz repudia y confunde?
>
> (Borges 1972, 62)

> [To relate with some reality the events of that afternoon would be difficult and perhaps unrighteous. One attribute of a hellish experience is unreality, an attribute that seems to allay its terrors and which aggravates them perhaps. How could one make credible an action which was scarcely believed in by the person who executed it, how to recover that brief chaos which today the memory of Emma Zunz repudiates and confuses?]
>
> (Yates–Irby 1971, 116)

Not only chronologically ordered time but also the condensed time of memory are placed beyond credibility by a text which 'goes ahistorical' (or 'transcendental'), opting for the atemporality of structures, of symbolic systems, of generic patterns and resonances.

Macherey himself is less troubled than Jameson by the so-called *implicit* 'reflexive meaning' of a Borges text:

> The narrative is inscribed on its reverse side, begun from the end, but this time in the form of a *radical* art; the story is begun at the end in such a way that we no longer know which is the end and which is the beginning, the story having wound around itself to produce the illusory coherence of an infinite

perspective. But Borges's writing has a value other than that of the riddle . . . . The stratagems of Borges all ultimately lead towards the possibility of . . . 'a vast polemic concerning the composition of a novel in the first person, whose narrator would omit or disfigure the facts and indulge in various contradictions which would permit a few readers – very few readers – to perceive an atrocious or banal reality'.

(Macherey 1987, 251, 257)

In what follows, I shall trace Borges' stratagems, in pursuit of a '*radical* art', conscious of the 'vast polemic' which has arisen between deconstructive and ideological reading-practices. Whether the 'very few readers' perceive the reality of 'Emma Zunz' as 'atrocious or banal' must depend, finally, on the degree to which they can tolerate Jameson's 'marriage of Marxian and Freudian analysis' (Dowling 1984, 78): that is, the 'dialectical shock' which, whenever the ideological is textualized, operates not always at the level of the conscious but within the generally more subversive layers of the *political unconscious*.

ON THE UN-SEME-LINESS OF THE PROPER NAME

'To read is to struggle to name' (Barthes 1974, xl). For Barthes, 'all subversion . . . begins with the Proper Name' (ibid., xli). So *who* is Emma Zunz? While the story's title invites us to centre our attention on Barthes' semic or 'character' code, we cannot fail to be disconcerted by his further claim: 'What is obsolescent in today's novel is not the novelistic, it is the character; what can no longer be written is the Proper Name' (ibid., xli). Emma Zunz promises to be both all-subversive and, yet, as a name, as a signature, unwritable.

In the context of the narratological enterprise of the formalist and structuralist generations, it is not in the least surprising that Barthes should write of the 'Proper Name', understood as a character, as being obsolescent. For the structuralist, it is the ordering, the *diegetical* patterning of fictional discourse, rather than any psychologizing, that determines the semic code. However much we might disagree with such 'transcendence' of the individual by the sign or conventional system of signs socially, it is somewhat harder to refute the structuralist view of character as that which amounts to a series of signs on a page *fictionally*. This is not the place for more than the briefest sketch of the theory of the roles or functions that characters may assume in fiction. However, we may recall that, in Aristotelian tragedy, 'the notion of character is secondary, entirely subsidiary to the notion of action'. Furthermore, 'it must not be forgotten that classical tragedy as yet knows only "actors" not "characters"' (Barthes 1984, 104). The shift in meaning from *persona* as a 'voice behind the mask' to *person* as 'being' is a relatively modern, arguably Romantic development. Rather than the subjectivity subsequently attributable to actOR, or the specific reification of an actION, formalist and structuralist theories focus on a different linguistic function: namely, on the participial actANT, a form which 'partakes of the nature of a verb and an adjective' and underpins those notions which construe character as 'describing action' (McGuirk 1987, 32–4).

If, in the story of 'Emma Zunz', such theories were to lead us to any syntagmatically constructed conclusion, it would probably be less towards sexuality than towards justice. At best, we might plot 'Emma Zunz''s trajectory within Propp's folk-tale morphology, recognizing the roles of, say, villain (Loewenthal), sought-for person (Emma) and her father (Emanuel Zunz); or within A. J. Greimas' actantial paradigm of donor/object/receiver/helper/subject/opponent. To play with these roles and with their interchangeability is to realize the possibility of situating Emma Zunz in all six, just as a different kind of narratological analysis might trace consistent syntagms of contractual, performative and disjunctive action throughout this Borges story.

The sheer intricacy of interrelated detail, within the plot, rewards the closest attention. As the interchangeability of Emma Zunz's actantial roles suggests, the *action* embodied by the 'named character' is not only 'endlessly' complex but also, as the text emphasizes, 'endlessly' resistant to interpretative closure, even at the level of the *non*-psychological. Roland Barthes' warning concerning that struggle to name constituted by the act of reading highlights, then, the inadequacy of the Proper Name – inadequate (or obsolescent) in so far as it fragments and dissolves into the multiple layers of meaning, of echo, of paronomasia and play, which make up its own text and its many intertexts.

NAMES, DATES, PLACES . . . UNREALITY EFFECTS

One of the most striking paradoxes of Borges' story concerns the use of proper names. Meticulously, teasingly, eruditely and humorously, Borges chooses *all* the proper names of the narrative so deliberately that the reader might easily assume that the naming process is anything but a struggle, merely a hermeneutic exercise, perhaps even a cryptogram whereby the reader–exegete first unravels the layers of scriptural resonance before the all too identifiable strands of biblical tradition are restored to their admittedly intertextual yet still recognizable master-pattern. Briefly, I wish to demonstrate the kind of naming, dating and placing patterns the text exploits.

On the fourteenth day of the first month of the Christian calendar (a transposition or echo of the fourteenth-cum-fifteenth day of the first month of the Judaic calendar, Nisan, and the most sacred feast of Passover, blood-sacrifice and deliverance of the first-born?) a young Jewish woman, after six years of separation from her father Emanuel, prepares herself to confront not his mere (secret) absence but the (textual) revelation of his death:

> luego, quiso ya estar en el día siguiente. Acto continuo comprendió que esa voluntad era inútil porque la muerte de su padre era lo único que había sucedido en el mundo, y seguiría sucediendo sin fin.
>
> (Borges 1972, 59)

> [then she wished that it were already the next day. Immediately afterwards she realized that her wish was futile because the death of her father was the only thing that had happened in the world, and it would go on happening endlessly.]
>
> (Yates–Irby 1971, 164)

To repeat 'endlessly' this moment (all other desire rendered futile) is the trajectory announced for itself, by the text, from the first page. In short, temporal succession gives way to narrative time, already (proleptically) 'aquel tiempo fuera del tiempo' (Borges 1972, 62)/'that time outside time' subsequently to be lived, inhabited, manipulated by Emma Zunz.

The scroll of revelation regarding the irrecuperable loss of the patriarch is furtively hidden in a drawer, enclosed (framed) for ever: henceforward, for Emma, knowledge coincides with action ('ya era la que era' (ibid., 59)/'she had already become the person she would be'). From this point, the story which unfolds emerges from 'la creciente oscuridad' (ibid., 60)/'the growing darkness'. Emma is separated not from Emanuel (for *that* name means 'God is with us') but from Manuel (Maier) – an incomplete, not-quite-sacred name of God. The pristine harmony of 'los antiguos días felices' (ibid., 60)/'the old happy days' when he was Emanuel Zunz, might be restored only putatively, only through a rever-berating, distorting echo, textually, through the *interaction* of Em[ma]nuel. The named actant, therefore, the sphere of action of the Proper Name, is split, pluralized, fragmented. Not, how-ever, limited to the binary play of Emma–Manuel, the fabric of patriarchy is woven from many strands, for weaving is also the trade of Emma's boss, Aaron Loewenthal: *Aaron*, who yielded to pressure, in Moses' absence, to worship the golden calf; *Loewenthal*, the valley of the lion; where the 'adversary the devil, as a roaring lion, walketh about, seeking whom he may devour' (I Peter 5: 8).

Not even with her best friend Elsa *Urstein* had Emma shared her secret knowledge – an 'original' script (Ur-text) which dates back beyond the 'stone of Ur' (*Urstein*), beyond the place of Abraham (or Abram), a 'model' patriarch who also indulged in a change of name. A change imitated here by *Maier* – the 'assumed' or 'false' name adopted now, in the bitterness (mrh/mrr) of loss of child, by Manuel, the absent father, as originally by *Mara*/ Naomi, the bitter, bereaved, biblical mother (Ruth 1: 19–21). Emma's father becomes *Maier* by name and embittered in life – even unto death, when consuming the barbiturate or bitter poison 'veronal'.

The timing of Emma Zunz's 'time outside time', her endless sabbath, then, is critical. That sabbath begins at nightfall on the Friday, and is preceded by a ritual act of purification: in this case, a visit to the swimming-pool, where a woman could not bathe if menstruating – whence Emma Zunz's subjection to a superficial examination and the 'vulgar jokes' of Elsa and the sisters *Kronfuss*. Head(*Kron*)-to-toe(*fuss*) inspection can hardly be novel to them, unlike the embarrassed, virginal Emma, in whom 'los hombres inspiraban aún un temor casi patológico'(ibid., 61)/'men inspired, still, an almost pathological fear'. This rite of initiation into the club of women, prelude to her physical initiation into the 'club of men', is sealed by the ritual spelling out of her name – 'tuvo que repetir y deletrear su nombre y su apellido' (ibid., 60)/'she had to repeat and spell out her first and her last name'. The invitation to repeat the name EMMA ZUNZ, to spell it out, is part of what Barthes describes as the reader's 'struggle to name'. The Jewishness of the name, the strict adherence to Judaic genealogy, the relative rarity of the inclusion of a woman in biblical genealogical registers, finally the unusual though specifically resonant form of the name *Zunz* – all these are deferred correspondences with the real world, all these are narrative and, of course, semantic strategies. I pause, then, for a moment, on the semantics of Emma Zunz.

zunz: most obviously, readable upside-down, an invertible palindrome – a self-enclosed sign, sufficient onto itself. Reversible, impenetrable. Obviously, too, the *tetragrammaton* – that four-letter (sacred?) name, yet another Borges version of the never-to-be-pronounced, the never-to-be-written. The apex of a four-based, quadrangular, Judaic textuality comprising: *drawers*, reminiscent of the secret drawers of the hidden apocryphal texts of non-canonical Scripture; *lozenges*, of Emma Zunz's memory, of her idyllic, orthodox childhood, the shape of tablets, classically inscribed by ten – or, in this case, by 'nine or ten roughly drafted lines', since, of course, no text is 'faithfully' re-presentable.

The 'frame-texts' will ever take different forms, be they 'los amarillos losanges de una ventana' (ibid., 62)/'the yellow lozenges, of a window' of the little house in Lanús (which conceal the half-remembered mother), the cinema stills, or the superficially concealing 'portrait of Milton Sills', the furtively silent, Hollywood, textuality of Emma's sublimated sexuality. (In 1923, Milton Sills starred in the film *Madonna of the Streets*, made, presumably, during 1922, the year of the story's action.) Not least, the 'frame-texts' of *zunz* are the *mirrors* in which 'se vió multiplicada en espejos, publicada por luces y desnudada por los ojos hambrientos' (ibid., 62)/'she saw herself published by lights and denuded by hungry eyes'; other frames are the *door* and then murky *entrance*, then the 'vestíbulo (en que había una vidriera con losanges idénticos a los de la casa en Lanús)' (ibid., 62)/'vestibule (in which there was a window with lozenges identical to those in the house at Lanús)', and, finally, through a vertiginous series of textual frames, the *passageway* and a *door* which closed behind her. At this very point of spatial arrival at the final unnameable, unwritable, four-letter word that the text never utters (namely, *cama*/'bed'), a parallel temporal vertigo occurs, up the spiral staircase of Emma's receding virginity – for 'los hechos graves están fuera del tiempo . . . porque no parecen consecutivas las partes que los forman' (ibid., 62)/'the arduous events are outside of time . . . because the parts which form these events do not seem consecutive'.

Apparently non-consecutive are the *semantic* parts which form the actantial sphere of Emma Zunz's name. Bearing in mind the consonantal nature of written Hebrew, the vowel sounds being supplied by the reader, the actant *zunz* draws on:

[znh] – to play the harlot; to commit idolatry
[znh] – to reject as abominable, to cast off, reject
[znv] – to attack from the rear; to stab in the back (metaphorical)
[zvz] – a silver coin, a *fourth* part of a shekel
[zzm] – a people from East of the Jordan, associated with Abraham of Ur
[– and so on]

At best, the semantic network, however rich, can but defer the relationship between the lexical item and the reality towards which it gestures – as I suggested earlier, the case of my own 'Z/Z'. It is provisionally, therefore, that I dwell on but one of the semantic possibilities – namely, [znh], 'to play the harlot' – which has an obvious textual 'sexual' echo in Emma Zunz's behaviour. But what of 'to commit idolatry'?

The end of Emma's orthodoxy is as multi-layered as that orthodoxy's construction. The more obvious elements of her *un*orthodox behaviour are her option for the Gentile, the Swede or Finn, the Arian tool which served her for justice, her self-abasement with the Nordic seaman, not from the father-associated South but from the *Nordstjärnan* ('out of the North', whence JHVH 'will utter . . . judgements against them' – Jeremiah 1: 14–16). Yet a series of binary tensions, of doubles, of bifurcating Judaic and Christian elements weave the fabric of her sexual encounter, her transition from the four-base of orthodox Judaism to the three-base, the Trinity, of Christian 'defilement'. The ciphers of transition – however instrumentally ('tool') – go beyond the 'Pier 3' of the *Nordstjärnan* and the three shots which kill Aaron

Loewenthal. For Emma even 'abstains' on the Friday, eating tapioca soup and vegetables (whereas Jewish sympathy, in the eyes of the Inquisition, for instance, was associated with eating meat).

Furthermore, harlotry and idolatry are brought together in the blasphemous association of Arian money and Christian bread (Holy Communion); 'romper dinero es una impiedad como tirar el pan'/'tearing money is an impiety, like throwing away bread' – the single 'acto de soberbia' (ibid., 63)/'act of pride' of which Emma repents on that day. The final reminiscence of non-orthodoxy I wish to pick up is that which links Emma Zunz with Jael, the non-Israelite woman used by Jehovah to avenge the whole Jewish nation, to assassinate Sisera, the oppressor of Israel, who, in the inverse of Borges' text, comes to her tent for water and is given not water but a violent, temple-shattering death (Judges 5: 24–31).

MIDRASH?

To some degree, my argument demonstrates Emma's transition from orthodoxy to heterodoxy, from Judaic purity to Gentile defilement (not, I stress, as an egocentric *prima donna* but, rather, after the style of a calculating pre-Madonna whose 'goy-toy' is the tool of her passage). Paradoxically, I have employed a consistently Hebraic system (or alphabet) to chart this 'passage'. Those of up-to-date deconstructive turn might well detect in such a paradox the inescapability of *Midrash and Literature*, the latest turn (or screw) of the Yale School, which seeks to re-insert all Western literature into that rabbinic tradition of *midrash* which 'designates both a genre of biblical exegesis and the compilations in which such exegesis . . . was eventually preserved . . . an extraordinary web of consciousness not easily matched in the Western tradition' (Hartman and Budick 1986, ix–x). Yet just how applicable might *midrash* be to 'Emma Zunz'? Just how might Borges have anticipated these remarkable claims of Geoffrey Hartman and Sanford Budick? An answer may emerge as we listen to the latters' statement of their concerns:

> What we are concerned with is a variety of 'open' modes of interpretation, a life in literature or in scripture that is experienced in the shuttle space between the interpreter and the text.

Abiding in the same intermediary space is a whole universe of allusive textuality (the history of writing itself, some say) which lately goes by the name of *intertextuality*. In this spacious scene of writing the interpreter's associative knowledge is invested with remarkably broad powers, including even the hermeneutical privilege of allowing questions to stand as part of answers. By confronting the undecidability of textual meaning, this species of interpretation does not paralyse itself. Instead its own activity is absorbed into the activity of the text, producing a continuum of intertextual supplements, often in a spirit of high-serious play. And even when we encounter play of seemingly outrageous kind we cannot dismiss it as mere self-indulgence, because the phenomena of intertextuality and supplementarity systematically achieve, to a remarkable degree, the very effacement of self. Here there are essentially no proprietary rights, nor, properly speaking, are there any individuals to be proprietors. So it is, we might say, with the midrashic exegeses of Rabbi Akiva, Reb Derrida, Reb Kermode; as with Reb Milton, Reb Agnon, Reb Borges: pseudepigrapha all . . . *Midrash* somehow engages in ever-new revelations of an originary text, while the question of origins is displaced into the living tradition of writing. Indeed, the passwords into our era, still hard for our uncircumcised lips, may well be the 'originary supplement' that Derrida and others began to trace out twenty years ago and which has lain inscribed in *midrash* for two millennia. In this emerging phase *midrash* is seen to affirm the integrity and authority of the text even while fragmenting it and sowing it endlessly.

(Hartman and Budick 1986, xi–xiii)

It will now come as no surprise, perhaps, that Hartman and Budick attribute the re-emergence, in modern times, of *midrash*, to one *Leopold Zunz* – though 'Zunz's appeal, ominously enough, was suppressed by the local authorities', they hasten to add! Local authority or *autoridad loca*(l) – the inscription of the specific madness of institutional hermeneutics with one 'l' of a difference. For *midrash* falls away from the 'dead' letter, the encased Scripture of an ever-'feigned' hand (or origin), towards lateral (not literal) readings. Transcribing rabbinical oral debate, *midrash*, for Susan Handelman (1987, 113), is 'non-mimetic', 'intra-linguistic', 'turned ever-inwards', syntactic delay, not a hermeneutics but a poetics of text-duality. As such *midrash* operates as far away from the initial letter (or 'verse') as possible.

Enticed by the possibility of pursuing 'Reb Borges' in his assumption of the midrashic exegetical mantle, I have risked, am risking, the writing of the 'Reb Ber —— '. Thus, I disclose the 'Preface' to Leeser's *The Twenty-Four Books of the Holy Scriptures*, 'carefully translated according to the Massoretic Text, on the basis of the English Version, after the best Jewish Authorities' (Bloch Publishing Company, New York, 1914), preceded by an epigraph from Deuteronomy, Misreh Torah, xxxi, 21: 'For it shall not be forgotten out of the mouth of his seed'. On the opening page of the 'Preface', not only do I read the name 'Zunz, whose work appeared in 1839', but also that of 'Löwenthal, and some anonymous writers, referred to occasionally in the notes appended to this work'. At the foot of the page, there is but one note, listing Zunz's aids (rabbis and doctors). The footnote continues: 'Occasionally . . . "Zunz" is named; at other times the special translators. The merit of the later translators consists therein that they have adhered to the letter of the text, and not rendered it freely, to avoid difficulties and to improve the style'. I further discover that Löwenthal himself, in 1846, supplants (usurps) the Zunz version.

To view Emma's undertaking as a *midrashic* re-inscription of a *non-*'adherence to the letter of the law' – in the Zunz tradition – is tempting. But I hasten to add, lest carried away by the appropriation of the Borges story for a Hasidic reading, that Emma's transition from orthodoxy leaves her stranded (ferociously) *between* alphabets. For her story is in the collection *El Aleph*, Borges' echo of the *first* letter of the *Hebrew* alphabet, about which Gershom G. Scholem, in *On the Kabbalah and its Symbolism*, warns us: 'to hear the aleph is to hear next to nothing, it is the preparation for all audible language, but in itself conveys no determinate, specific meaning' (1965, 30). 'Z/Z' doubles the text of 'Z' ('Thou unnecessary letter', *King Lear*). However, my reading of Emma's story hinges on the *last* letter of the modern, Western, Christian, alphabets, a re-inscription not in *audible* language but in an ever-undecidable, ever-bifurcating, deconstructible *écriture*, a 'Z/Z'.

ÉCRITURE FÉMININE

I have played with the narratological and with the semantic structures of 'Emma Zunz''s signifying strategies yet, each time, have striven to show the arbitrary nature and the obvious limitations of a given network of appropriative reading – however intricate, however rich. Consider, for instance, the possible conclusions which might be drawn from the fact that Borges has, demonstrably, lifted much of the plot of 'Emma Zunz' from the Old Testament – as well as many of its tropes and motifs. Is Emma Zunz, then, to be seen as latter-day Jewish heroine, thirsting for justice and a restoration of patriarchal harmony? The self-sacrificing daughter who, in the high tradition of Judaism's female responsibility for the salvation of the genealogy, places her father's name and honour before her own? Such patriarchal readings are dangerously limited and limiting, although Borges' text *does* play with patriarchal binary thought.

On the one hand, a Gilbert and Gubar approach to Emma as, alternately, angel and whore is productive. As the story opens, the arrival of a letter (however 'feigned') announcing the death of a father previously 'emasculated', *absent*, but still a shadow/presence in the life of his angel/daughter, triggers a new role for Emma. She now becomes the executor of her father's will in two senses: executor and executor; will as *testament* and will as *desire*. The letter is initially half-absorbed then hidden furtively in the drawer of Emma's latent sexuality, in the drawer which conceals her as yet still 'closeted', iconographic (Milton Sills), image of an impossible, idealized maleness. When Emma's decision to act is taken, the letter is destroyed, as she constructs her alibi, of course, but also as she sheds the guardian from its 'angel', releasing the rational, scheming, active 'whore'. Paradoxically, in exploiting the 'female' construction of her own body, her physical being, Emma is obliged, as a social being, to operate within the 'male' construction of her own society, namely the strong Judaeo-Argentine patriarchy of the story's setting. In the process, although her motivation 'He vengado a mi padre' (ibid., 65)/ 'I have avenged my father' is 'true' but never heard, the 'false' explanation 'Abusó de mí' (ibid.)/'he abused me' emerges as the only acceptable – sexually derived – explanation which such a patriarchy can encompass in a system it calls 'justice'.

In such a 'reforming' role, then, Emma Zunz could be seen not only as 'unsettling' Loewenthal (literally) but also as unsettling (by implication) social justice as a whole construct. In Jewish terms, her assumption of a strong role as a woman situates her within a 'reform' tradition – whence the legitimacy of this text as Ba*t*mitzvah – Emma's coming of age when, as a Jew, she becomes responsible for reading not only the text herself but also herself the text ('published by lights and denuded by hungry eyes'?).

On the other hand, however, again undermining *passion* and *resignation*, the story could be read as a denunciation parallel to Hélène Cixous' attack on the notion 'either woman is passive or she doesn't exist' (1977a, 118). Paraphrasing Toril Moi's description of Cixous' trajectory, Borges' story thus could 'in one sense be summed up as the effort to undo this egocentric ideology: to proclaim woman as the source of life, power and energy and to hail the advent of a new feminine language that ceaselessly subverts these patriarchal binary schemes where logocentrism colludes with phallocentrism in an effort to oppress and silence women' (Moi 1985, 105). The *un*natural, *dis*passionate, *non*-resigned Emma Zunz actively exploiting her culture (not her nature), her intelligence (not her sentiment), as well as her sexuality, would thus be construed as re-writing tradition (which might even account for the series of reversals of the Bible source-texts such as the asking for rather than being asked for water). I would argue, however, against the more extreme *écriture féminine* approach to 'Emma Zunz', that, as a protagonist, Emma is too implicated in the very discourse she seeks to reject. I would push her 're-writing' or 'deconstruction' of the logocentric discourse beyond a supplementing of the 'absent term' – that is, *her* name, *her* role in continuing, in guaranteeing a non-patriarchal version of justice. Beyond legal *gouvernement* to lethal *gouvernementalité* for, inevitably, Emma's resistance is part of the institutional order she inhabits. Emma Zunz must partake, still, of both *ego*centrism (for justice) and *phallo*centrism (for her alibi).

Where I would accept Cixous' analysis would be in the claim that feminine texts are texts that 'work on the difference' (1977b, 480), texts which 'strive in the direction of difference, struggle to undermine the dominant phallologocentric logic, split open the closure of the binary opposition and revel in the pleasures of open-ended textuality' (Moi 1985, 108). Consequently, I would re-affirm her claim, too, that 'the fact that a piece of writing is signed with a man's name does not in itself exclude femininity. It's rare, but you can sometimes find femininity in writings signed by men:

it does happen' (Cixous 1981, 52). Although the writings of Borges have been the object of more critical attention than any other Latin American writer, the narrowness of approaches, basically thematic, mythological and stylistic, has been surprising. The last few years have seen more attention paid to the poetics of his texts as more sophisticated theoretical perspectives are employed. Even when, for instance, a Bakhtinian analysis has been used (A. J. Pérez) exploiting the notions of carnivalization and the chronotope, criticism has seemed reluctant to extend the analysis to the realm of the sexual. Borges, it seems, is 'excluded' (canonically) from 'working on the difference', from the construction of a *sexual* chronotope, a scene of writing ('riting') where gender is constructed – and gender-stereotypes are de-constructed. A multi-voicedness can be shown to emerge from the Borges text, a heteroglossia which affirms not the presence of a speaking subject but the construction of an ever-differentiated, ever-deferred *écriture*; and – why not? – of an ever-differentiated, ever-deferred sexuality. The text 'works on the difference' of the opposition masculine/feminine, constructing *actants* which, as Hélène Cixous might say, are 'inherently bisexual'. Thus, 'Emma Zunz' operates that *'other bisexuality* which is multiple, variable and ever-changing, consisting as it does of the "non-exclusion either of the difference or of one sex"' (Moi 1985, 109). The danger of theorizing, however, about *écriture féminine* is that the writing refuses all static textuality, performs a 'vatic' sexuality: 'this practice can never be theorized, enclosed, coded – which doesn't mean that it doesn't exist. But it will always surpass the discourse that regulates the phallocentric system; it does and will take place in areas other than those subordinated to philosophico-theoretical domination' (Cixous 1980, 253). Those familiar with the work of Cixous may already have noticed the echoes, specifically the Old Testament echoes, between 'Emma Zunz' and *La Venue à l'écriture*, which opens thus: 'In principio adoravi'/'In the beginning I adored' (Cixous 1977a, 9). Here, for Toril Moi, 'Cixous casts herself ... as a prophetess, the desolate mother out to save her people, a feminine Moses ... "I am myself the earth, everything that happens on it, all the lives that live are there in my different forms"' (Moi 1985, 116).

Like Emma, Cixous constructs her 'voicing' out of a 'collapsed' presence, a written patriarchy, a deferred 'Testament': 'Writing or God. God the writing. The writing God' (Cixous 1977a, 30). As in the case of 'Emma Zunz', the power of the phallus is harnessed, integrated and surpassed. The phallocentric symbolic order is exploited *because* it is insufficient, inefficient; the writing becomes a 'rape-text' (ibid., 19–20) in 'submission to the phallic rule of language as differential, as a structure of gaps and absences' (Moi 1985, 119). But, as a supplement, the 'rape-text' becomes a creative, 'mother' text, undoing the gaps, distinctions and injustices of the patriarchal system.

After what Cixous claims for *écriture féminine*, the insufficiency – the downright clumsiness – of, say, Oedipal (Freudian and Lacanian) interpretations of 'Emma Zunz' are shown up as further limitations of the patriarchal symbolic order. Such (a Freudian) reading would suggest that Emma never passes beyond the 'blind guilt' of her first impression on receiving the letter; that she is condemned merely to repeat (and suppress) the primal scene of a violence her father did to her mother; that 'that will' (immediately seen as 'useless') to escape the present moment, to be already in an unreal 'tomorrow' of inaction and non-responsibility, is not *her* will but the Desire of the Father, wielding her as a mere instrument of revenge. In fact, such a reading is posed but momentarily, at once to be dismissed. For Emma, by her subsequent actions, moves out of the shadow of the Father . . . and out of a Freudian legacy. Moving beyond Freudian *sexuality* into active, effective de(con)structive *textuality*, Emma redresses the inadequacy of Freudian discourse – a discourse she must, however, re-enact – all the way to Loewenthal's obscenely gaping, bloodied, mouth – in order to re-write it.

The phallologocentrism which would situate Emma's 'action' in a binary *Nom-du-père/Non-du-père* of Naming/Interdiction is all too superficially plausible as an explanation of, a solution to, the Borges story. Such a reading would also suggest that Emma Zunz never emerges from, or breaks with, the symbolic order which, sexually, condemns her ever to re-enact ('endlessly') the thought '(no pudo no pensar) que su padre le había hecho a su madre la cosa horrible que a ella ahora le hacían' (ibid., 62–3)/'(she could not not think) that her father had done to her mother the horrible thing that was now being done to her'; which, scripturally, condemns her never to emerge from, to break with, the however fragmented system of patronymics.

But the text does not promote a univocal interpretation of Emma's motives along such lines. For it is the sole intervention of a distinctly patriarchal first-person (singular) narrator, at the initial, untextualized moment of Emma's act of coition – 'En aquel tiempo fuera del tiempo, en aquel desorden perplejo de sensaciones inconexas y atroces'/'In that time outside of time, in that perplexed disorder of unconnected and atrocious sensations' – asking rhetorically – '¿pensó Emma Zunz *una sola vez* en el muerto que motivaba el sacrificio? Yo tengo para mí que pensó una vez y que en ese momento peligró su desesperado propósito' (ibid., 62)/'did Emma think *even once* about the dead man who motivated the sacrifice? It is my opinion that she did think once and that in that moment she endangered her desperate proposition'.

And who asked him? Should his opinion function as the master-discourse any more than the Oedipal prohibition by which desire is channelled towards the prohibited for Jacques Lacan? Might we not take up and revise the cry of Deleuze and Guattari, in rejecting the interpretation of this first-person narrator? 'The Law tells us: You will not marry your [father] and you will not kill your [mother]. And we docile subjects say to ourselves: so *that's* what I wanted!' (Wright 1984, 162).

The advantage of a non-essentialist feminist analysis in not merely the anti-Oedipus, however. By stressing the way the marginal (feminine?) functions – *à la* Kristeva or Foucault – 'the *meaning* of the [text] is thrown open – the sign becomes polysemic rather than univocal . . . . The power struggle *intersects* in the sign' (Moi 1985, 158). And intersection in the sign of a power struggle, far from implying the interdictory shadow and the 'sacred' name of the Father, in an Oedipal splitting of the Emma–Manuel sphere of action, might now be seen to throw up, textually, the suppressed tetragrammaton, the ultimately unpronounceable (sacred) four-letter word which hides between EmMA and MAnuel: namely, 'MA-MA'. A *nom de mère* might thus emerge as strategically concealed counter to the refuted master-discourse. For what is left behind when this Christian, Hispanic, mother-text ('mamá') emerges? Not a fragmented 'Em' but, rather, a reconstituted, whole, Judaic 'EM', the Hebrew word for 'mother'. EMMA, it seems, is again situable (though perhaps, this time, not 'stranded') between cultures. She is inscribed *between* ancient, Old World, Judaism, and Argentine, New World, 'Semitism'.

That the application of certain *écriture féminine* insights to

'Emma Zunz' highlights and problematizes the inadequacy of notions of individual subjectivity, personal morality, the 'propriety' of a name, or even the 'nature' of woman, should be clear. For: 'If "femininity" has a definition at all in Kristevan terms, it is simply . . . that which is marginalized by the patriarchal symbolic order . . . and Kristeva's emphasis on marginality allows us to view this repression of the feminine in terms of *positionality* rather than of essences' (Moi 1985, 166).

SPECULUM – SPECULATE – SPECTACLES

Spéculum assaults not Freud but his blind-spot: the feminine. If I now speculate on a possible 'blind-spot' of 'Emma Zunz', it is merely to reflect on Loewenthal's spectacles. Generically, in terms of the detective genre (which Borges' text both reflects and deflects), the 'flaw' in Emma's construction of an alibi is the removal of Loewenthal's bespattered glasses. Why take them off after the killing, bloodied? In offering to detective (or reader) the flaw in a 'perfect' crime, 'Emma Zunz' invites further speculation, refuses the closure of its own text, supplementing the already read with the trace of further writing. No crime story is perfect since no text is perfect; since no re-presentation (of a 'truth') is, textually, possible. While it is tempting to speculate that Emma is expressing her own (secret) desire to be caught ('cogida'?), it is perhaps more textually relevant, in the *con*-text of her vaginal alibi, to return to Irigaray's speculum–phallus meditation on (male) gynaecological practice. For will Emma's 'story' suffice? Will she have to succumb (again) to the male desire to penetrate, 'to pierce the mystery of the woman's sex' (ibid., 82)?

Must the cold steel of his (surgical) speculum probe her innermost 'textuality' as the hot metal of her (liturgical) bullets have just rent the temple of his 'sexuality'? To argue that Loewenthal's spectacles constitute the 'flaw', the deconstructive turn, the functioning of an absent term in the present text of Emma's alibi, is to shift attention from oral to written and to the validity of truth and falsity statements on which Borges' text ends:

La historia era increíble, en efecto, pero se impuso a todos, porque sustancialmente era cierta. Verdadero era el tono de Emma Zunz, verdadero el pudor, verdadero el odio. Verdadero también era el ultraje que había padecido; sólo eran falsas las circunstancias, la hora y uno o dos nombres propios.

(Borges 1972, 65–6)

[Actually the story *was* incredible, but it impressed everyone because substantially it was true. True was Emma Zunz's tone, true was her shame, true was her hate. True also was the outrage she had suffered: only the circumstances were false, the time and one or two proper names.]

(Yates–Irby 1971, 169)

For what is truth but a version of (a vision of) male justice? In shifting specularity from 'seeing' to 'exploring female sexuality', 'Emma Zunz' speculates on the possibility of an un-closed file (Emma places the spectacles, it must be recalled, not *in* but *on* the filing-cabinet).

Luce Irigaray re-opens the file on Freud's 'tache aveugle d'un vieux rêve de symétrie' (1974, 1), that 'blindspot of an old dream of symmetry' whereby the 'little female' is assimilated into a version of 'little male' sexuality, thereby being 'explained away' in Oedipal 'truth'. 'Emma Zunz' re-opens the file both on that 'truth' and on all truth; invites, in Machereyan terms, a symptomatic reading: 'Evidently the function of the discourse of the narrative is to deliver *the truth*, but this is done at the cost of a very long detour, a cost which must be met. The discourse shapes a truth only by bringing itself into question' (Macherey 1987, 254). While the shaping of an alibi-truth is, rather obviously, delivered via the detour of three 'verdaderos' (*mea culpa, mea culpa, mea maxima culpa?*) in echo of Christianity, and of four 'verdaderos' (tetragrammatically) in *imitatio JAVE*, Macherey's notion of a discourse which 'brings itself into question' is exemplified, in a manner more strikingly relevant to 'Emma Zunz', by Mary Jacobus:

Freud's footnote to *Studies on Hysteria* amounts to saying that where hysteria is concerned it is impossible to over-read. The maze of signs, his metaphor for the hysterical text, invokes not only labyrinthine intricacy but the risk of self-loss. . . . Jane Gallop . . . intriguingly suggests that smell is repressed by Freud's organization of sexual difference around a specular image ('sight of a phallic presence in the boy, sight of a phallic absence in the girl') . . . . The female stench . . . is the unmentionable of misogynist scatology.

(1986, 229, 243)

'Emma Zunz', similarly, unsettles the patriarchal symbolic order inasmuch as man will only accept rational (under-read?) visible evidence, backed by the 'truth' of an alibi. Loewenthal's body, it must be stressed 'se desplomó como si los estampidos y el humo lo hubieran roto' (Borges 1972, 65)/'collapsed as if the reports and the smoke had shattered it' – an instance, perhaps of a Machereyan 'contradiction . . . which deforms the text'. *Sound* and *smell* (sound-barrier? smoke-screen?) met by a *look* of amazement and anger. Loewenthal's reaction is the textual embodiment of Jacobus' further claim:

> Feminine immediacy – predicated on the notion of an incompletely mediated relation between the female body, language and the unconscious – produces anxiety which must be managed by representation; that is by the privileging of visual representations in psychic organization . . . . Attempts to read therefore involve the (repressive) substitution of something – a figure – for nothing. At first the pattern serves simply to mirror the narrator's own specular reading, endlessly repeated in the figure of the eyes.
>
> (Jacobus 1986, 244, 246)

'Emma Zunz' is, then, an anti-'mirror-text': anti-'mirror-phase', anti-'mirror-stage', anti-Freud, anti-Lacan, anti-'cure' and anti-'readability':

> The gap between sign and meaning is the absence that the hysteric attempts to abolish or conceal by textualizing the body itself. Montrelay writes of the analyst's discourse as 'not reflexive, but different. As such, it is a *metaphor* not a mirror, of the patient's discourse' . . . metaphor engenders a pleasure which is that of *'putting the discussion of repression into play on the level of the text itself'* . . . . The ultimate form of this unmentionable pleasure would be feminine *jouissance*, or meaning that exceeds the repressive effects of interpretation and figuration.
>
> (ibid., 247–8)

After the murder – after Loewenthal has come (has been brought) to final, climactic, spurting – and before the telephone call, Emma prolongs her own *jouissance*, her own (proleptic) reading of the reaction of the Law. In the process, she renders her text 'unreadable'. The removal of spectacles, in 'Emma Zunz', assaults false speculation; is the text's bespattering of its own murdered (and murderous) vision.

I should like to end by suggesting that whatever our methodology, our mode of analysis – in this case, for instance, socio-political, narratological, semantic or psychoanalytical readings of 'Emma Zunz' – the danger, in our culture, of keeping woman outside representation, as Luce Irigaray has shown, is constant. And that 'the feminine has consequently had to be deciphered as forbidden [*interdit*], in between signs, between the realized meanings, between the lines' (1974, 20). There will always be oppositionary, 'master' discourses, however. But, as Jacques Derrida explains, the programmes of deconstruction and feminism have been similar: 'the resistance to deconstruction is exactly the same as that resistance which is opposed to women's studies [yet] there is always something sexual at stake in the resistance to deconstruction' (1984, 12) – and (un)consciously political?

The 'final solution', the ultimate obscene master-discourse – an insertion of naked maleness (*un/nu*) between crossed, inverted Zs (𖣣) – is unsettled, EM-end-ed, broken, by the re-reading of an over-inscribed, 'received', but no longer pronounceable ('sir')name: the *Ur*-text, the whore-text (flagrantly *hors-texte*) of anti-Semitic fascism.

WORKS CITED

Barthes, Roland. *S/Z*, trans. Richard Miller. New York: Hill and Wang, 1974.

—— *Image, Music, Text*, trans. Stephen Heath. London: Collins (Flamingo), 1984.

Borges, Jorge Luis. *Labyrinths*, trans. Donald A. Yates and James E. Irby. Harmondsworth: Penguin, 1971.

—— *El Aleph*. Buenos Aires: Emecé, 1972.

Cixous, Hélène. *La Jeune Née*. Paris: UGE, 10/18, 1975.

—— *La Venue à l'écriture*, avec Annie Leclerc et Madeleine Gaynon. Paris: UGE, 10/18, 1977a.

—— 'Entretien avec Françoise van Rossum-Guyon', *Revue des sciences humaines*, 168 (1977b), 480.

—— 'The Laugh of the Medusa', trans. Keith and Paul Cohen, in *New French Feminisms*, ed. Elaine Marks and Isabelle Courtivron. Brighton: Harvester, 1980 (p. 253).

—— 'Castration or Decapitation', trans. Annette Kuhn. *Signs*, 7.1 (1981), 52.

Derrida, Jacques. 'Women in the Beehive: A Seminar with Jacques Derrida', *subjects/objects*, 2 (1984), 12.

Dowling, William C. *Jameson, Althusser, Marx: An Introduction to the Political Unconscious*. London: Methuen, 1984.

Gilbert, Sandra M. and Gubar, Susan. *The Madwoman in the Attic: The Woman Writer and Nineteenth-Century Literary Imagination*. New Haven and London: Yale University Press, 1975.

Handelman, Susan. 'Jacques Derrida and the Heretic Hermeneutic', in *Displacements: Derrida and After*, ed. Mark Krupnick. Bloomington: Indiana University Press, 1987 (pp. 98–129).

Hartman, Geoffrey, and Budick, Sanford (eds). *Midrash and Literature*. New Haven and London: Yale University Press, 1986.

Irigaray, Luce. *Spéculum de l'autre femme*. Paris: Minuit, 1974.

Jacobus, Mary. *Reading Woman: Essays in Feminist Criticism*, London and New York: 1986.

Jameson, Fredric. *The Political Unconscious: Narrative as a Socially Symbolic Act*. London: Methuen, 1981.

McGuirk, Bernard. 'Structuralism II: Character Theory: *In the Cage*', in *Literary Theory at Work: Three Texts*, ed. Douglas Tallack. London: Batsford, 1987 (pp. 29–48).

Macherey, Pierre. *A Theory of Literary Production*. London: Routledge and Kegan Paul, 1987.

Moi, Toril. *Sexual/Textual Politics: Feminist Literary Theory*, New Accents. London: Methuen, 1985.

Norris, Christopher. *Contest of Faculties: Philosophy and Theory after Deconstruction*. New York and London: Methuen, 1985.

Pérez, Alberto Julián. *Poética de la prosa de J. L. Borges: hacia un crítica Bakhtiniana de la literatura*. Madrid: Gredos, 1986.

Scholem, G. Gershom. *On the Kabbalah and its Symbolism*. New York: Schocken Books, 1965.

Showalter, Elaine. 'Shooting the Rapids: Feminist Criticism in the Mainstream', *Oxford Literary Review*, 9 (1986). (*Sexual Difference*), 1–2.

Wright, Elizabeth. *Psychoanalytical Criticism: Theory in Practice*. London: Methuen, 1984.

Chapter 11

Post-

Back to the suture: on the un*seam*liness of patriarchal discourse in Susana Thénon's *Ova completa*

There will always be a *post-*. The Argentine Susana Thénon, in her 1987 collection *Ova completa*, highlights the recourse of contemporary women's writing to established patterns of patriarchal discourse. It has become commonplace, in the wake of the writings of Luce Irigaray, to trace the passage from mimeticism to mimicry in the undermining (or overwriting) of male canons. Yet a primary *caveat* is worth re-emphasizing: there can be no essentialism. When speaking of gender, therefore, or of sexual difference in the merely biological sense, I do not wish to import any genetic distinctions into my discussion of writing. I shall take it as read, as well as written, that the literatures under discussion are constructions. Which takes me from the physical to the metaphysical . . . but not so fast, since such a move itself may, and will, be shown to be a classically masculist trope in discursive practice. There are many possible intervening stages on the way and, in this instance, I shall dwell on the modes whereby a *machista* Argentine literary culture is subsumed into Susana Thénon's poetry (it takes two to tango) so that the male/female positions are re-locatable ever within the strategies of social d(omin)ance. The elaborate footwork, the side-steps, of her poems perform to the beat of her title/text *Ova completa*, itself an echo (parody) of masculine 'completeness'. Thus, *obra* will function not as 'l'œuvre' but as 'leurre', the work (or lure) of *his* (and now her) pomps and vanities.

The Devil may have danced in an empty pocket throughout 'Pre-' but, in a footnote to her collection's title, Thénon would make us wonder if male pockets are ever empty:

*OVA: sustantivo plural neutro latino. Literalmente: huevos
COMPLETA: participio pasivo plural neutro latino en

concordancia con huevos. Literalmente: colmados. Variantes posibles: rellenos, repletos, rebosantes, henchidos.

[*OVA: Latin noun neuter plural. Literally: eggs.
COMPLETA: Latin past participle neuter plural agreeing with eggs. Literally: topped up. Possible variants: full up, replete, brimming over, swollen.]

From the outset, it should be clear that Thénon's strategy is disruptive and playful, respecting neither strict etymologies nor restrictive plenitudes. In her rendering, the balls are burst or, in re-echo of Lacan, the eggs are smashed to reveal and to re-mould 'l'homme' as 'l'hommelette'. Her use of language and languages – Spanish, English, Latin, French or Espinglés – draws on classical and popular, cultural and *kitsch*. Riotously, she places her eggs not in one basket but rather in a punnet, a net of puns which at once enmeshes and undoes traditional poetic discourse.

The question, in the post-script *sine qua non*, concerns not merely the age-old problem of woman's representation by man but, inseparably, in the Susan Winnett formulation I outlined in Chapter 1, her finding a reading position outside, beyond, different from, masculist universalizing. The opening poem of *Ova completa* addresses the issue head-on, picking up and reworking the cliché fragments of a street-vendor's cry into a dialogic which unsettles both a standard image of woman, and a reader's capacity to accept it:

¿por qué grita esa mujer?
¿por qué grita?
¿por qué grita esa mujer?
andá a saber

esa mujer ¿por qué grita?
andá a saber
mirá que flores bonitas
¿por qué grita?
jacintos   margaritas
¿por qué?
¿por qué qué?
¿por qué grita esa mujer?

¿y esa mujer?
¿y esa mujer?
vaya a saber

estará loca esa mujer
mirá   mirá los espejitos
¿será por su corcel?
andá a saber

¿y dónde oíste
la palabra corcel?
es un secreto   esa mujer
¿por qué grita?
mirá las margaritas
la mujer

espejitos
pajaritas
que no cantan
¿por qué grita?
que no vuelan
¿por qué grita?
que no estorban

la mujer
y esa mujer
¿y estaba loca esa mujer?

ya no grita

(¿te acordás de esa mujer?)
        (Thénon 1987, 7–8)

[Why does that woman shout?/why does she shout?/why
does that woman shout?/*go and find out*/That woman, why
does she shout/*go and find out*/*look what lovely flowers*/why
does she shout?/*hyacinths marguerites*/why?/*why what?*/why
does that woman shout/and that woman?/and that woman?/
go and find out/*she'll be crazy that woman*/*look look at the little
mirrors*/will it be because of her steed?/*go and find out*/*and
where did you hear?*/*the word steed?*/it's a secret that woman/
why does she shout?/*look at the marguerites*/the woman/*little
mirrors*/*little birds*/which don't sing/why does she shout?/
which don't fly/why does she shout?/*which don't get in the
way*/the woman/and that woman/and was she crazy that
woman?/now she's not shouting/(do you remember that
woman?)]

The chosen framework of coy popular wisdom contained in rhetorical questioning allows Thénon's interventions to operate palimpsestically, providing a commentary on the very convention which is being mimicked. The key-words are simply repeated over and over again, as in many a song tradition: 'grita' (× 10), 'mujer' (× 13), and 'por qué' (× 12). Yet within and from the patterns of repetition there emerges an answer not to the question originally posed but rather to the bracketed (marginalized) question of the final line. The absence of an answer to '¿por qué grita esa mujer?' is, in fact, a stock feature broached overtly as such, in the opening sequence, by *'andá a saber'*. Since no direct reason can be given or expected, a series of speculations will ensue. The first eight instances of 'mujer' are accompanied by 'esa', reifying the object of the reader's attention as a yelling, flower-and-cheap-jewel-adorned creature whose presumed hysteria (*'¿estará loca?'*) might be explained in the most traditional of Hollywood styles – '¿será por su corcel?'. Now *'andá a saber'* might be said to operate as a throwaway 'but of course!' ('Don't all women pine for Prince Charming on a dashing white steed?'). A corrective intervention undermines such an assumption, however, in the form of the question:

¿y dónde oíste
la palabra corcel?
es un secreto   esa mujer.

The 'exotic' location of the word 'corcel' is highlighted and questioned but, ultimately, emerges out of a conspiracy – 'un secreto'. The gap between 'secreto' and 'esa mujer' is resonant: the blank space, I would suggest, inhabited by a shadow, the shadow of narrator, or focalizer, or vocalist, or reader-of-the-popular-tradition – or man. Preferring the silent place of concealment, it is none the less this voice that opts to shift attention to 'esa mujer', the deemed 'proper' object of contemplation, the 'normal' enshrinement of whim, of fantasy, of emotion. But another voice, another reader, is about to twist the genre to different ends. 'Esa' is suddenly replaced by 'la', breaking through the 'chuchería' trinketry of *'margaritas'*, *'espejitos'*, *'pajaritas'*, breaking free from trivial diminutives, the unproductive nature of which is stressed in *'no vuelan'*, *'no cantan'*, *'no estorban'*. 'La mujer' emerges, then, as an alternative to the reified image of 'esa mujer', is juxtaposed with it, leading to the pressingly relevant question, no longer hypothetical ('*¿estará?*') but real: '*¿y estaba loca esa mujer?*' The madness is displaced from woman to reader of woman, from false attribution to falsifying attributor. Consequently, the poem ends with a further twist to the tale: 'ya no grita' removes hysteria; '(¿te acordás de esa mujer?)' adds a sting to the tail. Did she ever exist and, if so, do you even remember her? The bracketed question is, of course, directed to and targeted at the putative male reader, who by now does not care, and at a newly alerted female (or non-traditional male) reader who may never be able to hear 'esa' again.

This first poem by Thénon effectively operates the strategy of questioning the 'gendering' of readership noted, in a different context, by Susan Winnett. I now wish to examine her further claim: namely, that pursuing 'a possible erotics of reading, we find a woman's encounter with the text determined by a broad range of options for pleasure' (Winnett 1990, 507). It should be obvious here that she is picking up Susan Sontag's very 1960s' plea for an erotics in preference to a hermeneutics of reading. And the replacement of analysis, textual and psycho-therapeutic, is one of the devices constantly exploited by Thénon:

> el struss
> uno de los grandes males
> que afectan a la womanidad
> antes se llamaba stress
> y antes strass
> o Strauss
> es como un vals trastabillado
> por la mujer sin sombra
> no hay drama
> está borracha
> borracha la puerca
>
> el struss
> > (ibid., 39)

[struss/one of the great evils/affecting womanity/before it was called stress/and before strass/or Strauss/it's like a tripping waltz/for the woman without shadow/there's no drama/she's drunk/drunk the sow/struss]

A glance at the titles of, say, Neruda's *Obra completa* reveals a varied list of song and dance rhythms: 'Barcarola', 'Sonata',

'Tango (del viudo)', 'Vals', and so on. In Thénon's poetry, too, song and dance figure and, usually, disfigure. The treatment of waltz, in this poem, is a striking case. The organizing centre of the text is the line 'o Strauss', a surrogate figure, Father of the Waltz, in whose Shadow, the steps of a supposedly 'erotic' dance are performed. But the pattern is spoilt, tripped up, 'trastabillado'. And who is at fault but 'la mujer'? The *faux pas*, however, is turned to startling effect, triggering a series of dislocations of the interdictory original lawgiver so that the path to Strauss is paved with good inventions, a stressful, strassful, strussful process. When turned inside-out, the rigid partnership of woman/man, dance/dominance is revealed as but the floor-show of public role-playing. The private reality is stark: 'uno de los grandes males/que afectan a la womanidad'. Might the cultivated bilingual humour throw up (on) 'grandes males' as overbearing *males*? The stress of 'la mujer sin sombra' derives from any attempt to step out of the shadow, into independence. The male hermeneutic demands analysis. The shadowy figure of man will always presume to dance with the woman seeking to break free; for without him, or his shadow, there can be no drama, no excitement. To think other is to enter the realm of condemnation: 'está borracha / borracha la puerca'/'Has she hit the bottle? – the slut!'.

'El struss', a nonsense, a no-sense word, gains context and meaning only in the absence of hermeneutic, in the absence of man, of me – and my shadow. The erotics of this poem involve dance and play, dance as play, as un-dance, un-done. In 'Choreographies', an interview-dance with Christie McDonald, Jacques Derrida responds to her question: 'How would you describe woman's place?':

> And why for that matter should one rush into answering a topological question (what is the place of woman [quelle est la place de la femme])? Or an economical question (because it all comes back to l'*oikas* as home, maison, chez-soi [at home in this sense also means in French within the self], the law of the proper place, etc. in the preoccupation with a woman's place)? Why should a new 'idea' of woman or a new step taken by her necessarily be subjected to the urgency of this topo-economical concern? . . . . This step only constitutes a step on the condition that it challenge a certain idea of the locus [lieu] and the place

[place] (the entire history of the West and of its metaphysics) and that it dance otherwise . . . . The most innocent of dances would thwart the *assignation à résidence*, escape those residences under surveillance; the dance changes place and above all changes women's movements, and of some women in particular, has actually brought with it the chance for a certain risky turbulence in the assigning of places . . . . Is one then going to start all over again making maps, topographies, etc.? distributing sexual identity cards?

The most serious part of the difficulty is the necessity to bring the dance and its tempo into tune with the 'revolution'. The lack of place for [*l'atopie*] or the madness of the dance . . . can also compromise the political chances of feminism and serve as an alibi for deserting organized, patient, laborious 'feminist' struggles . . . an incessant, daily negotiation – individual or not – sometimes microscopic, sometimes punctuated by a poker-like gamble; always deprived of insurance, whether it be in private life or within institutions. Each man and each woman must commit his or her own singularity, the untranslatable factor of his or her life and death.

(Derrida and McDonald 1982, 68–9)

For once – rare occurrence – a Derrida text demands little or no commentary, explicitly and politically pointing up the disruptive power and responsibilities of choreographies. The disruption of place, however, is indistinguishable from the disruption of language, as the Thénon poem has just shown. The 'place' of analysis, be it dance-floor, psychoanalyst's couch or literary text, must be subjected to stress if the neurosis is to be shifted away from the analysand-and-analyst construed as partnership, as sphere of action, rather than as static cure.

I pause but briefly to meditate on loss of unity as a (Western) metaphysical problematic. In the theocritical system, the Fall of Man and the Fall of Language have been ascribed names of place: Eden; Babel. Man separated from God, word separated from referent. Non-referentiality, therefore, is a broken mirror, reminiscent of but never able to reflect a given reality. At the level of man, an unending search for God ensues, an endless consultation of the mirror-image, God-made-man, man-made-God, a system of mutual reflection wherein binarism is portrayed as unity, self-love as love of God. In this relationship, narcissism or homoeroticism, the constant rhythm is the pursuit of direct reference, of access, of penetration, of arrival, of coming, of consummation, of unity, of restoration, of fusion – before a further Fall. The already always-guaranteed failure, the collapse into 'otherness', operates, too, at the level of language, the pursuit of meaning, the hermeneutical resistance to Babelic fragmentation and chaos. But where is woman? Consider the view of Julia Kristeva, in her 1981 essay 'Women's Time':

> when evoking the name and destiny of women, one thinks more of the space generating and forming the human species than of time, becoming or history . . . . Moreover, antipsychiatry . . . proceed[s] to the arrangement of new places, gratifying substitutes that repair old deficiencies in the maternal space . . . which innumerable religions of matriarchal (re)appearance attribute to 'woman', and which Plato . . . designated by the aporia of the chora, matrix space, nourishing, unnameable, anterior to the One, to God and consequently, defying metaphysics.
>
> (Kristeva 1981, 15–16)

The men's time/women's space problematic is crucial to my discussion and, just as I have shown time to be the resolution to masculist erotics in the Neruda poem, so I have chosen a Thénon text which 'works on the difference' between the psychic – and psychoanalytic – structures of time and space:

MURGATORIO

olé olé
olé olá
yo soy el nieto
de mi papá

olé olé
olé olá
voy al piscólogo
a investigar

por qué por qué
pour quoi pour quoi
la vie en rose
no es pour moi

tal vez tal vez
quizá quizá
esto hay que verlo en
profundidad

molta lettura
molta poesia
molta cultura
molta pazzia

Nevsky Stogorny
Drugoi Igrushky
Gogol Andreiev
Chejov Tiburshky

y cuando supe
mis perspectivas
ya me encontraba
en la intensiva

hombre de ciencia
hombre de mundo
oh gran maestro
oh viejo inmundo

todo supiste
todo pudiste
más ahora viste
que esto no es chiste

olé olé
olé olá
nadie con   testa en
el más
a

cá
         (1987, 73–4)

[olé olé/olé olá/I'm the grandson/of my dad/olé olé/olé
olá/I go to the *pys*chologist/to investigate/why why/pour
quoi pour quoi/la vie en rose/is not pour moi/maybe maybe/
perhaps perhaps/this must be seen in/depth/molta lettura/
molta poesia/molta cultura/molta pazzia/Nevsky Stogorny/
Drugoi Igrushky/Gogol Andreiev/Chejov Tiburshky/and

when I knew/my prospects/I was already/in intensive/man
of science/man of the world/oh great maestro/oh dirty old
man/you knew it all/you could do it all/but now you've
seen/that this is no joke/olé olé/olé olá/no one rep   lies
in/the closest/to/here]

Song and dance come together, again, to perform Thénon's re-
siting of that provisional theological space *par excellence*,
Purgatory. 'Murga', an informal, carnival group which chants
often obscene songs to such popular rhythms as the Uruguayan
candombe of the text 'under analysis', serves here to undermine
the inherited psychological 'Grand' narrative. The 'olé olé, olé
olá' mockery of respectable 'ab*ole*ngo', the broaching of the taboo
topic of incest, echoes the problematic 'locura' of the opening
poem. Here, however, the voice is consistently masculine, 'el
nieto de mi papá', who resorts to investigating, to deep analysis,
in pursuit of a happiness more locatable in a Piaf popular
song than in reality. The axial quartets of the poem play with
foreign-sounding, 'hi-falutin'' culture and authorities – though
hinging (*à la* Danny Kaye) on 'molta pazzia', or folly. In light of
this revelation, of the persona's true 'perspectivas' or prospects,
comes the lapse into intensive care. The great Freudian sh(ad)ow
is dethroned, debunked, turned upside-down in carnival-fashion
as 'oh viejo inmundo' – 'piscólogo' [*sic*] (*pys*-artist?). All-know-
ing, all-powerful, in theory; unable, not present, to answer this
query – 'What do I do, not about my past, but my here and
now?'; 'el más a cá', protracted present space, regardless of time,
of history, of lineage, is for ever the unanswerable question, the
confounding disruption, not a 'purgatorio' with the promise of
eventual release into the Divine (and all-resolving) Presence;
merely another obscene, 'murga-torio'. And *murga* is a c(h)ant
obscenely transferable from the context of street to the *con*-text of
the gynaecologist's consulting-room, where a schizoid analysis
splits 'con' from 'testa', interdicting the unity of body and brain,
disallowing the direct response.

For both male and female voices, Thénon's strategy undoes
metaphysical constructs of time, institutional con-tricks of psychology, and gender-based confidence. In so doing, it exemplifies
Kristeva's further claim:

A psychoanalyst would call this 'obsessional time', recognizing
in the mastery of time the true structure of the slave. The

hysteric (either male or female) who suffers from reminiscences would, rather, recognize his or her self in the anterior temporal modalities: cyclical or monumental .... The reader will undoubtedly have been struck by a fluctuation in the term of reference: mother, woman, hysteric . . . I think that the apparent coherence which the term 'woman' assumes in contemporary ideology . . . has the negative effect of effacing the differences among the diverse functions or structures which operate beneath this word .... [T]he real fundamental difference between the two sexes: a difference that feminism has had the enormous merit of rendering painful [is] productive of surprises and of symbolic life in a civilization which, outside the stock exchange and wars, is bored to death.

(Kristeva 1981, 18)

If 'woman' is reduced to any one, given, space – other than that of the consulting-room – it is often to that of her literal sex, the genital place/space which is at once rendered sacred and dissected:

LA DISECCIÓN

cosa casi sagrada
es una cosa casi sagrada
una cosa casi
casi sagrada
tan casi sagrada es esta cosa
que llama poderosamente la atención
la casi absoluta ceguera de la gente
para tener en cuenta que a fin de cuentas
es casi innecesario ver para creer en cosa tan casi
tan consecuentemente casi
sagrada
y es que además este elemento o cosa
ha sangrado
o casi
y podemos apreciarlo por la sombra de lo casi sangrado
sobre el suelo sobre el suelo sobre el mismísimo suelo
y retomando la demostración
tenemos esta cosa
una cosa bah el montón
de cosa casi medio sagrada

y además sangrada y por ende
y en ciernes casi *ad nauseam*
y en otro orden de cosas esta cosa
se resiste con casi todos sus botones
a ser casi descubierta
analizada remolida destripada
en sus causales últimos internos
mejor dicho casi internos porque la cosa en sí
no se deshoja fácilmente
sino capa tras capa
como los alcauciles
los inviernos
y el tiempo ah el tiempo ese factor
disyuntivo que casi aquí se agota
y por lo tanto nos impide
llegar al gran por qué
y al supercómo de esta cosa
casi sagrada
tam tam casi sagrada
tan casi casi
casi tan sagrada.

(ibid., 15–16)

[thing almost sacred/it's a thing almost sacred/a thing almost/almost sacred/so almost sacred is this thing/that it attracts powerfully the attention/the almost absolute blindness of people/to take into account that at all accounts/it's almost unneccesary to see in order to believe in a thing so almost/so consequently almost/sacred/and besides this element or thing/has bled/or almost/and we can appreciate it by the shadow of the almost bled/on the floor on the floor on the very floor/and resuming the demonstration/we have this thing/a thing bah the lot/of a thing almost half sacred/and moreover bloodied and therefore/and blossoming almost *ad nauseam*/and in another order of things this thing/resists with almost all its buttons/being almost uncovered/analysed reground disembowelled/in its ultimate internal causatives/rather almost internal because the thing in itself/does not easily lose its leaves/but layer by layer/like artichokes/winters/and time oh time that factor/disjunctive that almost here runs out/and therefore impedes us/from arriving at the

great why/and at the super how of this thing/almost
sacred/tam tam almost sacred/so almost almost/almost so
sacred.]

What is being probed in 'La Disección' is a space both literal and
metaphorical, an attempt to penetrate that platonic chora
which, to echo Kristeva, was the 'unnamable matrix which
defied metaphysics' (Kristeva 1981, 16). Unnamability is the key
to the poem's organization, for the literal 'subject' of the text is
never divulged, always hidden – too sacred to be uttered – as if
it were equivalent to the Tetragrammaton, the ineffable four-
letter holy name of YHVH/God. The interplay of 'cosa'/'casi'
undoes the plenitude of the object's being; its 'sacred' nature,
therefore, is constructed from the outside, from that 'attentive'
readership whose principal insight is its 'powerful' and 'almost
absolute' blindness ('ceguera'). So obsessed by an economy of
'cuenta'/'cuentas', that calculation comes to replace vision ('es
casi innecesario ver para creer') in the construction of what
begins to appear not so much Godhead as maidenhead (what
has changed since Rubén Darío?). The slippage from 'sagrada' to
'sangrado' proves to be the hinge of blasphemy as a masculist
theological trajectory is mimicked and mocked. For what is left
of guilt (again *mea culpa, mea culpa, mea maxima culpa*) but a
bathetic echo of 'cielo' – 'suelo', 'suelo' 'mismísimo suelo'? For
what bled on the Cross, read what bleeds at the crux; for four-
letter 'unnamability' hear (but do not read) not *Dios* but *coño*.
You doubters, you Thomases who would not believe without
putting your hand into the sacred wound are invited to listen,
and to see, again ('retomando la demostración'). Hear the
'mound' or 'mount' ('una cosa bah el montón'); see the opening
and flowering ('en ciernes') *ad nauseam*; listen to the resistance of
buttons ('en otro orden de cosas') – resistance to the order of
man? Recall, indeed, *Spéculum de l'autre* . . . but not of Irigaray's
'autre femme'; rather, of 'l'autre/homme'.

The fate of the 'cosa . . . a ser casi descubierta/analizada
remolida destripada/en sus causales últimos internos' is a re-
write of Luce Irigaray's analysis of gynaecology, in the hollowed
concave mirror of which the enquiring male often fails to see
'other' than his intruding self:

> porque la cosa en sí
no se deshoja fácilmente

sino capa tras capa
como los alcauciles.

'Alcauciles', artichokes, are stripped layer by layer to reveal a soft
and juicy centre; but, in Argentine slang, 'alcaucil' also means a
buffoon, a silly man. In Chapter 6, we saw Barthes warn readers
to eschew the apricot of interpretation lest at the lapidary kernel
they should break their teeth. Thénon, in turn, replaces Barthes'
many-layered onion with a less tearful, though equally multi-
layered, dissolving, pun.

Now what is 'el tiempo ah el tiempo' doing at the end, the
'resolution', of this poem? Could Thénon be mocking so overtly
the post-penetration metaphysic 'set up' and explored in the
masculist (Neruda) model? Perhaps not post-penetration; and
even if so, penetration is not the be-all-and-end-all. For Time is
called 'ese factor disyuntivo', the possibility of breaking away,
certainly, but never an answer of universal proportions 'al gran
por qué'. The 'supercómo de esta cosa' will remain but provisionally sacred ('casi sagrada') as the poem ends amidst the
ceremonial drum-beats of vestal virginity – or non-virginity
– who knows?

tam tam casi sagrada
tan casi casi
casi tan sagrada.

As for time, female subjectivity would seem to provide a
specific measure that essentially means repetition and eternity
from among the multiple modalities of time known through
the history of civilizations . . . there are cycles, gestation, the
eternal recurrence of a biological rhythm which conforms to
that of nature and imposes a temporality whose stereotyping
may shock, but whose regularity and unison with what is
experienced as extrasubjective time, cosmic time, occasion
vertiginous visions and unnamable jouissance.

This further commentary, coincidentally applicable, to 'La
Disección', is not mine but that of Julia Kristeva (1981, 16).

If, as I have attempted to show, Thénon's poetry performs
counter to the restoration of any one, originary, Edenic place
via a temporal trajectory which stresses disjunction rather than
the conjunctions of a 'historically' linear time, hers is a poetry
too, which revels in the fragmentation of Babel. In language,

otherness and dispersion, far from producing nostalgia or anguish, are exploited and celebrated. Linda R. Boone has written engagingly of a direct parody of a Neruda love-poem, 'Barcarola', namely, Arsenio Cué's 'Si tú te llamaras Babel y no Beba Martínez', in Cabrera Infante's *Tres tristes tigres*: 'In order to satisfy Arsenio's requirements for the perfect woman, Beba must become precisely what she is not: Babel, fluent in witty language of literary wordplay'. Unlike Thénon's poetry, however, Arsenio's language, for Boone, 'is identified as an anti-language ... aimed not toward communication but sheer playfulness' (1990–1, 33, 35). In Cabrera Infante's ingenious *mise en abyme*, the construction of an idealized transformation of Beba into Babel, yet another projection of male readership, is suggestively *culbuté* by being inserted in the (Anglo-Portuguese) banality of Arsenio Cué's name. Thénon's play, too, is both on and with, is both pun and fun, pleasurable steps within the choreography of difference:

AND SO ARE YOU

hay sacarina
la bandada de albatros
o yo qué sé
digo de albatros
dólares
*de albatros*dólares
nunca vi un pájaro pishar eso no quiere decir nada
los canadienses pishan aunque vos no los veas
y los peces
los peces pishan mar
vos sos poeta ¿no?
o Sappho made in Shitland
poetisa
¿no ves que es mujer?
vamos mujer
si no puedes tú con Dios hablar
¿para qué preguntarle si yo alguna vez?
te lo digo personalmente
en efecto
alguna que otra vez te he dejado de adorar
pero el inglés es más práctico
te ingeniás en todas partes

verbigracia en las pudendas
do it   don't
y aunque pronuncies mal
igual te entienden
do it   don't
o te expresás por señas
vieras cómo te arreglás
cómo aprendés a *do it*
cómo *don't* te acostumbrás
cómo hacés *do* lo que querés
it cómo
don't.

(ibid., 13–14)

[there is saccharine/*the flock of albatross/or what do I know/I say*
of albatross/dollars/of *albatross*dollars/*I never saw a bird pish*
that means nothing/Canadians pish although you don't see them/
and fish/fish pish sea/you're a poet, aren't you?/*Or Sappho made*
in Shitland/poetess/can't you see she's a woman?/*let's go*
woman/if you can't speak with God/why ask him if I sometimes?/
I'm telling you personally/in fact/some time or another I have stopped
loving you/but English is more practical/you show ingenuity
everywhere/*for instance in the pudenda/do it don't*/and although
you pronounce badly/they probably understand you/*do it*
don't/or you express yourself by signs/you should see how
you get by/how you learn to *do it*/how *don't* you get the
habit/how you make *do* what you like/*it* how/*don't*.]

Dialogics operate strongly in the title 'And So Are You', anticipating the question 'vos sos poeta ¿no?'. The poet attempting
self-definition depends heavily on the reader/interlocutor – and
vice versa. The saccharine-sweet legacy of the post-Baudelairian
image of a *poète par définition* of 'L'Albatros' ('prince des nuées
. . . exilé sur le sol'), is at once evoked and derided by Thénon's
'de albatros/o yo qué sé'. Intrusively, 'dólares' thrusts writing
forward as profession rather than as confession; 'Confiteor de
l'artiste', for Thénon, involves an economy of art, *'albatros-*
dólares', a rejection of *l'art pour l'art* purity, illustrated by the
four-line bi-lingual play on *'pishar'*. The grossness of tactic
renders 'for the birds' too facile a definition of poet:

vos sos poeta ¿no?

o Sappho made in Shitland
poetisa
¿no ves que es mujer?

The interplay of 'pish' and 'shit' besmirches the ready-made label ineptly attached to the 'poetisa'-inheritor of Sappho. Poet-ess thus becomes the unacceptable term; rejected as forcefully as was the reified 'esa mujer' and, again, in a pastiche of popular art, subverting a famous *bolero*:

¡Ay! mujer, si tú puedes con Dios hablar
Pregúntale si yo alguna vez
Te he dejado de adorar.

[Oh! woman, if you can speak with God/Ask him if I ever/stopped adoring you.]

The 'undoing' of the inherited bolero-perception of woman – a creature who needs to corroborate male declarations of love by reference to masculine authority *par excellence*, the Great-Man-in-the-Sky – says simply: 'Who needs all that? I'm telling you *"en efecto"*, here and now, watch this space, hear this voice. And while we're at it, I have on occasion stopped loving you!'. The sudden shift sideways, to the apparently lateral thought, in English, of the '*do it   don't*', is subtly relevant. For woman as capricious creature of whim, of 'now I love you, now I don't', is not just portrayable in the saccharine poetry of the *bolero* line, where her yes/no is dressed up. Undressed, too, she may playfully change her mind – '*verbigracia en las pudendas*' (eloquent sexuality?); and across language-barriers, regardless of pronunciation, even by sign-language. The final lines of the poem are a bonanza of vertiginous word-play, of pun as fun: 'te arreglás'/ 'get by', 'have your period', 'get made up', and so on. All is a chaotic learning process of 'aprendés', 'acustumbrás', '*do*', '*don't*', '*it*', 'cómo', 'lo que querés' – desire, what you will, or will not (have done to you) – '*don't*'.

The heteroglossic and transcultural, as pseudo-intellectual commerce, are not by any means automatically liberating. One of the things 'done' to poets, even 'woman' poets, is to be anthologized. This particular version of having a label hung round the neck is hilariously broached by Thénon:

LA ANTOLOGÍA

¿tú eres
la gran poetisa
Susana Etcétera?
mucho gusto
me llamo Petrona Smith-Jones
soy profesora adjunta
de la Universidad de Paughkeepsie
que queda un poquipsi al sur de Vancouver
y estoy en Argentina becada
por la Putifar Comissión
para hacer una antología
de escritoras en vías de desarrollo
desarrolladas y también menopáusicas
aunque es cosa sabida que sea como fuere
todas las que escribieron y escribirán en Argentina
ya pertenecen a la generación del 60
incluso las que están en guardería
e inclusísimamente las que están en geriátrico

pero lo que me importa profundamente
de tu poesía y alrededores
es esa profesión – aaah ¿cómo se dice? –
profusión de íconos e índices
¿tú qué opinas del ícono?

¿lo usan todas las mujeres
o es también cosa del machismo?

porque tú sabes que en realidad
lo que a mí me interesa
es no sólo que escriban
sino que sean feministas
y si es posible alcohólicas
y si es posible anoréxicas
y si es posible violadas
y si es posible lesbianas
y si es posible muy muy desdichadas

es una antología democrática
pero por favor no me traigas
ni sanas ni independientes.

(ibid., 69–70)

[you're/the great poetess/Susana Etcetera?/delighted/I'm Petrona Smith-Jones/ I'm associate professor/at the University of Paughkeepsie/which is a teeny-bitsy south of Vancouver/ and I'm in Argentina on a grant/of the Whorefar Commission/ to compile an anthology/of women writers on the road to development/developed and also menopausal/although it's a known fact that come what may/all the women that wrote and will write in Argentina/already belong to the generation of the sixties/including those in the nursery/and even including those in old folk's homes/but what is deeply important to me/about your poetry and its surroundings/is that profession – oooh, how d'you say it?/ profusion of icons and indices/what do you think of the icon?/do all women use it/or is it a macho thing too?/because you know that in reality/what interests me/is not only that they write/but that they are feminists/and if possible alcoholics/and if possible anorexic/and if possible raped/and if possible lesbians/and if possible very very unhappy/ it's a democratic anthology/ but please don't bring me/any sane or independent women.]

Again, the resistance to fixed identity refuses the tired process of 'naming' of the academic interview. What emerges instead is a Rabelaisian feast of perceptions and misperceptions; of cultural difference and condescension (working both ways); of institutions and subversions which, of a sudden, switches from Petrona Smith-Jones and her Putifar Comissión to that no less restrictive missionary band, the radical feminist ghetto-mongers. I take for granted that further commentary on this poem would be superfluous, save to point out the heightened awareness in Thénon's text of the dangerous power which any and all institutions design for 'íconos e índices', instruments which are humorously and healthily eroticized as fetish-gadgets of both men and women. The academic interview itself – when the two cultures involved are North and South – might be subjected to a 'dependency' reading of the lop-sided cultural encounter, the illusion of a multi-voicedness which, in fact, excludes dialogue. An uneven, politically correct 'exchange' (where 'Third World' is avoided in the phrase 'on the road to development') leads only to the new imperative, the 'please don't bring me' (polite) order of a new imperialism, the key note of which is a lack of place for the uncolonized. In short, 'la antología' is always a choice; but a choice which merely parades as 'democrática'. Politically, what system can tolerate persons both sane and independent? Completeness, or closed system, is anathema to the disruptive workings of *Ova completa*. Susana Thénon's anthology is entitled not *Obra completa/Complete Works* but *Ova completa/Complete Ova* (*eggs*) – and will be, for some, no doubt, completely *ova* the top. In her open system, words are abused, in reversal of language-systems' traditional strategies of power. Thénon, the classicist, the translator from ancient Greek, the translator of Rainer Maria Rilke, the multi-lingual, none the less attempts to break free of the constraints, to come out of the closet, of language:

OVA COMPLETA*

Filosofía significa 'violación de un ser viviente'.
Viene del griego *filoso*, 'que corta mucho',
y *fía*, 3a. persona del verbo fiar, que quiere decir
'confiar' y también 'dar sin cobrar *ad referendum*'
Ejercen esta actividad los llamados *friends*
o 'Cofradía de los Sonrientes'
los fiadores – desde luego –,
los que de veras tienen la manija y los que creen tenerla
en la descomunal mezquita de Oj-Alá.

Una vez consumada la filosofía
se hacen presentes por orden de aparición:

la taquería el comisario el juez de la causa
el forense el abogado de oficio el reportero gráfico
el secreto del sumario Max Scheler una familia vecina
un psiquiatra dos guardias

Ya adentro, hay:

1 que perdió entrambas gambas 1 sacerdote
1 indiferente 1 sádico 1 calcomaníaco de Racing
1 (UN) ejemplar del Erasmo Ilustrado para Niños

Ya más
ya bien adentro:

el recuerdo de una frase famosa el olvido de esa
frase famosa al que sigue el olvido de todo lo
famoso y lo que no lo es salvo tu culo

Filosofía significa 'violación de un ser viviente'

cuando tu pena es condonada 26 años después
retomás su ejercicio o te lo ejercen

* OVA: sustantivo plural neutro latino. Literalmente: huevos

COMPLETA: participio pasivo plural neutro latino en
concordancia con huevos. Literalmente: colmados.
Variantes posibles: rellenos, repletos, rebosantes,
henchidos.

(ibid., 31–2)

[Philosophy means 'violation of a living being'/It comes from
the Greek filoso, 'very cutting',/and fía, 3rd person of the verb
fiar, which means/'to trust' and also 'giving without charge
ad referendum'/Carrying out this activity are the so-called
friends/ or 'Confraternity of Smilers'/trusters – of course – ,/
those who have the shackles and those who think they have
them/in the extraordinary mosque of Oj-Alá [if only]/Once
philosophy has been consummated/the following present
themselves in order of appearance:/the police-station the
justice of the peace the trial judge/the pathologist the solicitor
the graphic reporter/the secret of the Max Scheler summary
a neighbouring family/a psychiatrist two policemen/Further
on there are:/1 which lost both legs 1 priest/ 1 indifferent
1 sadist 1 Racing transfer-swopper/1 (UN) example of the
Illustrated Erasmus for Children/And more/even further
in:/the memory of a famous phrase the forgetting of that/
famous phrase followed by the forgetting of everything/
famous and whatever isn't except your arse/Philosophy
means 'violation of a living being'/when your punishment is
condoned 26 years later/ you take up their exercise or they
exercise it for you

* OVA: Latin noun neuter plural. Literally: eggs.

COMPLETA: Latin past participle neuter plural agreeing
with eggs. Literally: topped up. Possible variants: full up,
replete, brimming over, swollen.]

To read the discourse of love, after Thénon, tends to render the
passage from Eros to the erection of an all-embracing world-
view a preposterous enterprise. Much the same can be said
for her puncturing of the inflated ideologies which she detects all

around and throughout history, in her own 'Latin' culture but, equally, in a Graeco-Roman legacy of thought-policing. A 'filoso' cutting-edge is employed to dissect and dismember many a body or confraternity ('Cofradía') of (Make-)Believers, fake believers, unmasked (pre-Rushdie) in 'la descomunal mezquita de Oj-Alá'. Not accidentally, the axis of change from debunking 'Grand Theory' to mocking petty institutionality is the line 'Una vez consumada la filosofía'. Consummation, the summit of masculist self-regard, is promptly followed by a post-coital parade of male bodies: 'taquería', 'comisario', 'juez', 'forense', 'abogado', 'reportero gráfico' and so on. In arch-surrealist fashion, a comically incongruous list divulges 'entrambas gambas' – where else? who else? – '1 sacerdote', alongside the bored, the sadistic, the football-transfer collector. The further in you go, the closer the inspection, the more urgent the need to remember (or to forget) 'una frase famosa', the nearer you get to – the contemplation of your own (infamous) ass.

The total effect of all this verbiage is to (un)cover a stark primal scene of intellectuality construed as incarceration and torture: 'Filosofía significa "violación de un ser viviente"'. Enigmatically, the poem ends. Twenty-six years of punishment, daily exercise sinisterly other than the compulsive repetition of routine: the passage from 'su' to 'te' throws the switch from the exercise of incarcerating philosophy to the philosophy of exercising torture, the clear implication of 'o te lo ejercen' – which brings this discussion of Thénon's poetry to a near-contemporary confrontation with politics:

PUNTO FONAL (TANGO CON VECTOR CRÍTICO)

'la picana en el ropero
todavía está colgada
nadie en ella amputa nada
ni hace sus voltios vibrar'

¡ESO ES DECLAMACIÓN!
(ibid., 47)

[PHONAL POINT (TANGO WITH CRITICAL SLANT)

'the prod in the wardrobe/is still hanging there/no-one amputates anything on it/or makes its volts vibrate'/THAT IS DECLAIMING!]

Alfonsín's first law, a guillotine to prevent military personnel 'acting under orders' from having to face due legal processes, was designated PUNTO FINAL. The instruments of torture, then, and the memories of torturers, are to be hidden away, in the Argentine psyche, as easily as the sadly dormant (*pace* Miguel Cantilo) guitar of the popular tango:

> la guitarra en el ropero
> todavía está colgada
> nadie en ella canta nada
> ni hace sus cuerdas vibrar.

> [the guitar in the wardrobe/ is still hanging there/
> no-one sings anything on it/or makes its strings vibrate.]

The play 'final'/'fonal' occurs at the intersection of politics and art, of direct ideological reference and the intertextual echo of tango. While I have argued throughout this treatment of Thénon's poetry that her word-games disrupt masculist metaphysics, narrow erotics and linear temporality, I would end by stressing her own heightened awareness of the danger inherent in a writing, or a reading, which is too dependent on the ludics of language. It is my recent experience that feminist critical practice is often politically the most subversive. But Thénon is ever prepared to subvert her own practice as exemplified in *Ova completa*:

ROUND 15

> ah sí
> fácil
> *word games*
> tampón de voces tales
> mimpide
> tra
> gar

> más fácil que no hacer
> o hacer nada
> como el tío de dios

> como el tío de dios
> que no hizo nada

volar delalf abeto

me ahogo.

(1987, 75)

[oh yes/easy/word games/tampon of such voices/stops
me/swall/owing/easier than not doing/or doing nothing/
like God's guy/like God's guy/who didn't do anything/to fly
from thealph abet/I smother.]

The spontaneous, arguably facile, way word-games stifle the
personal voice which, even in the most extreme heteroglossia,
will struggle to re-affirm its presence, threatens to render Susana
Thénon as open as Jacques Derrida to accusations of self-
indulgent *jouissance*. Yet in 'Round 15', she goes down ('me
ahogo') struggling. Her attempts to break free of the constraints,
to come out of the closet of language, 'volar delalf abeto', have
been exemplified by her own poetic practice in an undeniably
feminist *Ova completa*. If the text creates a new kind of reader, s/he
must be the judge of whether Thénon's challenge has been 'más
fácil que no hacer/o hacer nada' – in fact must decide, too, on what
she 'gags'.

It will still, and always, be necessary, however, to seek to
avoid preposterous (reading) positions. Positions, for instance,
of repetitive, colonial transfer, as provoked in 'Poema con traduc-
ción simultánea Español–Español'/'Poem with Simultaneous
Translation Spanish to Spanish':

desembarcaron
en 1492 a.D.
        (pisaron
        en 1982 a.D.)
jefes esperaban
en pelota
genuflexos . . .

Cristóforo gatilló el misal
        (Christopher disparó el misil)
dijo a sus pares
        (murmuró a sus secuaces)
coño
        (fuck)
ved aquí nuevos mundos
        (ved aquí estos inmundos)

quedáoslos
  (saqueadlos)
por Dios y Nuestra Reina
  (por Dios y Nuestra Reina)
AMÉN
  (OMEN).

  (ibid., 28)

[They disembarked/in 1492 AD/(they trod/in 1982 AD)/chiefs
were waiting/stark naked/genuflecting/ . . . /Cristóforo triggered the missal/(Christopher fired the missile)/said to his
peers/(whispered to his followers)/*coño*/(fuck)/see here new
worlds/(see here these filthies)/keep them/(sack them)/ for
God and our Queen/(for God and our Queen)/AMEN/
(OMEN).]

If the somewhat less than celebratory pre-quincentenary gift of
Prime Minister Thatcher to the Galtieri regime came ten years
too early, at least the unseemly rush across the South Atlantic,
again to see and sack new worlds, allowed Thénon the time
(she died in 1990) to situate the *translatability* of inseparably eccle-
siastical and military post-colonialism as, also, operative between
Spanish and Spanish, between Spanish Americans and Spanish
Americans. I shall show, in the last chapter, and by analysis of
Guimarães Rosa's 'Seqüência', the workings of difference
between and within personal/libidinal frontiers. Here, Thénon
shows up the virtual taboo subject of *intra*-colonialism. Within
the political/ideological frontiers of Spanish America, there
would appear to be a need *not* (only) for translation of the
message of resistance against cyclical colonizing aggression into
the language (English) of its latest perpetrators but (also) for the
repetition, in difference, to the often indifferent (Spanish
American) other. To any and every Latin American who has said,
since 1982, 'What *we* need is a Margaret Thatcher', the poem
pleads 'coño' (and only in brackets '(fuck)' for the Anglo-Saxons
who never listen until it suits them): 'ved aquí nuevos mundos
. . . quedáoslos . . . por Dios y Nuestra Reina – AMÉN'.

For in the wings, always opportunist, are the listeners – on the
inside as well as on the outside – who will (mis)interpret the plea,
hear differently the same words. Prayer will easily be (mis)read
as imprecation, invitation – '(ved aquí estos inmundos)' . . .
'(saqueadlos)' . . . '(por Dios y Nuestra Reina)' . . . '(OMEN)'.

From *within*, too, comes the subversion, the ominous call for outside intervention by those who have always (all ready) been poised to pounce, and to sack – '(fuck)'.

WORKS CITED

Boone, Linda R. '"Si tú te llamaras Babel . . . "': Love Poetry, Parody and Irony in *Tres tristes tigres*', *Siglo XX/20th Century*, 8.1–2 (1990–1), 31–40.

Browning, D. C. *Everyman's Dictionary of Quotations and Proverbs*. London: Dent, 1962.

Chatman, Seymour (ed.). *Literary Style: A Symposium*. London: Oxford University Press, 1977.

Cixous, Hélène. 'Entretien avec Françoise van Rossum-Guyon', *Revue des sciences humaines*, 168 (1977), 479–93.

Derrida, Jacques and McDonald, Christine V. 'Choreographies [Interview]', *Diacritics*, 12 (1982), 66–76.

Kristeva, Julia. 'Women's Time', *Signs: Journal of Women in Culture and Society*, 7.11 (1981), 13–35.

McGuirk, Bernard. 'From Mirror-State to Mirror-Stage: Reflections on *Modernismo* and *Modernidad*', *Romance Quarterly*. 36.3 (1989), 315–23.

Showalter, Elaine. 'Shooting the Rapids: Feminist Criticism in the Mainstream', *Oxford Literary Review*, 8.1–2 (1986) (*Sexual Difference*), 218–24.

Thénon, Susana. *Ova completa*. Buenos Aires: Sudamericana, 1987.

Winnett, Susan. 'Coming Unstrung: Women, Men, Narrative, and Principles of Pleasure', *Publications of the Modern Language Association of America*, 105.3 (1990), 505–18.

Post-postscript: space, self, other
Latin America and the 'third term'

The era and dimension of the third term are the time, the space and the other we inhabit. Consciously or not, and whether the filter of our awareness be Einstein or Peirce, Bakhtin or Derrida, the provisional binaries in which we are locked are constantly unsettled by the relativities, the interpretants, the dialogics, the differences whereby the play, the shuttle effects, are to be conceived before the dualities, the seductive polarities of our thoughts, the parentheses of our disciplines. In reconceiving the relationships between Latin America and Europe, the risks of relativism can be countered, then, by the rhythms of relativity. But, first, the question of history:

> In 1488, a Senegalese prince, named Bemoin, arrived in Portugal to request military assistance in a civil war. As legal orthodoxy regarded all forms of government as identical, Bemoin was received with enthusiasm by the Portuguese ruler, John II, given a knighthood and provided with a fleet of 20 caravels commanded by a nobleman called Pero Vaz.
>
> Here, however, Bemoin's triumphant engagement with the forces of civilisation ended. Some miles off the African coast he was murdered and thrown over the side, whereupon the task force returned to Portugal. Although Vaz later alleged that Bemoin was plotting against him, the explanation for this piece of perfidy has a much deeper cultural resonance. Translated to Africa, Bemoin was merely an upstart black barbarian – properties which happily invalidated any promises of help he might have been given back in Lisbon.
>
> The spectre of Bemoin survives to haunt much of *European Encounters with the New World*, a little metaphor for European

self-centredness and the frequently confused attitudes that Europeans were prone to demonstrate in their dealings with native races.

(Taylor 1993, 5)

It is not my purpose to propose a reading of the story of Bemoin. I need only underline a text, or context, of threefold interest: (1) the public – that of sovereignty; (2) the private – that of Pero Vaz's power; (3) the particular (my main focus) – that of the narrative specificity of a confrontation of history and textuality, of ideology and epistemology, of materialism and theory.

The text in which I think I am is still that Anglo-Saxon institution, or institutionality, of the present *fin de siècle*, in which I operate as a literary theorist and Latin Americanist, and the inequalities of which I sought to locate at the beginning of this book. The context, eventually, will be my wish to situate a Brazilian writer, João Guimarães Rosa, in the challenging line of thinkers of the third term. My initial aim, however, will be to problematize and characterize, even to personalize, the principal current debate of the institution in which I write: namely, *Post-Structuralism and the Question of History*, as expressed in the title of a book edited by Attridge, Bennington and Young:

> The *question* of history is ... *excessive* with respect to history: this worrying excess no doubt accounts for the repeated calls to 'get *back* to history' and for the accusations that history is what post-structuralism *lacks*. Such attacks invoke history, or History (the capital letter transforming a problem into a magic word) as a given which post-structuralism has somehow, culpably, managed to ignore .... Once this question is opened, it is possible to discern the fundamental complicity which allowed structuralism to cohabit with history.
>
> (Attridge, Bennington and Young 1988, 8–9)

It remains, therefore, to open the question of *space* – space *in* time, *of* the other. And the opening of the question of the other will always operate as excess and trace. I shall juxtapose with the narrative of Bemoin's impact on Europe (and that of Europe's impact on Bemoin) the opinion of Alexander von Humboldt on the decisive effect which America has exercised upon Europe:

> never has a purely material discovery ... produced so extra-ordinary and lasting a moral change. To the late 20th-century

historian this might seem an elementary deduction. In discovering another world, you discover yourself. By incorporating
new phenomena into an existing taxonomy you change,
however marginally, the framework by which you classify
those phenomena. In fact, the new continent seemed to
demand a new literary form, based on observation rather than
canonical prescription, such were the complexities that had to
be rendered into intelligibility. The twitch on the linguistic
thread went further than this, however. Language – 'the
instrument of empire', according to a prescient Renaissance
grammarian – was to the Enlightenment philosophers a symbol
of Western bamboozling of the natives. Lying, as one of
Voltaire's figurative savages puts it, 'is an art of Europe'.

(Taylor 1993, 5)

The relationship between language and lying as instruments of
empire, parallel to what might be said of Bemoin, of Humboldt,
or of history as a discipline, was developed more than a decade
ago by the Uruguayan critic Ángel Rama. In Europe, the legacy
of Rama's thought on the *founding* of Latin America is slowly
being absorbed and propagated, an antidote to inappropriate
utopian notions and a reminder, in his words, that the history
of *la ciudad letrada*, from the remodelling of Tenochtitlan to the
designing of Brasilia, has been 'un parto de la inteligencia': in
other words, a *brain-child*. As if America were a text to be written,
from *tabula rasa* emptiness – and upon a 'vide papier' which
prompts me to reformulate Mallarmé, 'ce n'est pas avec des
pierres qu'on fait une citée mais avec des *mots* – generations of
Europeans and Eurocentrics have come to write the pages
of Latin American culture propagating twin illusions: first, that it
is ever possible to begin *ex nihilo*; second, that any repetition of the
theological formula *in principio erat Verbum* disguises an ulterior
ordering presence or power. The indelible imprint on Ángel Rama
of Michel Foucault's *Les Mots et les choses* is again clear and, thus,
the city is construed not as the locus of mere *gouvernement* but
as that of *gouvernementalité*. For generations of urban, bourgeois,
writers – of narratives, fictions, or histories with or without
capitals – the sign is to be seen as ever more distant from its
referent, causing a construction of national, romantic ideologies,
fleshed out with the mythemes of nostalgia, pride in the past and
its conservative values. Rama situates this deliberate ideologizing
or *trans-culturation* (the key title-word of a later book) in the

passing from clerical to lay control of the writing implement. Thus, 'the city was sited and traced according to the ground plan and drawing that were made for it on paper' (Rama 1984, 9) describes not merely the founding of Lima by Pizarro in 1535, but traces the epistemologically irreversible equation of: *sword = cross = pen*.

Where Rama is relatable to the *question* of history is in his refusal to fall victim to the notorious misreading of the post-structuralist insight that there is nothing outside the text. For the manipulation which occurs within 'the lettered city' is ever identified by him as both ideologically and oneirically utopian: 'The dream of an order served to perpetuate power and to conserve the socio-economic and cultural structure which that power guaranteed. And, further, it was imposed on whichever discourse opposed that power, obliging it to pass, first, through the dream of another order' (ibid., 11). The impact of *La ciudad letrada*, then, was the tellingly simple polemical insistence that, in any society, the 'letrados' are to be seen as *implicated*, as wielders of the historical (dis)course, never its merely passive or observant transcriptors. The legacy of Ángel Rama will no doubt meet constant resistance from that Latin American literate hegemony whose best interests demand that they hide behind a naive, reflectionist view of the discourse of history, sociology and literature. Their survival as 'helpless', 'unembroiled' but parasitic feeders on the body politic derives from an *a priori* refutation of Rama's thesis. Concomitantly, their European equivalents may be said to feed parasitically on the otherness of Latin America, on its exoticism, its utopian potential or exploitability – and the line of precursors is impressive, from Montaigne to Humboldt, from Keyserling to Kissinger: all occupiers of Latin American *spaces*. My meditation on the spaces not of Latin America *in* Europe but on the interpenetrated spaces of Latin America *and* Europe returns to a Portuguese handling of the problem, first through Camões and then in a text by Fernando Pessoa. The former will point to a Renaissance response to other worlds somewhat subtler than the arguably more feudal dispatching of Bemoin. The latter may be read as a subtle criticism of that by now familiar tendency to 'go transcendental' which has bedevilled so many textual (and real) encounters of the Eurocentric self with its other. Conceived thus, any *other* space becomes, inevitably, a dangerous lure, a *locus amoenus*.

By definition, the *locus amoenus* is a classically derived, literary device, the 'pleasant place', of reality or dream, of idyll or revel, of illusion or delusion. The notion of 'place' is however, already, always *textual*: a construction, readily subjectable to deconstruction(s), from the primitive to the psychoanalytical. It might even, therefore, be construed as a prim(aev)al scene, in which are played out the fantasies, aspirations, fears and suppressions of an individual writer, culture or tradition. The link between the primaeval and the primal is, thus, deliberate. For the *locus amoenus* is part of a 'back to nature' simplicity, and, at the same time, part of a forward-looking, utopian complexity which drives ever 'beyond the pleasure principle', ever beyond mere dalliance to a *higher* reality principle.'It is thus in a markedly post-Freudian critical perspective that I situate myself at the very moment I situate Europe's textualizing of the African, the Latin American, the Indian or any other encounter with otherness. In Camões' *Lusiads*, such transcendence takes a visionary form. Tethys, the sea goddess, in the final canto of the poem, seeks to fulfil Venus' ambition of bringing forth, from the union of Portuguese and nymphs, a new and vital progeny, able to surpass mortal, political ambition, 'mere' empire. Though traditionally interpreted as Camões' vision of a Christian realm of harmonious love, the obvious *dissatisfaction* with mortal possibilities suggests, too, an alternative, pagan reading: namely, the coming-together – on a metaphorical Isle of Love – of conquest (possession), *jouissance* and transcendence of death, the Freudian triad of an eternal sexuality. If the metaphor of the island be taken not as C. M. Bowra found it, as 'worse than an anti-climax' (1945, 119), but as the endlessly deferred, non-consummated, therefore never mortal, resistance to climax/death, then the *heroic* trajectory of Camões' use of the *locus amoenus* becomes apparent. For Camões the *humanist* (rather than the theist) sought transcendence not in the passage from reality into fantasy but in the incorporation of the fantastic into the real, the virtual. Just as, historically, the textualizing of all encounters will provoke readings which, in Machereyan parlance, reveal *symptomatically* the intercultural layers of the construction of colonial discourses, similarly, contemplation of the *locus amoenus* will always operate at an inter-textual level. For in markedly self-conscious fashion, the greatest of Portuguese poets since Camões, Fernando Pessoa, habitually echoes and exploits poetic – and ideological – traditions such as

the one discussed here. The bilingual Pessoa draws not only on
Portuguese and English heritages, but also on the mainstream
devices of European poetry since classical times:

Não sei se é sonho, se realidade,
Se uma mistura de sonho e vida,
Aquela terra de suavidade
Que na ilha extrema do sul se olvida.
É a que ansiamos. Ali, ali
A vida é jovem e o amor sorri.

Talvez palmares inexistentes,
Áleas longínquas sem poder ser,
Sombra ou sossego dêem aos crentes
De que essa terra se pode ter.
Felizes, nós? Ah, talvez, talvez,
Naquela terra, daquela vez.

Mas já sonhada se desvirtua,
Só de pensá-la cansou pensar,
Sob os palmares, à luz da lua,
Sente-se o frio de haver luar.
Ah, nesta terra também, também
O mal não cessa, não dura o bem.

Não é com ilhas do fim do mundo,
Nem com palmares de sonho ou não,
Que cura a alma seu mal profundo,
Que o bem nos entra no coração.
É em nós que é tudo. É ali, ali,
Que a vida é jovem e o amor sorri.
                    (Pessoa 1980, 160–1)

[I know not whether it is dream or reality,/or a mixture of
dream and life,/that land of sweetness which/on an island far
to the south is forgotten./It is the one we long for./There,
there life is youthful and love smiles. Perhaps inexistent palm-
trees,/distant alleys unable to be,/shade or rest may they give
to the believers/that that land can be had./Happy, we? Ah,
perhaps, perhaps,/in that land, at that time. But once dreamt
it loses value,/just to think of it has tired thinking,/under the
palm-trees, in the light of the moon,/is felt the cold of it being
moonlight./Ah, in that land also, also evil does not cease,

good does not last./It is not with islands at the world's end,/nor with palm-trees of dream or not,/that the soul cures its deep ill,/that good enters the heart. It is in us that everything is. It's there, there,/that life is youthful and love smiles.]

The opening of Pessoa's poem serves as a reminder of Antoine Compagnon's claim: 'to write, since it is always to rewrite, is no different from citing . . . to read or to write is to perform an act of citation' (1979, 34). Thus, the fabric of the first stanza is woven from by now familiar threads or lines. To any Portuguese reader, the forgotten island in the south instantly recalls the *Lusiads* and the Island of Love. Even for us, in the present act of writing or reading, Veloso's cry re-echoes in the poem, inviting once again the curious pursuit of some resolution to a Renaissance dilemma, the paradoxical relation between *ser* and *parecer*, between 'being' and 'seeming', between *sonho* and *vida*, between 'dream' and 'life'. Ironically, the words held back to the very end of the first sentence are belied by the irrepressible, familiar resonances that go before; for 'se olvida'/'is forgotten' becomes an impossibility, given the clarity of exposition and re-evocation of this particular 'terra de suavidade', of this particular instance of the *locus amoenus*. The lack of forgetfulness, of oblivion, is confirmed in the blunt and generalized 'É a que ansiamos'; for 'ansiamos' means not only 'we long for' but also 'we fret for', 'are anxious for'. The crucial transition from the opening first-person singular verb to the first-person plural presumes to bring the 'island' out of a specific into a universal consciousness, one associated, moreover, with youth and love. What had been, initially, conceived in *spatial* terms now assumes a *temporal* dimension, too. The retrospective evocation of a place free of ageing, full of love and laughter, recalls the first, backward-looking element of our earlier definition, psychologically, of the *locus amoenus*. The next stanza immediately broaches the second element; the forward-looking 'Talvez'.

Whether you exist or not, palm-fronded images – probably never virtualizable – at least give substance to those who believe in you. The desire for protection ('shade') or consolation ('rest') functions as a resistance against that intuition of mortality/ *Thanatos* which lies beyond the principle of ageless love/ *Eros*. Whereas 'É a que ansiamos' (anxiety) was expressed as an affirmation, 'Felizes, nós?' (contentment) remains for ever hypothetical, an unanswered interrogative – unless, still, within the realm of 'maybe', the sphere of sigh ('Ah') and the repeated 'talvez, talvez', the place and the time firmly distanced, in 'naquela', 'daquela', pick up and echo the far-off land of line 3, 'aquela terra'.

Though the construction of a convoked, never virtual, dream-land, in the first two stanzas, has been most fragile, the very effort of dreaming it has proved burdensome to thought. Previously comforting shade turns to shadow, the source of light is now the moon – a chilling moonlight, a chill realization; there can be no permanent suspension of duration, the undermining of youth and well-being by age and ill. In the final stanza, therefore, the very idea of a *locus amoenus* as having any relevant external existence is dismantled. A series of negative particles ('não', 'nem', 'não') interrupts the flow of thought, obstacles to the construction of either palm-trees or dreams, hammer-blow reminders of the irrelevance of utopianism – but only in so far as it is traditionally constructed, *outside* the self. The anti-dualist, full-blown existentialism of the final two lines performs a commentary on the tradition and the psychology of the *locus amoenus*. Camões' attempted re-integration of the fantastic, the erotic, the dreamt, into the principle of reality, political, temporal, mortal, is re-read, re-vised, re-vived. An existentialist *misprision* swerves away from the humanist vision, but, at the same time, firmly rejects the Romantic heritage of mere disaffection at the loss of Eden. For the Romantic poets in general, dualism reigned, the gap of alienation loomed wide (as it was soon to do for Karl Marx). While Fernando Pessoa's attempted re-integration of inner and outer experience is hardly expressed socio-politically, at least the generalized use of 'ansiamos' and 'É em nós que é tudo' makes no class distinction between the 'paltry' and the 'noblest', say, of Byron's *Childe Harold*. By no means has the *locus amoenus* been abolished. Rather does Pessoa's poem subject it to a process of deconstruction, whereby the metaphor is revealed as containing both a present and an absent term, existence (at the level of dream) and inexistence (at the level of experience). The interplay between the two levels constitutes the poem, the rhythm encapsulated in 'Talvez . . . inexistentes'/'Perhaps . . . inexistent'. But the poem is kinetic, never static, indulging the trace and supplement of whichever term is *momentarily* absent. Might it be that Fernando Pessoa, in his poetic practice, has intuited and anticipated the insight of

Jacques Derrida of my locating mosaic: 'Play is the disruption of presence . . . . Play is always play of absence and presence, but if it is to be thought radically, play must be conceived of before the alternative of presence and absence. Being must be conceived as presence or absence on the basis of play and not the other way round' (Derrida 1978, 292)? The *locus amoenus*, then, is still at – and in – play.

Let us now play within the spaces of a playful text, the microstory of the Guatemalan contemporary writer Augusto Monterroso:

SINFONÍA CONCLUIDA

– Yo podría contar terció el gordo atropelladamente – que hace tres años en Guatemala un viejito organista de una iglesia de barrio me refirió que por 1929 cuando le encargaron clasificar los papeles de música de La Merced se encontró de pronto unas hojas raras que intrigado se puso a estudiar con el cariño de siempre y que como las acotaciones estuvieran escritas en alemán le costó bastante darse cuenta de que se trataba de los dos movimientos finales de la *Sinfonía inconclusa* así que ya podía yo imaginar su emoción al ver bien clara la firma de Schubert y que cuando muy agitado salió corriendo a la calle a comunicar a los demás su descubrimiento todos dijeron riéndose que se había vuelto loco y que si quería tomarles el pelo pero que como él dominaba su arte y sabía con certeza que los dos movimientos eran tan excelentes como los primeros no se arredró y antes bien juró consagrar el resto de su vida a obligarlos a confesar la validez del hallazgo por lo que de ahí en adelante se dedicó a ver metódicamente a cuanto músico existía en Guatemala con tan mal resultado que después de pelearse con la mayoría de ellos sin decir nada a nadie y mucho menos a su mujer vendió su casa para trasladarse a Europa y que una vez en Viena pues peor porque no iba a ir decían un *Leiermann** guatemalteco a enseñarles a localizar obras perdidas y mucho menos de Schubert cuyos especialistas llenaban la ciudad y que qué tenían que haber ido a hacer esos papeles tan lejos hasta que estando ya casi desesperado y sólo con el dinero del pasaje de regreso conoció a una familia de viejitos judíos que habían vivido en Buenos Aires y

* organillero

hablaban español los que lo atendieron muy bien y se pusieron nerviosísimos cuando tocaron como Dios les dio a entender en su piano en su viola y en su violín los dos movimientos y quienes finalmente cansados de examinar los papeles por todos lados y de olerlos y de mirarlos al trasluz por una ventana se vieron obligados a admitir primero en voz baja y después a gritos ¡son de Schubert son de Schubert! y se echaron a llorar con desconsuelo cada uno sobre el hombro del otro como si en lugar de haberlos recuperado los papeles se hubieran perdido en ese momento y que yo me asombrara de que todavía llorando si bien ya más calmados y luego de hablar aparte entre sí y en su idioma trataron de convencerlo frotándose las manos de que los movimientos a pesar de ser tan buenos no añadían nada al mérito de la sinfonía tal como ésta se hallaba y por el contrario podía decirse que se lo quitaban pues la gente se había acostumbrado a la leyenda de que Schubert los rompió o no los intentó siquiera seguro de que jamás lograría superar o igualar la calidad de los dos primeros y que la gracia consistía en pensar si así son el *allegro* y el *andante* cómo serán el *Scherzo* y el *allegro ma non troppo* y que si él respetaba y amaba de veras la memoria de Schubert lo más inteligente era que les permitiera guardar aquella música porque además de que se iba a entablar una polémica interminable el único que saldría perdiendo sería Schubert y que entonces convencido de que nunca conseguiría nada entre los filisteos ni menos aún con los admiradores de Schubert que eran peores se embarcó de vuelta a Guatemala y que durante la travesía una noche en tanto la luz de la luna daba de lleno sobre el espumoso costado del barco con la más profunda melancolía y harto de luchar con los malos y con los buenos tomó los manuscritos y los desgarró uno a uno y tiró los pedazos por la borda hasta no estar bien cierto de que ya nunca nadie los encontraría de nuevo al mismo tiempo – finalizó el gordo con cierto tono de afectada tristeza – que gruesas lágrimas quemaban sus mejillas y mientras pensaba con amargura que ni él ni su patria podrían reclamar la gloria de haber devuelto al mundo unas páginas que el mundo hubiera recibido con tanta alegría pero que el mundo con tanto sentido común rechazaba.

(Monterroso 1981, 31–3)

FINISHED SYMPHONY

['I could tell the story', broke in the fat man hurriedly, 'that a little old local church organist told me three years ago in Guatemala about how in 1929 when he was given the job of classifying the musical manuscripts of the church of La Merced he suddenly came across some strange papers which feeling intrigued he began to study with his usual care and which because the marginal notes were written in German it took him some time to realize were the last two movements of the *Unfinished Symphony* so I could imagine how he felt when he saw the clear signature of Schubert and that when he ran out into the street feeling very excited to communicate to everyone his discovery they all laughed and said that he had gone mad and that he was trying to pull their legs but because he knew what he was talking about and was certain that the two movements were as excellent as the first two he didn't give up but rather swore to dedicate the rest of his life to make them admit the validity of the discovery because of which from then on he devoted himself to seeing systematically every musician in Guatemala with such bad results that after falling out with most of them without saying anything to anyone and above all not to his wife he sold his house and moved to Europe and that once in Vienna well it was worse because *they* said that a Guatemalan *Leiermann** was not going to tell *them* how to find lost works and above all not Schubert's whose specialists filled the city and why would those papers have gone so far away until almost despairing and with no more than the money for his return ticket he met a family of old Jews who had lived in Buenos Aires and spoke Spanish and they looked after him very well and got very nervous when they played the two movements as best they could on their piano viola and violin and who in the end tired of examining the papers on every side and of smelling them and looking at them against the light were obliged to admit first in an undertone and then shouting They're by Schubert! They're by Schubert! and they burst into inconsolable tears each on the other's shoulder as if instead of the papers being rediscovered they had just then been lost and that I'd be surprised that still

* organist

crying although now more calm and after talking together on one side and in their own language they tried to persuade him rubbing their hands together that the movements despite being so good added nothing to the merit of the symphony as it was now and on the contrary it could be said that they reduced it because people had got used to the legend that Schubert tore them up or didn't even write them sure that he would never improve on or equal the quality of the first two movements and that the fun was in thinking if the *allegro* and *andante* are like this how might the *scherzo* and *allegro ma non troppo* be and that if he respected and really loved the memory of Schubert the most intelligent thing was to allow *them* to keep that music because apart from the fact that an inter-minable polemic was going to be unleashed the only one who would lose by it would be Schubert and that then convinced that he would never achieve anything with philistines and still less with Schubert's admirers who were worse he embarked on his return journey to Guatemala and during the crossing one night when the light of the moon was falling full on the foamy side of the boat with the deepest sadness and tired of fighting against the bad *and* the good he took the manuscripts and tore them up one by one and threw the pieces overboard till he was not absolutely sure that nobody would be unable to find them again at the same time' – concluded the fat man with a certain tone of affected sadness – as large tears burned his cheeks and whilst he thought bitterly that neither he nor his homeland could claim the glory of having returned to the world pages which the world would have received with such joy but which the world with such common sense rejected.]

Far be it from me, as in the case of my approach to that encounter with history, narrativity and, no doubt, fiction, implied in the story of the Senegalese Bemoin, to propose a reading of the micro-story as Augusto Monterroso's Guatemalan updating of intercultural transfer. Rather, inspired for the most part by the brilliant insights of Mark I. Millington's treatment of the text and drawing attention to the resounding recent debates it has set off (*Siglo XX/Twentieth Century*, 1995), I prefer to enlist some of those concerns and to list a series of issues most related to my eventual objective of highlighting the workings, the lurkings of the 'third term':

- a fable of exchange, of intercultural transfer?
- a theory of transcultural reading?
- cultural production conceived of as a property right?
- differential 'locations' of power (à la Albert Memmi): *inside, outside, between*?
- Latin America reading Europe reading Latin America reading Europe – and so on?
- the story reading Vienna/Schubert reading the old man reading culture – and so on?
- the institutional problem of a provisional binary: a Latin American versus a European 'criticism'? A Latin American 'criticism' *in* Europe (cf. the interpenetration of academic 'Latin Americanism', in the United States and Europe, by Latin Americans – an example not of difference *between* but of difference *within*)?
- a complication *within* binary terms, the tracing of 'fault lines' in differences of economies, cultures, resources, interests?
- related differential pressures within respective 'national' institutions, e.g. belated 'Cultural Studies' in the United States dressed up as 'New Historicism'; belated 'post-structuralism' in the United Kingdom apologetically reapproaching history ('History'); Argentine 're-writings' of literary history; Brazilian play (preoccupation) with translation?
- 'Europe' as but one of many spaces from which to read Latin American literature, further multiple differentiation *within* another provisional binary: that of hegemonic (positivist) versus marginal (theoretical) institutional approaches?
- the Homi Bhabha problematic of theory's status as (just) another Western export? (can 'method' ever be smoothly transferable?)
- or Fredric Jameson's problematic of the critic's viewing, through the microscope, his or her own eyeball?
- Robert Young's disarming and sober suggestion that there can be perhaps no *unlearning* of privilege (a further, and no less false, utopianism)?
- Gayatri Spivak's proposition that knowledge is never adequate to its object?
- an extreme example of 'brutal othering' (the knowledge of the little old man *is* real but, in Vienna, unacceptable)?
- 'othering' as aggressive marginalization, the dismissal, rejection or belittling of the other in an attempt to build the self as sovereign subject or culture?

- the question of *who* is permitted to produce knowledge?
- interpenetration as an alternative whereby 'identity' is structured dialogically?
- a counter to monological 'mastery', precluding simple dichotomies or comfortable assumptions of smooth access(ibility)?
- a demonstration that no reader is ideally placed, that there is no such location; that a so-called 'insider' to a culture will always have multiple locations within it; that access to a certain privilege is none the less restricted in scope and capacity for knowledge?
- a meditation on the possibility that different critical practices may not *re*place, but creatively *dis*place, one another in the process of *negotiating* with the other?
- and, uncomfortably, returning to two examples of the function of difference not only between but also within cultures, a reminder that the brutal othering suffered by the old man derives first from the other Guatemalans who laugh at him – that the narrative function of the Jews, now in Vienna but before that in Buenos Aires, is double (duplicitous), as they accept Schubert but reject the old man?
- a lesson, not least, in the subversive power of textuality? A 'text' without punctuation, without breaks, without separations between sentences, encounters, cultures, negotiations – belied, in reading, by the infinite *puncta* of cultural differences of the 'story' it narrates?

It may suffice to suggest that Monterroso's micro-story raises again the theoretical issues with which I began this discussion. A potentially abstract debate on the third term, on relativities, interpretants, dialogics and differences, irrefutably shifts to the political and ideological dimensions of intercultural transfer, translation, transgression. 'Sinfonía concluida' is notably resistant, as was the case with Fernando Pessoa's poem, to the dangers of 'going transcendental' in the encounter with the other. In the conceiving of 'spaces', however, any construction of a habitable, livable, pleasurable location will run the risk of becoming that dangerously utopian *locus amoenus* to which so much of this discussion has been devoted. The principal quality of 'aquela terra de suavidade' – that land of sweet *dreams* – was its capacity never to alter. Might the binary echo of a Peter Pan's *Neverneverland* be audible thus in the Guatemalans', in the Vienna Jews', reluctance to admit glimpsed change? Against one set of echoes may be set another. Any reminiscence of the long-sought land of milk and honey of the Judaic tradition might, for instance, be juxtaposed with the refusal of the Argentine Jews of Monterroso's Vienna to allow *anything*, be it symphony or journey, to be finished. For, notwithstanding a non-teleological strain of Jewish mysticism to which I shall refer through Emmanuel Levinas, the shadow of disastrous 'final' solutions (readings) of Holocaust is cast long.

Glimpsed change suffuses the texts with which I choose to suspend and project the present discussion. As at the outset, however, I am going to offer not an interpretation, only an *inter-penetration*, of the Millington *mosaic* of different voices:

- 'the act of cultural enunciation, the *place of utterance*, is crossed by the *différance* of writing or *écriture*' (Homi Bhabha)
- 'the word in language is half someone else's' (Mikhail Bakhtin)
- 'what is disclosed is what is concealed, that is the *fact* of concealment' (Marjorie Garber).

What, then, of Brazil? In a word (with three words in advance of its articulation, the self-same word thrice spoken prior to its utterance as object), a text of João Guimarães Rosa. In the short story 'A terceira margem do rio'/ 'The Third Bank of the River', the title signals *not* impossibility but necessity. The most quintessential binary, in referential terms – river banks – must still encounter another measurability, a relativity. Echoing the division of its self as object into a flowing challenge to its own confining binaries, the water of the river is (first) textualized in three terms: 'o rio-rio-rio' . . .

Sou homem de tristes palavras. De que era que eu tinha tanta, tanta culpa? Se o meu pai, sempre fazendo ausência: e o rio-rio-rio, o rio-pondo perpétuo . . . . Chamei, umas quantas vezes. E falei, o que me urgia, jurado e declarado, tive que reforçar a voz - '*Pai, o senhor está velho, já fez o seu tanto . . . Agora, o senhor vem, não carece mais . . . . O senhor vem, e eu, agora mesmo, quando que seja, a ambas vontades, eu tomo o seu lugar, do senhor, na canoa . . .* ' E, assim dizendo, meu coração bateu no compasso do mais certo. Ele me escutou. Ficou em pé. Manejou remo n'água, proava para cá, concordado. E eu tremi, profundo, de repente: porque, antes, ele tinha levantado o braço e feito um saudar de gesto – o primeiro, depois de tamanhos anos decorridos! E eu não podia . . . . Por favor, arrepiados os cabelos, corri, fugi, me tirei de lá, num procedimento desatinado. Porquanto que ele me pareceu vir: da parte de além. E estou pedindo, pedindo, pedindo um perdão.

Sofri o grave frio dos medos, adoeci. Sei que ninguém soube mais dêle. Sou homem, depois dêsse falimento? Sou o que não foi, o que vai ficar calado. Sei que agora é tarde, e temo abreviar com a vida, nos rasos do mundo. Mas, então, ao menos, que, no artigo da morte, peguem em mim, e me depositem também numa canoinha de nada, nessa água, que não pára, de longas beiras: e, eu, rio abaixo, rio a fora, rio a dentro – o rio.

(Guimarães Rosa 1981, 31–2)

[I'm a man of sad words. About what was it that I had such, such, guilt? If my father, always being absent: and the river-river-river: the river – growing perpetual . . . . I called, several times. And I spoke, what urged me, sworn and declared, I had to strengthen my voice: – '*Father, you are old, you've done your utmost . . . Now come, there's nothing left to do . . . Come, and I, right now whenever it be, with both wills, I'll take your place, yours, in the boat! . . . '* And, so saying, my heart beat to the surest rhythm.

He heard me. He stood upright. He dipped oar in the water, headed the prow this way, in agreement . . . And I trembled, deeply, suddenly: because, before, he had raised his arm and made a greeting of gesture – the first, after so many years gone by! And I couldn't . . . Out of fright, hair on end, I ran, I fled, I got out of there, in a headlong dash. For as long as he appeared to come at me: from beyond. And I am asking, asking, asking for a pardon.

I suffered the grave cold of fears, I fell ill. I know no one knew more of him. Am I a man, after that failing? I am what wasn't, what will be silenced. I know that now it's late, and I fear cutting life short, in the flat of the world. But, then, at least, in the article of death, let them take me, and put me in a little boat of nothing, in that water, which doesn't stop, of long banks: and I, down-river, out-river, in-river – the river.]

The mournful discourse of guilt, of lost patriarch, the indelibly Judaic heritage of Freud, of Harold Bloom, of George Steiner, of Levinas? And of how many Brazilian *novos cristãos*? Of how many

Spanish American *conversos*? Undoubtedly a trajectory of non-arrival, of non-finding – but not accidental. For the imperative of ethics pervades the text. [It is not sufficient to situate the discourse of the third term in the *merely* referential, linguistic realm of 'o rio-rio-rio, o rio'] For the third bank is never other than virtual, the *necessary* (however unattainable) objective of search, of enquiry, rabbinically echoing in 'pedindo, pedindo, pedindo' which, in the shift from object ('rio') to trajectory ('pedindo') does not equal the final term, 'perdão'. Mathematically $\neq$, the 'does not equal' sign of differential relations bears the weight and the burden of a realization which proves worse than death: namely, the situation of self in the space of non-teleology. In the process of transition, the opening three-term, one term of 'o rio-rio-rio, o rio' has been subjected to a process of change, of becoming. For now, as was the case in Fernando Pessoa's exploration of self in other in space, Guimarães Rosa's meditation introduces the kinesis of instability to the virtually untranslatable 'rio abaixo, rio a fora, rio a dentro'. Adverbial relations, relativities, serve to unsettle the referential or emotional support of the river(-system) as a (notionally) habitable space. It will always have the third bank – the bank of potential. And so the textualizing – fictionally, narratively, historically – of the third term echoes both poetically and ethically through Latin American, European, Latin American *spaces* as the play of the interpenetration of self in other in self extends ever across, ever *trans*(Atlantically) only as a soon-to-be-unsettled term of provisionality. Play before presence and absence, before self, before other?

Returning to my opening statement, 'the era and dimension of the third term are the time, the space and the other we inhabit', I am struck by the manner in which Guimarães Rosa's text *performs* an 'unsettling of the provisional binaries'. In what 'space' is the action of encounter to be situated? Not, it seems, *between* the 'banks', nor even *within* the single term 'o rio'. For if the word is 'half someone else's', it is only conceivable (situatable) within a dialogics. Before even arriving at the word – in this case 'o rio' – we must pass through the shuttle effect of 'o rio-rio-rio' – and into what have we entered? What is to be encountered? Nothing directly, no sudden pardon, but ever the rhythm of the absent term's ('fazendo ausência') *becoming* perpetual ('pondo perpétuo') . Before 'perdão', then, will ever intervene the triple, the echoing, 'pedindo', 'pedindo', 'pedindo'. And will there ever be an end (an illusory teleology) between the self and the object; between, even, the self and the word; between, here, 'eu' and 'rio'? If we are to know of that trajectory we must pass from 'eu', through 'rio abaixo', through 'rio a fora', through 'rio adentro' – *down*-river? *beyond* the river?? (drowning) *in* the river??? For the trajectory of the third term offers no guarantee of arrival, survival.

'In Search of the Third Bank of the River: Reflections on the Burden of the Past in Contemporary Brazilian Culture', Nicolau Sevcenko's seminal meditation on the cultural unconscious, situates the presence of magic 'as one of the matrices of the Brazilian cultural tradition. A threshold which we never cross, and which even now we do not confront. A symbolic prison, so to speak, on the bank of the river, the edge of a sea or cliff, from which bridges are not built and from which we cannot set off back to the interior whence we came, because of the conviction that reality lies neither at the beginning nor at the end, but in the middle of the crossing. It is now an advantage for this restrictive imperative of magic to be laid bare, but how many alternatives for the imagination are there flourishing on the third bank of the river?' (Sevcenko 1992, 83). Sevcenko himself proposes several alternatives, none more memorable than that of the songwriter Caetano Veloso's 'Clarice' of 1968:

> Clarice never reveals any preferences nor displays a single inch of her body, which is maddeningly desired, yet remains always completely concealed. The men, sick with desire, spend their lives wondering what mystery it is that makes her keep her body and heart in absolute seclusion. Until the day when the man she secretly loves departs in a ship for the distant sea, destined never to return. On that day, as the ship draws away from the port, at the sea's edge, Clarice removes all her clothes, indifferent to the population of the village, until she is completely naked, so that her beloved can see her like this and remember her forever, remaining eternally faithful to her. The man who never had her where she always was, will have her forever where she has never been.
>
> (Sevcenko 1992, 84)

The haunting beauty of Clarice's gesture can hardly mask, indeed also lays bare, a libidinal economy which I shall enter in a brief juxtaposition of two very different positings of the power of the river; first, in the Mexican Juan Rulfo's short story 'Es que somos muy pobres'/'The Fact is We're Very Poor' (1953), and, second, in Guimarães Rosa's 'Seqüência'/'Sequence' (1962). Both might be seen as engaging dialectically with economies inseparable from nascent adolescent sexuality. Both might serve to illustrate the claims I made in my 'Fore-word: locating inequality', in respect of William Ray, regarding post-structuralism's interest in the propensity of two texts to function as a mutual purge as, in dialectical engagement one with the other, the stories open each other up, using the logic of the other's system of (co-ercive) authority to point to that system's shortcomings.

In the case of the Rulfo text, the river functions in, and as, a predominantly materialist horizontal:

> Aquí todo va de mal en peor .... Y apenas ayer, cuando mi hermana Tacha acababa de cumplir doce años, supimos que la vaca que mi papá le regaló para el día de su santa se la había llevado el río ... mi papá con muchos trabajos había conseguido a *la Serpentina*, desde que era una vaquilla, para dársela a mi hermana, con el fin de que ella tuviera un capitalito y no se fuera a ir de piruja como lo hicieron mis otras dos hermanas las más grandes .... Y eso ahora va a estar difícil. Con la vaca era distinto, pues no hubiera faltado quién se hiciera el ánimo de casarse con ella, sólo por llevarse también aquella vaca tan bonita .... Y Tacha llora al sentir que su vaca no volverá porque se la ha matado el río .... Por su cara corren chorretes de agua sucia como si el río se hubiera metido dentro de ella .... El sabor a podrido que viene de allá salpica la cara mojada de Tacha y los dos pechitos de ella se mueven de arriba abajo, sin parar, como si de repente comenzaran a hincharse para empezar a trabajar por su perdición.
>
> (Rulfo 1975, 145–9)

> [Here everything is going from bad to worse .... And only yesterday, when my sister Tacha had just had her twelfth birthday, we learned that the cow that my papa gave her for her saint's day had been swept away by the river ... papa had worked hard to get *la Serpentina* since she was a calf, to give her as a present to my sister, so she would have a little capital and not turn to whoring as did my other two older sisters. ... And that's going to be difficult now. With the cow it was different, because there'd have been no lack of someone to

want to marry her, if only to take away as well that really lovely cow . . . . And Tacha is crying now that she knows that her cow won't come back because the river has killed it . . . . Down her cheeks run rivulets of dirty water as if the river had got inside her . . . . The rotten smell that comes from over there spatters Tacha's wet cheeks and her two little breasts move up and down, without stopping, as if suddenly they were beginning to work towards her perdition.]

Though a socialist realist pathos is undoubtedly at work in the text, and though an economic factor might be at the base of a superstructure of sexual relations dictated by dowry or damnation, the social determinism is never, to rephrase Geoffrey Bennington, *'excessive* with respect to history' (1994, 8). The sparseness of Rulfo's treatment of Tacha's (and the narrator's) realization of the inseparability of the libidinal economy from the neo-feudal class structure rescues the text from the excesses of, for instance, the early Marxian mode of a Jorge Amado. Already, though somewhat tentatively, the text focuses not only on the river *between* Tacha and her future but also on the river *within* Tacha's potential for 'rotting' . . . in the voice, and nose, of the sibling narrator. The undeclared maleness of gaze and smell, and of sensual response, approximates the narrator both to the father's presuppositions of Tacha's fate and to the preying sexuality of the marauding 'hombres de lo peor'/'the worst type of men' who had led the sisters into the *pirujería* of their Ayutla ('o no sé para donde') whoring.

The differences performed by a Mexican and a Brazilian riverflow of libidinal economies are at play both within and between respective traditions and specific texts:

SEQÜÊNCIA

Na estrada das Tabocas, uma vaca viajava . . . . Nem hesitava nas encruzilhadas . . . ao rumo que reto a trazia, para o rio, e – para lá do rio – a terras de um Major Quitério . . . . Seguia, certa; por amor, não por acaso . . . . Apressava-se nela o empolgo de saudade que adoece o boi sertanejo em terra estranha, cada outubro, no prever os trovões . . . . Seu cavalo murça se aplicava . . . ligeiro. Sabia que coisa era o tempo, a involuntária aventura . . . . Deu patas à fantasia . . . . Do ponto, descortinou que: aquela. A vaquinha . . . .

Aí, subia também ao morro, de onde muito se enxergava:
antes das portas do longe, as colinas convalares – e um rio
. . . . O rio, liso e brilhante, de movimentos invisíveis. Como
cortando o mundo em dois . . . a vaquinha chegava à beira . . .
a vaca vermelha o transpondo, a esse rio . . . o filho de seo
Rigério . . . . Hesitou, se. Por certo não passaria, sem o que ele
mesmo não sabia – a oculta, súbita saudade. Passo extremo!
Pegou a descalçar as botas. E entrou – de peito feito. Àquelas
qüilas águas trans – às braças. Era um rio e seu além. Estava,
já do outro lado . . . . Iam-se, na ceguez da noite . . . . O mundo
entre as estrelas e os grilos . . . . Onde e aonde? A vaca, essa,
sabia: por amor desses lugares . . . Chegava, chegavam. Os
pastos da vasta fazenda . . . . A casa de um Major Quitério
. . . . A uma roda de pessoas. Às quatro moças da casa. A uma
delas, a segunda. Era alta, alva, amável. Ela se desescondia
dele. Inesperavam-se? O moço compreendeu-se. Aquilo
mudava o acontecido. Da vaca, ele a ela diria: . . . 'É sua'. Suas
duas almas se transformavam? . . . Amavam-se.

(Guimarães Rosa 1981, 56–60)

[Along the Tabocas road, a cow was walking . . . . She didn't
even hesitate at the cross-roads . . . on the route that would
lead her straight to the river, and – beyond the river – to the
land of a Major Quitério . . . . She ambled confidently on, out
of love, not haphazardly . . . . Tugging her on was the tether of
homesickness which afflicts the ox from the bush-country in
foreign pastures, every October, at the hint of thunder . . . . His
flint horse galloped . . . lightly on, aware of time's involuntary
adventure . . . giving hoofs to fantasy . . . . From there he could
discern that . . . that little cow . . .

He went up the hillside, from where a great deal could be
seen: at the threshold of the faraway, the white-lilied hills –
and a river . . . . The river, smooth and glistening with invisible ripples, as if cutting the world in two . . . The cow was
approaching the bank . . . the red cow crossing it, this river.
Senhor Rigério's boy . . . held himself back. Certainly he
wouldn't cross without what he himself didn't know . . . the
secret, sudden longing. Extreme step! He stooped to take off
his boots. And he waded, chest first, into those quil water trans
– with arm-strokes. It was a river and its beyond. He was
already on the other side. On they went, in the blindness of the

night . . . . The world between the stars and the crickets . . . .
Where and where to? The cow, she knew: out of love for these
places . . . . One arrived, both arrived. The big-farm pasture
. . . . A Major Quitério's house . . . . At a ring of people. At the
four house girls. At one of them, the second one. She was tall,
fair, friendly. She unhid from him. Were they unexpecting
each other? The boy understood himself. This changed what
had happened. About the cow, he to her would say: 'She's
yours'. Were their two souls transforming? . . . . They loved
each other.]

The Brazilian critic Else Vieira, whose creative feel for post-
modern translation aesthetics I touched on in relation to 'double
appropriation' in my broaching of 'Post-, trans-, intra-' relations,
has recently extended her analyses from translation to an engagement with this João Guimarães Rosa short story. In a far-reaching
meditation on 'Seqüência' (in press), Vieira ingeniously appropriates the text as 'moving forward towards the past', positing
just the kind of 'complicity which allowed structuralism to
cohabit with history' that Bennington has proposed as the way to
deal with 'worrying excess' (1994, 9). Worrying excess is often
attributed, in materialists' critiques, to any or all workings of the
libido in economically driven relations. And it is such a hang-up
that I shall address in reading 'Seqüência'.

The division of estates and of patrimony, the economic
boundaries of respect and fear, are relativized disingenuously by
the cow's (nature) and the boy's (culture) difference of approach
to the dividing river. Certainty, desire and the *sertanejo* lure of sea-
son are opposed to hesitation, reticence, *saudade* and the law of
reason: 'Thou shalt not transgress'. The taking of the 'extreme
step' cannot be textualized without the breaking-through, too and
simultaneously, of a language-barrier, a naked penetration of the
shiver–river, a reference-preference and, in the transgressive
betrayal of father's land for other's hand, of a *traditore–traduttore*
reversal. For if, in a traditional epistemology, translation *between*
languages runs the risk of treachery, in the *particular* libidinal
economy of 'Seqüência', transgression invests in the risk-taking of
translation *within* a language: 'E entrou – de peito feito. Àquelas
qüilas águas trans – às braças'. Full frontal surrender to an other,
an other's territory, language. 'Where and where to?' Easily after
the breaking of the waters, the crossing of the *Pubi*/con opens
the Guimarães Rosa text (Joyce-like) to an ending – and a

consummation – of ungrammaticalities: 'Ela se *dese*scondia dele. *In*esperavam-se?'. And in making a gift of the cow which is not his to give but was, perhaps, his inheritance, he puts his future in the past in order to remake the present. Returning to my 'Post-, trans-, intra-' relocation, 'a *trans-jectory* of movement both *across* frontiers and through the *up*lift of self in other, other in self' has become operative. Economy and libido are (become) inseparable.

And what of the risk of eroticizing the I–you encounter? Shocking ideologically, perhaps, to those who have not yet become accustomed to the meeting of other in self, and vice versa? Does it seem erotic because it is exciting? Strange *without* being brutal? A distant echo, too, of Levinas? 'Nothing is further from Eros than possession' (Levinas 1969, 265). I concede that there will be those who will still suggest that I, too, along with Levinas, with Irigaray and the rest, am dangerously eroticizing the encounter with other, the space of self in other/other in self. They might feel, too, uncomfortable with my discourse of the third term, my text of juxtaposed quotations, my always repeated but already altered (Mosaic) mosaics, *my* mosaic:

> Giving oneself, that giving – a transition which undoes the properties of our enclosures, the frame of envelope of our identities. I love you makes, makes me, an other. Loving you, I give myself you. I become you. But I remain, as well, to love you still. And as an effect of that act. Unfinishable. Always in-finite.
>
> Luce Irigaray

The place of an aporia is at the border, before a door, threshold line, or the approach of the other as such.
Jacques Derrida

> The very fact of questioning ... identity means it is al-ready lost. But by the same token it is precisely through this kind of cross-examination that one still hangs onto it. Western [but how *far* Western? identity] walks a tightrope.
>
> Emmanuel Levinas

Jewgreek is greekjew: but greekjew is
Egyptian.

Geoffrey Bennington

> The spectre of Bemoin [the Senegalese] survives
> to haunt . . . *European Encounters with the New
> World.*

D. J. Taylor

PPS

Those suspicious of the encounter with the other, as I have
expressed it here, as being dangerously eroticizing, might also be
unhappy with the hardness (the splinters, the cutting edge) of the
mosaic. Perhaps a softening of the metaphor, an alternative, a
quilt – an endlessly expandable *patchwork* quilt – will ease the
acceptance. For such a quilt would be the product of one hand or
many, a carefully spaced, a placed but often a *dis*placed writing,
a creativity. Such a quilt would serve either to lie on, or under,
to be wrapped in or to be cast off according to temperature
(latitudes/attitudes), according to (dis)position or other shifts –
variations; to be used alone or with another/others – according
to what I might call 'positionality'. But the patchwork quilt
will always be, after all, only a *cover*, a cover of the site (*locus*) of
encounter. Not, however, a *locus amoenus* – only a place, a space,
spaces, potentially amenable . . . in Portuguese both 'aconche-
gante' and 'acolchegante' – which, however, untranslatable,
might suggest a space of welcome, of coming together.

WORKS CITED

Attridge, Derek, Bennington, Geoffrey and Young, Robert. (eds). *Post-
Structuralism and the Question of History.* Cambridge: Cambridge
University Press, 1988.

Bennington, Geoffrey. *Legislations.* London: Verso, 1994.

Bowra, C. M. *From Virgil to Milton.* London: Macmillan, 1945.

Compagnon, Antoine. *La Seconde main; ou, Le Travail de la citation.* Paris:
Seuil, 1979.

Derrida, Jacques. *Of Grammatology,* trans. Gayatri Spivak. Baltimore, Md:
Johns Hopkins University Press, 1976.

—— *Writing and Difference,* trans. Alan Bass. London: Routledge and
Kegan Paul, 1978.

—— *Aporias.* Stanford, Calif.: Stanford University Press, 1993.

Guimarães Rosa, João. *Primeiras estórias*. Rio de Janeiro: Livraria José Olympio Editora, 1981.

Irigaray, Luce. *Elemental Passions*, trans. Joanne Collie and Judith Still. London: Athlone Press, 1992.

Levinas, Emmanuel. *Totality and Infinity*, trans. A. Lingis. Pittsburgh, Pa: Duquesne University Press, 1969.

Millington, Mark I. 'The Question of Reading Crossculturally', *Siglo XX/20th Century*, 13.1 (1995), 13–39.

Monterroso, Augusto. 'Sinfonía concluida', in *Obras completas (y otros cuentos)*. Barcelona: Seix Barral, 1981 (pp. 31–3).

Pessoa, Fernando. *Poesias*. Lisbon: Ática, 1980.

Rama, Ángel. *La ciudad letrada*. Hanover: Ediciones del Norte, 1984.

Rulfo, Juan. *El llano en llamas*. Barcelona: Planeta, 1975.

Sevcenko, Nicolau. 'In Search of the Third Bank of the River: Reflections on the Burden of the Past in Contemporary Brazilian Culture', *Travesía: Journal of Latin American Cultural Studies*. 1.1, (1992), 69–85.

Taylor, D. J. 'Westward ho!', *Sunday Times: Books*, 21 February 1993, 5.

Vieira, Else Ribeiro Pires. 'Translation, "Sequence", (W)Rite of Passage', in *Retranslating Latin America: Dimensions of the Third Term*. ed. with Bernard McGuirk, Nottingham Monographs in the Humanities. Nottingham: University of Nottingham Press, (in press).

Index

Bernard Gui, as the French
called him, or Bernardo Guidoni
or Bernardo Guido . . . his gray
eyes . . . often flash with
ambiguous light, shrewd both
in concealing thoughts and
passions and in deliberately
conveying them.

Umberto Eco